Storytelling in Queer Appalachia

Storytelling in Queer Appalachia

Imagining and Writing the Unspeakable Other

**Edited by
Hillery Glasby,
Sherrie Gradin,
and Rachael Ryerson**

WEST VIRGINIA UNIVERSITY PRESS / MORGANTOWN

ISBN

Cloth 978-1-949199-47-5

Paper 978-1-949199-48-2

Ebook 978-1-949199-49-9

Library of Congress Cataloging-in-Publication Data

Names: Glasby, Hillery, editor. | Gradin, Sherrie L., editor. | Ryerson, Rachael, editor.

Title: Storytelling in queer Appalachia : imagining and writing the unspeakable other / edited by Hillery Glasby, Sherrie Gradin, and Rachael Ryerson.

Description: First edition. | Morgantown : West Virginia University Press, 2020. | Includes bibliographical references and index.

Identifiers: LCCN 2019052204 | ISBN 9781949199475 (cloth) | ISBN 9781949199482 (paperback) | ISBN 9781949199499 (ebook)

Subjects: LCSH: Sexual minorities—Appalachian Region.

Classification: LCC HQ73.3.U62 A6778 2020 | DDC 306.760974—dc23

LC record available at https://lccn.loc.gov/2019052204

Book and cover design by Than Saffel / WVU Press

*To all the queers out there—past, present, and future,
wherever they call or find home.*

Contents

Part III
Both/And:
Intersectional Understandings of Appalachian Queers

Part IV
Queer Media:
Radical Acts of Embodiment and Resistance

Acknowledgments

The editors thank West Virginia University Press for generously providing a space and opportunity for queer Appalachians and queers living in Appalachia with a place to connect and share stories.

Thank you to our anonymous reviewer and Will Banks for feedback and added perspective on audience.

Thank you to Kate Birdsall, Danielle DeVoss, Julie Taylor, and the Cube at Michigan State University (run by the writing, rhetoric, and American cultures department) for their support with index planning. Thank you to Paula Durbin-Westby for the final indexing. The editors also thank the Ohio University College of Arts and Sciences Humanities Research Grant.

We appreciate all of you who read these essays and for taking the time, we hope, to amplify the voices and stories within its pages.

Last but not least, we sincerely thank our contributors, who were all deeply committed to adding valuable voices and experiences to the conversation on the intersection and tensions between Appalachian and queer—and other—identities. You are the lightning bugs of the hollers, the majestic peaks of the mountains, and the rich soil of this place.

Introduction

Hillery Glasby, Sherrie Gradin, and Rachael Ryerson

For a decade I had bought into the dominant narrative in LGBTQIA spaces that because I am queer I could never live back home. I was told—in not so many words—that I could not have my queerness and my mountains, too, that I would not be safe there, that I would not be able to survive, much less thrive. This is a common experience for those of us who have left the small towns and rural areas where we grew up.

—Garringer (2017, 80)

Appalachia as a geographic, mythic, and cultural place is multifaceted and impossible to understand as monolithic or singular. Queer identities and experiences are equally multifaceted and nonmonolithic; they are crossed by and created within economics, destructive land practices, political turmoil, and stereotyping. This collection of essays, imaginings, zines, and photographic records takes up what it might mean to live, embody, and/or perform queerness in Appalachia through personal reflections, researching, teaching, learning, composing, and rhetorical positions and selves. What weight is born by being both queer and Appalachian? What might it mean to be queer in Appalachia? What might it mean to be "quare" in Appalachia? What might it mean to actively queer Appalachia? What might it mean to live or write as queer in Appalachia after the 2016 election process, the results of which seem to have ushered in a new sense of vulnerability and fear for many LGBTQ+ persons (who might also be undocumented, of color, disabled, and/or Muslim)? While work in Appalachian studies and queer studies have produced interesting and important work that is quite rich, we want to contribute to the writings of queers about queerness in Appalachia through this eclectic set of queer renderings because we believe that Appalachian queerness remains underrepresented, misunderstood, sometimes muted, and sometimes invisible. The contributors to this volume are doing everything they can to make queer visible, make queer viable, make queer thrive in Appalachia, and allow

Appalachia to thrive in queers. Although we first imagined this collection as more narrowly about composition studies and pedagogy, our call seems to have traveled through social pathways into the Appalachian hills and hollers, calling forth work from a more eclectic set of writers and scholars and, we now assume, an equally eclectic audience. We think the book is better for this diversity. It works directly against any simple, static, or stereotypical academic relationship to or understanding of Appalachia. The contributors to *Storytelling in Queer Appalachia: Imagining and Writing the Unspeakable Other* are scholars, social workers, riot grrrl activists, teachers, students, practitioners and scholars of divinity, and crossers of boundaries. Some of us were born in Appalachia, and some call it home after arriving from other climes. Whatever the case, the marks this land and culture leave on us are deep and contested.

Appalachia can be a place of isolation—geographically, economically, linguistically, and culturally; boundaries between insiders and outsiders are clear and felt. For queers in the region, being made to feel like an outsider—suspicious—in the context of insiderness creates a certain kind of alienation and loneliness, a sense of being what Trinh Minh-ha calls "elsewhere, within here." The alienation lingers as a displacement, the feeling of existing in one space while always recalling another, more familiar home space. As Minh-ha (2011) explains, "the traveling self is here both the self that moves physically from one place to another, following 'public routes and beaten tracks' within a mapped movement; and, the self that embarks on an undetermined journeying practice, having constantly to negotiate between home and abroad, native culture and adopted culture, or more creatively speaking, between a here, a there, and an elsewhere" (27). Appalachian queers who leave Appalachia, especially those who leave because of their queerness, experience a unique form of displacement, a certain kind of exile, forming a queer (Appalachian) diaspora, often finding themselves in places that, although accepting of their queer identity, are not always accepting of their Appalachian identity.

Notions of exile and diaspora are rooted in transnational studies and globalization, belonging primarily to the experiences of those who have been driven out of or felt compelled to leave their home country because of persecution, war, despair, economic collapse, and ethnic cleansing. Individuals, families, and whole communities are left spread across the world—isolated, lonely, made to feel alien in other places than what is known as home. Their exile, although hopeful for a safer, better life, can be laced with pain, instability, and longing. In her book *Alienhood: Citizenship, Exile, and the Logic of Difference*, Katarzyna Marciniak (2006) describes exile as "a performative condition, one that evokes a sense of shifting, or quivering, identity location—an experience of liminality and undecidability that destabilizes the traditionally static notion of national identity" (27). Certainly there is much at stake when one crosses national borders, whether through processes that provide documentation or as an undocumented transnational.

In his analysis, "The 'Diaspora' Diaspora," Rogers Brubaker (2005) discusses the uptick in applications of notions of diaspora beyond its Greek, Armenian, and Jewish roots and previous theoretical discussions bound to academia. He identifies patterns in the proliferation of diasporic applications, noting three main criteria: dispersion, homeland orientation, and boundary maintenance, all of which seem fitting to the (queer) Appalachian diasporic application we invoke. As Brubaker describes it, *dispersion* is "forced or otherwise traumatic dispersion; more broadly as any kind of dispersion in space, provide that the dispersion crosses state borders"; *homeland orientation* implies "the orientation to a real or imagined 'homeland' as an authoritative source of value, identity and loyalty [. . .] maintaining a collective memory or myth about the homeland"; and *boundary maintenance* consists of a sense of hybridity, "the preservation of a distinctive identity vis-à-vis a host society" (6).

We do not imply that a queer Appalachian moving from West Virginia to Illinois experiences the same dangers, poverty, illness, language barriers, and anti-immigrant rhetoric as does a refugee from Syria. We see these understandings of "unbelonging," exile, and diaspora as generative in understanding the experience of queer Appalachians who are either dislocated—separated from their home region and geographical landscape to find acceptance, validation, and queer community—or made to feel like outsiders in their own region due to their queerness. Leaving Appalachia to be more safely and fully out as LGBTQ+ may bring one identity into the light, but often at the cost of forcing another identity into the shadows, since some Appalachians face scrutiny and discrimination based on the assumptions and stereotypes about their dialects and home culture. These struggles are not limited to queer Appalachians who leave home, since queer Appalachians who remain are also made to feel like strangers in their own region.

In his keynote address at the 2014 Annual Appalachian Studies Conference, Silas House describes how queer Appalachians are reminded of—and made to feel—their difference at home:

> Often I hear people talk about how accepting Appalachians are of people who are different. "He's just a little bit quare," people in my community sometimes said when referring to a person they accepted as part of their

world but who didn't quite fit in, whether he was socially inept or actually queer in the most modern sense of the word. I'd be interested to hear how many of you are familiar with that colloquial word "quare"? Will you raise your hands? Of course it's a colloquial distortion of the word "queer." That's easy to figure out. As a people, Appalachians have always had "quare" folks amongst them. Always, these people were only accepted with some wariness. Consider the quare women who changed the region at the settlement schools. They were eventually folded into the community, but not without skepticism. Not without having to prove themselves the extra mile. Anyone who is different—whether it be by their origins, their actions, their race, or their orientation—has always been accepted only with a fair amount of suspicion. That is a kind of halfway acceptance, and an acceptance that demands the quare not be too awfully visible. The common phrase among the homophobe is: "Just don't rub it in my face how gay you are" [. . .] Homophobia lurks in the hollers, and slithers along the ridges of Appalachia. The reason why is because Appalachia is in America. What is happening here is happening throughout the rest of the country. (2014, 109, 110)

In response, House calls for a "New Appalachia," where collective discrimination and subtle homophobia are acknowledged, discussed, and fought—among neighbors and in community classroom conversations. Rather than continuing the "exodus," out-migration, and "exile" of young (queer) Appalachians seeking better economic opportunities and acceptance, he imagines Appalachia as a place where they feel wholly themselves, at home, in the place they love. Rather than seeing queer(nes)s as separate or apart from Appalachia, we hope to show how queers are *a part* of Appalachia, "shap[ing] the region as it shapes them" (Sohn 2006, 5). The writers in this volume reveal those connections and draw parallels between queer pride and empowerment and regional pride and empowerment, the closeness of (found) family and community formations in opposition to the mainstream at the heart of both.

The underrepresented, muted invisibility that gives rise to this collection has multiple points of origin, including the fact that much of Appalachia is also rural, geographically and geopolitically. Rurality complicates queer identity, queer community, and queer experiences. Rural queers often combat stereotypes that associate their ruralness with backwardness, ignorance, and dirt(iness) and their queerness with urbanity. Scott Herring (2010) finds that "the rural . . . is shelved, disavowed, denied, and discarded in favor of metropolitan sexual cultures such as New York City, San Francisco, or Buffalo. In each the rural becomes a slur" (5). As a result of this characterization, queers who occupy rural places are left out of what J. Halberstam (2006) describes as "the metronormative story of migration from 'country' to 'town' [which] is a spatial narrative within which the subject moves to a place of tolerance after enduring life in a place of suspicion, persecution, and secrecy" (36–37). These narratives characterize, foreclose, and silence rural queer identities, especially those refusing to assimilate to heteronormative, homonormative, metronormative ideals. This story suggests that rural queers have no stories of their own, or at least not ones worth hearing, reading, and viewing.

Yet rural queer texts can be found, as Herring (2007) demonstrates in his analysis of the quarterly journal *Radical Faerie Digest* (*RFD*), an analysis that shows how, in the 1970s, the journal "was one of the first anti-heteronormative, anti-urban, and anti-middle-class journals to appear as a challenge to and a critique of . . . normalizing urban gay culture" (341). These early issues of *RFD* imagine other ways of queer being and belonging, and they value the regional, the rural, and the nonmetropolitan (Herring 2007, 367). In his book, *Another Country: Queer Anti-Urbanism*, Herring (2010) explores queer rural texts, finding that their rural stylistics foreground an anti-urbanism that counters queer metronormativity. Fairly recent publications, such as Blevins and McElmurray's (2015) *Walk Till the Dogs Get Mean: Mediations on the Forbidden from Contemporary Appalachia*; Garringer's (2017) " 'Well, We're Fabulous and We're Appalachians, So We're Fabulachians': Country Queers in Central Appalachia"; Gorman-Murray, Pini, and Bryant's *Sexuality, Rurality, and Geography*; Gradin's (2016) "Can You See Me Now?: Rural Queer Archives and a Call to Action"; Gray's (2009) *Out in the Country: Youth, Media, and Queer Visibility in Rural America*, all provide a place for queer and Appalachian writers, artists, teachers, and scholars to dwell. As mentioned already, this volume captures and illustrates queer Appalachia through a variety of genres, queer positionalities, and identities. Some veer toward the visual, some toward the academic, some toward storytelling, and some toward reflection on living, teaching, and researching as queers in hostile yet familiar territory.

This collection of essays mixes traditional and queer(ed) elements of storytelling, personal essay, personal reflections, Appalachian writing/composing— a coming to voice alongside or as a way of doing the more traditional academic work of theorizing and analyzing. We find such composing practices—practices that seem too sexual, too excessive, too personal—critical to the queer work and meaning of this volume. As others have argued, queer being is inextricably linked with language, with composition, with expression and meaning making, and this connection has led scholars like David Wallace (2011) to suggest we "allow for writers to be more personally present in their texts and for inclusion of a wider range of discourse practices, particularly the genres, vocabulary, dialogue, and syntax often used by members of marginalized groups" (11). Queer scholars and writers have already moved in that direction, with Jonathan Alexander and Jacqueline Rhodes (2011) crafting texts that demonstrate the queer possibilities of composition. For example, their *JAC* article, "Queer: An Impossible Subject for Composition," pairs a scholarly, theoretical discussion of queer theory and composition with lyrics from the Eurythmics song "Sweet Dreams," narrative asides, single-sentence paragraphs, multiple genres, the word *fuck*, and their sex/uality. These authors compose and gesture queer(ly) in the very form of their text, enacting their claims that "If queerness means more than just one more static representation of 'diversity,' containable in its knowability, then it must *move* in multiple directions at once, embracing multi-modality, multi-genre texts, and even, when available or perhaps necessary, multi-media . . . we want to make room for the kinds of writing—and the kinds of subjects—that challenge such composure, that offer rich, capacious, and (yes) excessive ways of thinking and writing" (Alexander and Rhodes 2011, 183). In response, our collection seeks to queer genre and identity, invoking a sense of hybridity and the esprit of voice.

We have clustered essays into four sections: "The Heart over the Head: Queer-Affirming Epistles and Queerphobic Challenges," "Queer Diaspora: Existence and Erasure in Appalachia," "Both/And: Intersectional Understandings of Appalachian Queers," and "Queer Media: Radical Acts of Embodiment and Resistance." Amanda Hayes's "A Letter to Appalachia" opens our first section, but in its demand "to listen up" it also introduces the whole body of work that follows. As its title indicates, this contribution is an epistle, a time-honored rhetorical form for establishing more intimate connections with those close to us and wider audiences and publics. The epistle in the hands of women has often been a rhetorical gesture that establishes a close relationship while critiquing oppressive power (think Sarah Grimké). Following in this tradition comes Hayes's "A Letter to Appalachia," in which she demands that we closely examine our own hypocrisies and biases against all that seems queer. She engages us in a discussion of queerness and difference with an imagined yet very real audience of family, friends, neighbors, teachers, and readers by evoking the old Appalachian definition of queer—simply *different*. As a beautiful storyteller and rhetorical scholar of Appalachia who moves through standard academic prose and her home Appalachian dialect, Hayes connects that old-time Appalachian understanding of queer to family, current political climates, and her sexual and gender identities. Not only does she challenge Appalachian stereotypes, like the unquestioned conflation of Appalachian-ness with white-ness, she challenges Appalachians themselves. For example, she cannot recon-cile the strength she sees and knows in Appalachian women with a majority vote against a strong woman for president and instead for a man known for his disrespect and mistreatment of women and other minority groups. The form of the letter allows her to be confrontational with her fellow citizens and us as readers about antiqueerness and homophobia because it allows for her story to emerge while calling for the stories of her fellow Appalachians to yield their own queerness. Along the way she manages to show us how to enact cultural change through storytelling, framing common rhetorical ground, and informal teaching. Her closing salutation, "Give my love to the family," reverberates with sincerity and is rich with queer irony.

Like Hayes's letter, Justin Dutton's essay, "Challenging Dominant Christianity's Queerphobic Rhetoric," explores ways to make central Appalachia a more welcoming environment for all persons—Appalachian natives, citizens, and tourists alike. Dutton offers an alternative story of and challenge to the queerphobic mountain Christianity that has done great harm to Appalachian queer people. His alternative story and challenge suggest that Christian con-cepts of deep love and acceptance complement Appalachian culture and can be a means by which queerphobic folk learn about queer lives and listen to queer stories. His contribution demonstrates that the Appalachian traditions of pride in place and telling stories—traditions that hold much sway in moun-tain Christianity, historically and currently—present Appalachian Christians with the unique opportunity, often denied to those who desire or seek to pre-serve the historic and current status quo in other forms of the faith, to move beyond queerphobia into a state of Christ-like love that continually expands. For Dutton, being queer in Appalachia means being in the "toxic closet," which reminds readers why reconciling Appalachian (Christian) culture with queer culture remains such important work. Like Hayes, Dutton sees such work hap-pening from inside Appalachia, from his people. In other words, when it comes to developing new understandings of the world—a process made famous by a first-century Jewish man who challenged the comfortable religious and politi-cal status quos of his time—mountain Christians have advantages that cannot be claimed by other Christian traditions, even those that seem similar on the surface. We chose to open with the section "The Heart over the Head: Queer-Affirming Epistles and Queerphobic Challenges" and its two contributions be-cause they are simultaneously a calling out, a calling to action, and a calling to the heart that the following essays try to enact.

The next section of the collection, "Queer Diaspora: Existence and Erasure in Appalachia," begins with Adam Denney's lyrical essay, "A Drowning in the Foothills." Denney's chapter starts at Lake Cumberland, a large reservoir within a 101-mile stretch of land in southeastern Kentucky, an important ecological, economical, and recreational resource to the region. The waters of Lake Cumberland are full of many stories, quite literally because underneath its surface are the remnants of communities and farms that were vacated in the 1950s when the US Army Corp of Engineers dammed the region. Local narratives probably include tales of those who drowned alongside the foothills, either unable or unwilling to leave. To drown at/for home is a familiar feeling for many queers in the Bible Belt. Within this affect of drowning, this essay mobilizes a departure. "A Drowning in the Foothills" negotiates the times when holding one's breath is an act of both resistance and survival in the face of hostile environments. The essay explores specific geographical sites/historical moments while weaving stories of personal queer experiences to create new imaginations of self and land. By reinvestigating the natural vis-à-vis the personal, Denney uses a blended methodology of scientific inquiry and storytelling to create a provocative exploration of life and death—and queerness—in this region.

In his essay, "A Pedagogy of the Flesh: Deconstructing the 'Quare' Appalachian Archetype," Matthew Thomas-Reid moves us from the mythic waters of Lake Cumberland to Appalachian classrooms, where the "boy who is good to his momma" excels in the arts and becomes the sweet submissive pleaser in a performance allowing no fully embodied identity. In other words, he can be *quare* (pronounced "kwar") as in strange, unusual, or colorful, but not *queer* (pronounced "kwir") as in a sexual being. Thomas-Reid further contends that although this separation of the spirit and the flesh proliferates in K–12 settings, it can be mended through (opportunities for) storytelling. Narratives for and by queer youth are missing in schools, and there is more than the academic at stake; in our classrooms right now, queer bodies are starving themselves, cutting themselves, and drugging themselves. Using a blend of familial, personal, and student narratives in a queer phenomenological approach, this author advocates for a pedagogy in Appalachia that embraces the narratives of the flesh, the voices of fully formed queer identities liberated from the quare constructs that favor cultural safety by promoting queer folk in Appalachia as sexless curiosities. This pedagogy aims to disrupt quare archetypes by allowing the flesh to be communicated through explicitly embodied queer narratives.

"Pickin' and Grinnin': Quare Hillbillies, Counterrhetorics, and the Recovery of Home," Kim Gunter's chapter, also begins with narrative, with a story of her father's response to her uncle's verbal homophobia in a feed store. Indeed, this chapter is scholarly and personal, combining queer theories with queer stories that mirror the alienation, the sense of being neither here nor there that so many Appalachian queers experience. Gunter, a self-described country dyke, also troubles binaries like urban/rural and blue-collar/white-collar while insisting that queer rhetorical analyses also consider how class and place can reveal antiqueer, anti-Appalachian discourses. In a series of vignettes, Gunter weaves together autobiography, queer composition, and rhetorical studies to highlight the disconnects she experiences among competing yet overlapping identities as Appalachian, academic, and queer. Moreover, she sees a similar negotiation of identities, performances, and places in the experiences of her (queer) writing students. In response, she calls for an intersectional approach to classrooms, scholarship, and people that allows for these identities to simultaneously exist and be heard, to enable counterrhetorics, counterpublics, and counter-world-making. Her essay describes agentive life after deconstruction, the possibilities of quare counterpublics, and applications of a reconstruction of self to the composition classroom as a public response to those personal experiences.

Opening our third section, "Both/And: Intersectional Understandings of Appalachian Queers," Lydia McDermott's essay, "The Crik Is Crooked: Appalachia as Movable Queer Space," beautifully merges the personal with the academic, the private with the public, combining story with theory to explore multiple senses of queerness in/out of Appalachia; queer for McDermott, includes what Halberstam (2005) calls "an outcome of strange temporalities, imaginative life schedules, and eccentric economic practices" (1). As an imagined space, Appalachia is queer—queer as a "crik is crooked." McDermott asks and explores whether *queer* can be deployed as a verb of subversion—whether Appalachia also moves and subverts. In response, she combines personal anecdote, family history, pedagogical practices, and queer theorization in a quilted form to disturb the academic ground she regularly walks. As well as a powerful story, McDermott's essay is a powerful family history, which moves her (us) queerly through the hills of Pennsylvania; to Athens, Ohio; to Washington state; and finally back to a queer state of mind and memory where we feel, with McDermott, our "feet sunk into the Appalachian ground, the hills and hollows."

In their essay, "Are Y'all Homo?": Mêtis as Method for Queer Appalachia," Travis Rountree and Caleb Pendygraft also describe their experiences in/out of Appalachia. Like so many in this collection, these authors begin with storytelling because they believe stories are foundational to Appalachian and southern queer culture and because retelling them is a powerful narrative tool that honors and gives voice to the identities and people of a given place and time. In the spirit of cultural rhetorics scholars and for the sake of queering the genre conventions and methods of scholarly writing, the coauthors begin with story, individually relating their version of the same event: a somewhat terrifying experience of being researchers and strangers in a small Appalachian town and being asked at a local restaurant/bar, "are y'all homos?"; their "yes" response led to a warning that they had better leave before certain locals showed up and caused trouble. Yet from this experience, Rountree and Pendygraft offer a methodology for (queer) person-based research grounded in the rhetorical concept of mêtis, which calls for responding to rough situations with cunning, wit, and wisdom. The second half of the chapter theorizes mêtis to suggest a performative precarity and a performative disidentification as methods for other queer scholars and queer research in Appalachia. The authors see mêtis as not only an embodied intelligence but an enacted strategy that can protect queer folx in the queerphobic places where they might work.

Focusing on their experiences as the former director of a university LGBT center that serves campus and community in a rural part of the country, delfin bautista's chapter, "Queering Trauma and Resilience, Appalachian Style!" highlights the challenges and resiliencies of queer narratives in southeast Appalachian Ohio. bautista observes the preponderance of queer narratives, especially in popular media, that are set within the city, and they—as so many do in this collection—call for more queer narratives from and of rural places. As a person who moved to Athens, OH, from Miami, FL, they have worked to create their own home in a rural area that also hosts a state university, and from there they recast the queer stories and lives of students negotiating being displaced because of their queerness. Not surprisingly, LGBTQ+ students fear for their safety, face discrimination and abuse, and lack access to a larger rainbow community. Like Gunter, bautista argues that an intersectional approach might offer the support these students need and bridge gaps between the Ohio University campus and community, and specifically these LGBTQ+ folks.

The fourth and final section of the collection, "Queer Media: Radical Acts of Embodiment and Resistance," opens with Tijah Bumgarner's chapter, "Working against the Past: Queering the Appalachian Narrative," in which she explores through queer art, films screened at the Appalachian Queer Film Festival, and student work how master narratives of Appalachia are being reworked by artists, citizens, and students. Together, these folx and Bumgarner imagine and represent a more diverse Appalachia that challenges the usual dueling banjos/ *Deliverance* tropes. By focusing on minor narratives and voices often elided or erased, this chapter subverts silencing homogeneous grand narratives, such as those that render themselves invisible while shoring up devastating extraction industries and mountaintop coal removal. Bumgarner calls for an intersectional approach within the "rooted" framework of Appalachia to argue against such homogeneous tropes. As Appalachia transitions into an economically postcoal landscape, its cultural landscape is in transition, making room to dive (queerly) into the cultural gaps created by this transition. This essay argues that art is most beneficial in representing the differences and diversity in the region within the cultural gaps.

Savi Ettinger, Katie Manthey, Sonny Romano, and Cynthia Suryawan's chapter, "Writing the Self: Trans Zine Making in Appalachia," highlights the connections between the material making of zines and their lived queer experiences at Salem College, a small women's college. This essay focuses on the theoretical and pedagogical contexts and practices that led to a creation of a zine project at Salem College that features writing by and about trans authors. The chapter is structured as vignettes of an interview between a cis professor and three trans students. Although Salem College is not openly accepting of trans students, many of the students there do not self-identify as women. The cis and trans writers of this chapter offer the Salem College Writing Center as a queer space in the vein of "third space"—a space in between the classroom and the outside world, in between the public and the private, in between the professional and the personal. In this space students have room to interrogate their identities in the context of writing, tutoring, and making in Appalachia. By offering vignettes from multiple student zine authors and the director of the Writing Center, this story offers a theoretical approach to navigating story as queer theory while investigating tensions between the institution and individuals for both students and faculty and the place of academic third spaces as queer havens, all within the larger context of a women's college in Appalachia. This essay includes the link to their zine, titled "Trans Embodiment."

Finally, we close the collection with a powerful tribute to Bryn Kelly, a transgender artist and activist who killed herself, leaving behind a deep and painful absence for many in the queer community. In their essay "Queer Appalachia: A Homespun Praxis of Rural Resistance in Appalachian Media," Gina Mamone and Sarah E. Meng revive our hearts and create a space of evocative queer power and subjectivity in their tribute to Bryn. Their chapter details the birth and blossoming of an online community called Queer Appalachia. Since 2015, the digitized space of Queer Appalachia has provided a place to share stories of resistance and resilience and mobilize against legislation villainizing queer communities and policing queer bodies. Through social media, Queer Appalachia has become a contemporary zine, an online place to call to one another over the mountains of our closets and a counter to the violence that isolation wreaks on the lives of too many queers. Queer Appalachia offers a rural, accessible, queer space/place that celebrates representation and visibility at the crossroads of queerness and Appalachian culture. This chapter shares these stories through images taken from their Instagram page, images that illustrate survival and tell tales of wildcrafting Appalachian queerness, foraging for pieces of ourselves within the intersections of coal mines and class, race and religion, food justice and colonialism. With nearly 4,000 social media followers and a publishing contract offer, Queer Appalachia is building an online space for these stories while helping community members find each other.

The Editors' Place: Queers in Appalachia

It is ethical and important, we believe, to acknowledge that we are not queer Appalachians. We are queer(nes)s in Appalachia, but we are not *of* Appalachia. We are queers living in Appalachia. We are outside-insiders—"elsewhere, within here," as Trinh Minh-ha puts it. These stories are not ours to tell. We are privileged and humbled to have been given this opportunity to curate and archive the extraordinary stories of those who negotiate and experience Appalachian queerness. To that end, we say something about who we are in relation to Appalachia and to queerness.

Hillery

A few months after moving from Athens, OH, to East Lansing, MI, to start my position at Michigan State University, my partner and I attended a concert hosted by The Ten Pound Fiddle, a local folk music scene/community. It was chilly outside, and it poured rain that night. The show was held indoors, with no alcohol served. Right off the bat, it felt very different from any folk show I'd been to in southeast Ohio; honestly, it felt different from *any* folk or bluegrass show I'd ever been to. As more people entered the concert room, and I watched them chatting among friends, that feeling changed. I realized it was the first time I felt at home since leaving Appalachia, despite having lived in Lansing fifteen years prior. There were people in their seventies with long silver ponytails, homemade dresses—patchworked with colorful and playful patterns—worn over pants, and a strong sense of friendship and community all around us. I found myself, again, among a tight-knit community and in the presence of the banjos and fiddles.

We took our seats and a hush fell over the room. Run Boy Run began to play, and on hearing that first string plucked, I couldn't help myself: I began to cry. After the third or fourth song, my wife nudged me and asked, "Are you going to cry through the whole thing?!" And I basically did. Tears rolled down my cheeks until intermission. I cried because I missed Athens. I missed the community I had formed there, the friends who had become family. I cried out of longing. Because it sounded like hilltops, hollers, ridges, and criks. Banjos and fiddles have become lush, green sounds of home.

I am a Midwestern queer, but my heart beats for Appalachia. Since I have moved away, I feel a sense of loss similar to those described in these stories. Although I left Appalachia, it has not left me. This collection was a way for me to reconnect, to recollect, and re-collect—as I have been apart from Sherrie and Rachael, two important pieces of my found queer family—and to go home again. A part of me will always imagine myself back in the foothills of Appalachia, exploring the people, music, beer, caves, rocks, and rivers of the Hocking Hills. I may have moved away, but I will never move on.

Sherrie

I was born in Wyoming and have spent fifty-two years of my six decades living in rural America from the Rocky Mountain West, to rural New England, to Mississippi's deep South, to Appalachian Ohio for the past eighteen years. I am not from Appalachia, but I am (mostly) home, and queer, in Appalachia. I live up in the hills outside a small village off two-nine holler, and just a few miles from the old Sunday Creek Coal mine, where Ohio's worst coal mine disaster took the lives of eighty-two men on November 5, 1930. My water source is Sunday Creek, which runs nearby, bright orange from years of acid runoff.

My neighbors hunt and fish. They live on family-owned land as multigenerational families, including cousins; when every new generation comes of age, gets married, and begins having children, a piece of the family land is set aside and another simple trailer house or modular home is added. They accept me into their hills and as their neighbor. I know they know I'm a bit different from them, a bit quare, yet they come to my aid when I need help and I to theirs when they need help. Side by side we've pulled four-wheelers out of mud holes, hauled trees out of the road, and returned each others' coon dogs at the end of an errant hunt. They are here for me no matter how quare, and I hope the same would be true no matter how queer, but I leave those grounds untested in times of Trump. This dog don't hunt trouble today. Maybe tomorrow.

Rachael

I'm not from Appalachia, as I was planted and grown amid the wheat, cattle, and red dirt of Oklahoma. After living in southern Ohio for seven years, in the foothills of the Appalachians and forty minutes north of the West Virginia state line, I have come to call Appalachia home. I am surprised by how much this place and its people recall rural, rugged, religious memories of Oklahoma. Down there in cowboy, cattle country, in the buckle of the Bible Belt, heart-warm people hold tightly to tradition, family, and the land, and this little country girl did, too.

I was rooted in that place, and it deeply affected how I thought and felt about myself and the world around me. In fact, it wasn't until I moved away from Oklahoma to Appalachia, and found a queer family here, that I began to openly tell people that I am queer. Close friends in Oklahoma knew of my bisexuality, but I didn't call myself queer, and I certainly didn't come out to my blood relatives.

Here's why: I attended a Temptations concert with my aunt at the Hard Rock Casino in Tulsa. We noticed two women dancing in front of us, one standing behind the other with her arms wrapped around her beloved. Against the backdrop of five men dancing and singing in sparkly green suit jackets, I watched this couple dance in sincere embrace, and it warmed my heart. At the young age of fourteen, I had a flash of pride that these women openly displayed their affection for each other in a public space *in Oklahoma*. Yet where I felt warmth and love, my aunt felt disgust and revulsion. Loudly she said, "You two should get a room. That's disgusting." I remember being shocked, and palpably feeling the great distance and disparity between my worldview and my aunt's. This experience and others like it marked me, leading me to disregard and not factor into my identity the relationships I would have with women in the years to come.

Yet in two unlikely places, Appalachia and academia, I was fortunate to find a queer family and home that gave me the safe space and love I needed to fully embrace my queer identity. I am a rural queer living and loving in Appalachia, and that is what I see this collection offering to queers within/ without Appalachia: a place where the rural and the queer *can and do* coexist.

BIBLIOGRAPHY

Alexander, Jonathan, and Jacqueline Rhodes. 2011. "Queer: An Impossible Subject for Composition." *JAC* 31, 177–206.

Blevins, Adrian, and Karen Salyer McElmurray, eds. 2015. *Walk Till the Dogs Get Mean: Meditations on the Forbidden from Contemporary Appalachia*. Athens: Ohio University Press.

Brubaker, Rogers. 2005. "The 'Diaspora' Diaspora." *Ethnic and Racial Studies* 28, no. 1, 1–19.

Garringer, Rachel. 2017. " 'Well, We're Fabulous and We're Appalachians, So We're Fabulachians': Country Queers in Central Appalachia." *Southern Cultures* 23, no. 1, 79–91.

Gorman-Murray, Andrew, Barbara Pini, and Lia Bryant, eds. 2013. *Sexuality, Rurality, and Geography*. Lanham, MD: Lexington Books.

Gradin, Sherrie. 2016, March 31. "Can You See Me Now?: Rural Queer Archives and a Call to Action." *Pearsoned.com*. http://www.pearsoned.com/pedagogy-practice/can-you-see-me-now-rural-queer-archives-and-a-call-to-action/. Accessed September 15, 2017.

Gray, Mary L. 2009. *Out in the Country: Youth, Media, and Queer Visibility in Rural America*. New York: New York University Press.

Halberstam, Judith. 2005. *In a Queer Time and Place: Transgender Bodies, Subcultural Lives*. New York: New York University Press.

Herring, Scott. 2007. "Out of the Closets, into the Woods: RFD, Country Women, and the Post-Stonewall Emergence of Queer Anti-Urbanism." *American Quarterly* 59, no. 2, 341–72.

———. 2010. *Another Country: Queer Anti-Urbanism*. New York: New York UP.

House, Silas. 2014. "Our Secret Places in the Waiting World: or, A Conscious Heart, Continued." *Journal of Appalachian Studies* 20, no. 2, 103–21.

Marciniak, Katarzyna. 2006. *Alienhood: Citizenship, Exile, and the Logic of Difference*. Minneapolis: University of Minnesota Press.

Minh-ha, Trinh. 2011. *Elsewhere, Within Here*. New York: Routledge.

Sohn, Katherine Kelleher. 2006. *Whistlin' and Crowin' Women of Appalachia: Literacy Practices since College*. Carbondale: Southern Illinois University Press.

Wallace, David L. 2011. *Compelled to Write: Alternative Rhetoric in Theory and Practice*. Logan: Utah State University Press.

PART I

The Heart over the Head: Queer-Affirming Epistles and Queerphobic Challenges

CHAPTER 1

A Letter to Appalachia

Amanda Hayes

My dear fellow Appalachians,

The letter is a time-honored tradition. Not many of us write them much these days, but plenty of us have old family letters saved in drawers or between book pages. Open letters specifically do something that I think of as particularly Appalachian: they don't draw boundaries around who's allowed to do the reading. If you're one of my fellow Appalachians, great. If you aren't, that's fine, too. Because writing, to me, is an exercise not only in creating connections to readers but also in shaping my voice. Mine is a little complicated, maybe, by the fact that it's shaped by Appalachia (a discourse that by nature is blurry and hard to define) and academia (a discourse that takes pride in being rigidly defined). Yet I no more want to cut off part of my voice than I do part of my audience. In my experience, letters can accommodate all of these. That's why, when I think about how I want to say something I think is really important, writing a letter springs to mind. And what I have to say now is important.

It's time to talk about queerness.

Talking about queerness is going to involve talking about some things I never much heard discussed with strangers when I was growing up—gender identity and sexuality. But we've got to talk about it now. There's too much at stake. Specifically, I want us to talk about the stories we tell—or don't tell— ourselves about queerness and why telling them and *listening* to them matter now more than ever.

There's a few different ways to think about queerness. There's an old Appalachian definition of queer: queer is, simply, *different*. Usually not in a good way. He or she "is a bit queer" was something I can remember hearing before I ever heard anything like he or she "is *a* queer." But I think there's a connection between both uses. I'm sure you've all heard the term (or maybe been called, or called someone else) "a queer" in relation to someone's sexuality or the way/shape/form they don't fit your definition of their gender. Therefore, *queerness* includes not just sexuality—bluntly, who we think someone wants to screw—but also whether we think they're acting the way they're supposed to act as a man or woman. But I think this idea, of someone who isn't doing their gender work being "a queer," extends directly from the older concept of being queer—essentially being different from normal.

This definition connects with the concept of queerness I've learned in academia. There's a whole subject called queer studies; people who study it think about what queerness means and reject that it is something negative. Queer studies offer a way of thinking about identity, social pressures, about how we define *anything* as normal . . . or not. Elise Dixon (2017) explains that queer theory "work[s] to resist normativity because our concepts of 'normal' are social constructs used to reinforce and bolster the power of the most privileged. Resisting normativity allows us to question why some things are normal and some things are not, which opens up space for exploration, interrogation, and dialogue." In other words, queer theory is about asking *why* what we think is normal *is* normal; it looks for how "normalness" exists to empower some and disempower others. The normality that gets questioned can be about sexual orientation, but also about anything we take for granted—gender, social values, even ways of communicating and interacting. So even if you're straight and cisgender (meaning, you identify just fine with what society says you should be for your gender), you're still part of the way of thinking that creates and assigns queerness. So if you think "queerness" has nothing to do with you—think again. For all our sakes.

I want us to be clear on what I'm asking for: questioning what we take for granted, questioning how we build identities around "us" and "them," looking for the weaknesses in those perceptions, and asking who benefits from us having those worldviews. Because, hint: I don't think we benefit. Of course, you might not know when I say *us* and *our*, who I'm talking about. You might not know that when I say "my fellow Appalachians" that I mean you. I understand that; I've noticed it's a lot harder to articulate who "we" are than who is not "one of us." We don't often think of ourselves as "being" anything in particular, let alone something called Appalachian. If you live within the 205,000-square-mile expanse that incorporates the Appalachian mountain chain and foothills—a region that stretches through twelve states, from New York to Mississippi ("The Appalachian Region" n.d.) then you are Appalachian by geography. But the people I'm addressing in this letter aren't just those who live here; they are those who, like me, are Appalachian culturally, by identity . . . we who have had these hills stamped onto our souls in some way.

Maybe you don't want to think of yourselves as Appalachian. I get that, too. So many movies, songs, jokes, even sometimes teachers have told you that being Appalachian (or hillbillies, rednecks . . . we can get into the shades of meaning in these terms another time) is a bad thing. Alternatively, maybe you have an ornery streak, and people's derision has made you double down on that identity, making you want to be exactly what the stereotype says a redneck hillbilly ought to be because fuck them, right?

Speaking of stereotypes, there's a particular subset of you I want to talk to in particular: those who might be thought of as the privileged within the marginalized. Let me be clear: Appalachian identity is not, by definition, "white." People of color have been here longer than anyone else, they've contributed more than most to what is considered quintessentially Appalachian. (The banjo? It's African in origin.) Still, I'm addressing this conversation to those of you who consider yourselves white. And I want to talk specifically to those of you who think of yourselves as straight and cisgender. You're the men who seem to have no problem with what acting like a man requires. Same for women. I'm addressing you because, let's be honest, you're the ones the rest of the country is saying got us into this mess. I ain't saying whether I agree with that or not. In general, I think Appalachia gets blamed for lots of things that aren't its fault, such as poverty, substandard medical care, and the lack of educational funding. But I also can't deny that I hear a lot of things from my fellow Appalachians, particularly the ones in the group I've just described, that I just plain don't understand. That's got me worried.

Maybe you know what mess I'm talking about: the state of our politics and what that says about us. I'll tell you what it looks like it says about us: that Appalachia is racist, sexist, unfeeling, and inexplicably happy to elect people who will destroy our land and take away our health care. Is that who we are? I want to talk to you because I don't know if *you* know who you are. If the 2016 election cycle has told me anything, it's that we need to have a serious conversation about who we are and what we stand for. Because it looks to me like too many of us decided to embrace the worst in ourselves and elected people who would embrace that, too. Not all of us, of course. But enough that, like I said, it's got me worried.

See, I'm worried because I thought I knew something about the people I come from.

I'm sure you're thinking right now, "Pffft. I know who I am, and even if I didn't, ain't no way someone like you is gonna tell me." Fair enough. The truth is, I don't know you, not specifically. The you I'm addressing is my sense of a portion of people I grew up with and around, people who identified (or would have, if they'd ever been called on to defend their identities the ways that queer-identified people are all the time) as straight, white, cisgender, and country as all hell. And as I said, so much of what I thought I knew about you got blowed out of the water in November 2016. So we're going to reconnect right now. How about this: I'll tell you some things about who I thought we were and how I thought we got that way. Then you can do your own thinking about who you are and how you got to be that way. Sound fair?

Let me start with some of the things I thought I knew. For one, I thought we of all people were cool with strong women. I know, of course, that everyone's different (something I think we would all do well to remember more often). Still, I thought we were generally a people who could understand that bucking mainstream definitions of "normal" could be a good thing, particularly if what we're rejecting is a limited sense of what women can and can't do. I'm focusing on femininity, for the moment, because it's the gender category that's been the most complicated for me by our own recent behavior. See, I'd paid enough attention to the television growing up to sense a story about what a woman was supposed to be. Magazine and television women were sparkly, skinny, expensively dressed . . . but not vocal. Not proactive. They weren't what I tended to see within my own family and community. I read an essay recently that made a point about gender and sports; as Roper and Polasek (2014) point out: "Sports are sites for reaffirming attitudes and beliefs about gender differences. The characteristics commonly associated with sports—strength, power, dominance, competitiveness, aggression—are socially defined as masculine traits/qualities. As a result, female participation in sport presents numerous challenges" (159). Except, my experience in school was very different from what this quote describes. More girls played sports than didn't, from elementary up through high school. Not playing sports made me something of an outcast, in fact. The sports situation wasn't gender-neutral at my school by any means—types of sports were divvied up by gender, with volleyball exclusive to girls and football to boys. While both genders played basketball, each gender had its own team. Yet, "Be aggressive, be, be, aggressive!" was chanted just as often at girls' sporting events as at boys', and both boys' and girls' games were well attended. The girls were told by parents, coaches, and teachers to be more competitive, more dedicated, more determined . . . more like boys, if the quote above is to be believed. But I don't think any of my classmates or their coaches and parents thought what they were doing was telling the girls to be more like boys. They were just telling them to be strong, a trait that crossed gender boundaries in many ways.

See, I grew up with strong women. Mentally and personally strong: they thought what they thought and would say so, sometimes whether or not you actually asked. But I don't just mean strong like that. They were physically strong. My momma used to haul firewood for our wood-burning stove. Because I wanted to be just like her, I "helped" by carrying the littlest twigs from the woodshed. At other times, my helping made more problems. One summer when I was five or six, we got low on water during a drought, so we hauled out the old washing machine in my grandparents' basement (a wringer-warsher, they called it). I watched momma feeding clothes through the wringer, two rolling pin-things that pressed the excess water out so the clothes would dry faster. One morning, momma had an appointment to get her hair cut, and I was helping grandma. When she wasn't looking (though I didn't know she wasn't looking—she would've stopped me if she had been), I fed a sock through the wringer, and it took my fingers with it. Three of them, to be precise. My pointer finger escaped, only to be torn nearly off as the three beside went on through the wringing press. My brother, who was on the other side of the machine, saw my fingers coming through and had the seven-year-old presence of mind to try to push them back out the way they'd come, only to inadvertently hit what he didn't realize was the wringer's release button.

I pulled my hand back and stared. I thought, at the time, that I was seeing my bone—and I damn well knew that was *bad*. (I was later told that what I'd seen was more likely my tendon.) I started to scream.

My grandma was another one of those strong women: capable, resilient, and gracious. She didn't often yell; in fact, the only time I remember her doing it was when she yelled at me now to *stop screaming*. What she also didn't do was drive, though I don't doubt for a minute that if she truly believed there was no recourse, she'd have gotten me in the car and driven me the thirty miles to the hospital, in defiance of the law. Or, quite possibly, stitched me up herself at home. But first, she tried calling my mom. This was before cell phones, of course, but in those days momma did like everyone and went to Fern to get her hair cut just down the road a ways, so grandma knew she'd be within reach of a home phone. She got ahold of her at Fern's and told her she needed to come home, because I'd got my hand caught in the wringer. I don't remember hearing the conversation, but I know grandma had to have been calm because momma had no idea the seriousness of the situation until she got home. She told me later that she'd thought I would just be bruised—she, as a child, had caught her arm in the wringer, too, and some bruising was the worst of it—she would come home, comfort me a bit, then go back and finish getting her hair cut. Instead, she discovered I'd nearly taken my damn finger off. But of all the things I remember of that day, I don't remember her panicking. She knew what to do. We got to the hospital and got me stitched up. Afterward, she cleaned my wound twice a day because I couldn't stand to look at it myself, thinking the stitches looked like spiders' legs sewn onto my hand. And I never helped with the wringer-washer again.

Why am I telling you this? Because I'm shocked at how many of you were so quick to fear the possibility of a woman president. Now I know, you're right about now going, "It wasn't that! She was corrupt! Her emails!" Yeah, I got it. But be honest—we can be honest here—that wasn't all there was to it. If it was, I would have heard more complaints among my neighbors about her politics than I did about her gender. ("She couldn't keep her husband at home, how's she supposed to run the country?" Or, "One good gossip session and she'll spill all our secrets" . . . ironic, given the current administration's relationship with Russia.) Nor, I suspect, if she had been a man would her detractors have made quite so many threats that involved violently shutting her up, through imprisonment or worse (Bordo 2017).

It amazes me how much the people around me made gender and Clinton's "failure" to play her gender role the focus of their dislike. ("If she'd have worried more about her family and less about her politics, we wouldn't have this problem"—the problem being that she seemed likely to win.) She was too vocal, she wouldn't submit to other people's opinions when she disagreed, she worked too hard (Carpentier 2016)—*excuse me, have you met your mothers?* To those who felt this way, I say that unless your experience is vastly different from my own—and of course it may be—then I'm truly ashamed. You of all peoples should have been able to weigh the merits of those candidates without gender getting in the way. What I mean by that is, I didn't think I was the only one that grew up with strong women. In fact, I thought more of us did than not. So why was the backlash against a potential woman president so great here, of all places?

Think about this: *The Hunger Games* showed the world a different perspective on Appalachia, through the character of Katniss Everdeen. Katniss is a woman who is also a damn rock. She hunts, she knows plants, she's not afraid of getting dirty, she fights and is ready to die to protect people (especially her family), she's a strategic thinker, and above all, she ain't looking for love. She isn't emotional; she isn't a romantic. Rather, she seems to think of it as a distraction she simply doesn't need—all these boys falling for her? Fine, but they had better stay out of her way; she's got work to do. In Lana Whited's (2012) review of the book, she points out how truly Katniss is a "heroine of the hills" (328) exactly because of these characteristics. I was even more delighted to read West Virginian Rachel Parson's review: "Katniss Everdeen is everything a girl from Appalachia hopes and has to be . . . Katniss had my attention immediately because I knew her—I was her, and am her" (qtd. in Poe 2015). Journalist

Jim Poe (2015) also pointed out that "Katniss is archetypal for Appalachian women in particular;" he quotes professor Elizabeth Baird Hardy, who added, "They just connect so much to her, because they know her; and if they're not Katniss, then their mamas, their grandmamas or their aunties are." It's true for me, too. Katniss is what I've always been led to believe an Appalachian woman should be.

This is a vision of femininity that, while only recently emerging in mainstream American culture, has deep roots regionally. The Cherokee were badass women: fighting, nurturing, political leadership—they did it all. And the Scotch-Irish immigrants imported some badass women, too, both in person and in legend. For example, there's a story in the Celtic epic *Táin Bó Cuailnge* (The Cattle Raid of Cooley) where a man is bragging on his wife, Macha, saying she is so strong and so fast that she could beat any of the king's horses in a race. His wife, pregnant at the time, begs the king and their onlookers not to make her prove it in her condition and appeals to their sympathy for their mothers. This doesn't work (part of the story's lesson is that these people should have listened, because they come to regret that they didn't). Macha races, wins, births her children (twins) on the field, and pronounces a curse on the onlookers, who fittingly go on to regularly suffer labor pains themselves, a punishment also visited on the next nine generations of their families (Kinsella 1969). Moral: women's voices have power. (And respect your mommas.)

Yet so many of you seemed unwilling to follow Macha's advice, instead supporting candidates who, you've got to admit, are no great respecters of your mommas. Especially if your momma's got a pussy worth grabbing. (Sorry, that was contrary of me. I come from contrary people, you understand.) It seems to me that something is not connecting here. We are looking at these strong women in our lives, yet somehow still accepting an outdated gender narrative—that women are weaker, more corrupt, less capable of leadership—even though many of us have personal experience to the contrary. *We aren't learning from our own stories, you see.* Instead, we're accepting the story that gets told to us by the people who benefit from us believing it: the people who would lose power if more women had it. We're siding with the people who feel entitled to police our identities, and what's worse, we're policing each other's.

So you women who see yourselves in Katniss: tell somebody who's not from here that you wore a camo gown to your high school prom or as a bridesmaid in your sister's wedding. (I know some of you did; I've seen the pictures and been to the stores where you bought those dresses.) Look at their face when you say it. Here's the thing: outside of Appalachia, the vision of femininity you applaud in Katniss and recognize in yourselves and those around you, the idea of women as hunters, as fighters, as strong and earthy in the way Appalachian women are pushed to be—it's just plain queer.

I'm generalizing here for the sake of discussion, and I know there's gonna be people out there just dying to tell me off for it. I'm not trying to simplify and categorize all Appalachian women, just trying to make a point about the cultural dynamics I grew up with, because there's things to be learned from these dynamics that I don't think many of us, including me, fully have yet.

The gendered cultural dynamics I'm describing aren't just about women—they matter for men, for our definition of *manliness*, too. Maybe, for example, you're a man who embraces all things redneck, à la *Duck Dynasty*, the things you know "elites" and city-types just don't get. "Well, I don't care what anybody thinks of me," you might be saying. "I'm gonna be who I am." Isn't it nice to live in a place where who you are is accepted, even applauded? Because around here, calling yourself a redneck, wearing camo, and driving a pick-up truck with a "Make America Great Again" sticker doesn't make you an outsider. Around here, it simply makes you normal. When your identity matches what your community tells you is the norm . . . well, that's called privilege. Do you realize that? From what I'm seeing, it's a privilege too few of you allow for those who are truly different, a privilege you assert every damn time you call someone a queer.

Here I was thinking that in Appalachia, we want to earn our respect, that we don't hold with unearned privilege. But I guess you're fine with it, if it's working in your favor.

See, neither gender roles nor attitudes toward sexuality are set in stone. They're what peoples decide they should be and consequently how they act based on what they're taught to see as normal or expected. In academic terms, it's called social construction. What one society "constructs" as gender-appropriate or sexually sanctioned isn't always the same in others. For example, what many of us here seem to be accepting of as normal feminine behavior—that a woman can ride, hunt, drive trucks, yet also nurture, rock the babies, and even dress up nice—isn't what is appropriately feminine to others. This isn't to say that there is necessarily equality or freedom from gendered behavior expectations for women here; most women would probably also be expected to cook the deer they just shot and skinned. But there is somewhat more availability of activity, a chance for women to do some of the things otherwise considered "masculine" without being slapped down for it. Just the other day, a boy in the grocery store told me how excited his girlfriend was for the upcoming weekend because they was going turkey hunting. Now I know that not all women would see this as a hot date, inside Appalachia or elsewhere. But it strikes me as relevant that it is an option here. Would more women in, say, Manhattan, want to go turkey hunting if that was considered an appropriate feminine pursuit? Maybe. But it's not.

In other words, I always thought the accepted norms of feminine behavior were wider where I grew up than in many other places. I think it's a good thing if they are. Yet this somewhat wider notion of "acceptable" feminine behavior doesn't necessarily extend to respecting women's capabilities as leaders. (A woman wants to play ball, ride a bronco, hunt deer, and drive a tractor? Fine. A woman wants to be president? Lock the bitch up.) That's a cultural problem. But there's another one I want us to think about: any wider allowances for women don't seem to be extended to men. I was talking with a friend of mine, a rural Appalachian woman from Kentucky, about how women could do things that might in other cultures be gendered male and still be accepted; she pointed out that she was equally free to hunt, fish, pick flowers, and read poetry without seeming to be "unwomanly." I asked her if she ever felt men were treated differently, and after a moment, she said, "Yeah, that's true. A man can hunt and fish, but if he wants to read and write poetry, for a lot of people, it's like, 'What the fuck?' " Again, I know we're talking in generalities here. Appalachia has produced some fine male poets, and could produce more if we'd let it. But I'm talking about the things that are likely to get you accepted, or excluded, in the halls of an Appalachian high school or talked about at the local firemen's fair. I don't know many people who would be eager to talk about their sons taking up poetry. This is a bit ironic, since plenty of us would be tickled if our sons played music or told good stories; these are received differently, as less girly. Part of the concern might be about practicality—how do they expect to make a living writing poems?—but gender can't be discounted. Todd Snyder (2014), an Appalachian rhetoric scholar from West Virginia, has explained the typified masculine gender norms for what gets dubbed the Appalachian hillbilly: "He is expected to be a *man*. Expected to work. Work hard. Expected to have a sexual appetite for women. . . . He is expected to protect. He *damn well* better be tough. Emotionless. Emotionless because this is the way things are and the way things are always going to be" (3–4). Like Snyder, I am worried about how too many of us react when someone, male or female, "gets out of line," and I'm particularly worried about those who are reacted upon. It's not enough to say "that's just how things are" because how things are just plain ain't working any more. I don't know that it ever did. So it's time to take a new look at what we can learn from our stories—not just the ones we're told, but the ones we tell ourselves.

On that note, let's talk about Carter Sickels. I don't know Carter personally.

I only know him the way that you know me—because he wrote a piece of himself onto some pages and put those pages out for me to read. And because he told me his stories, I've come to think of my own a little bit differently. I initially connected to his stories about growing up in Appalachian Ohio, told in his essay "Bittersweet: On Transitioning and Finding Home" (2015), because he described going to his grandparents' house as going "down home" (73), which is the exact same way I was brought up to describe my own grandparents' place. To this day, if I tell anyone in the family that I'm going down home, they'll know exactly where to find me. But Carter's experience is far different from mine another way: Carter was assigned female at birth and transitioned to male as an adult. As a girl child, Carter was considered too masculine even among people who typically accept somewhat more "boyish" behavior in girls. He was never allowed to feel comfortable at family and community gatherings, and as a result eventually moved away, something he thought was necessary to be himself. It wasn't until later he started to realize how much of who he was also grew from the place he'd been told he didn't belong.

When I first read Carter's story, I remember feeling enraged on his behalf, specifically because he felt he couldn't stay on the land he loved. The land was part of him, too, but for many years he got the message that being both Appalachian and either gay or trans was impossible. The people who made him feel this way did so by asserting their unearned privilege: they claimed the right to say what was normal about gender, identity, and sexuality and what was not. The idea that someone, anyone, has the right to say who can and cannot be part of this land seems totally anathema to me. In writing this, I've come to deeply suspect that my rage is rooted in both my aversion to unearned privilege but also on the ways Carter's right to his own identity, his individualism, was attacked.

Through his outsider status, Carter later found commonality with those fighting against the environmental degradation caused by the coal industry: "they were already used to being on the outside—they'd been stereotyped as ignorant hillbillies for hundreds of years, and had to fight to be seen and heard and recognized. Now they also had to stand up to people in their own community" (77). Just like Carter, these people were gaining firsthand experience in being "queered" by family, friends, and neighbors who supported the coal industry. Their shared outsider status helped Carter see how they also defied mainstream gender norms: "I spoke with grandmothers turned environmentalists; I followed a long-haired pistol packing woman into the woods; I listened to a tough, country man dressed in camouflage explain that he was worried about his granddaughter getting sick from the water, and as he talked, his eyes dimmed with tears" (76). It's a shared experience that brought Carter in touch with his Appalachian identity in a way he hadn't felt able to be before. From them he learned, "Don't be afraid of who you are; don't back down" (77), even if it's your own people trying to make you. The story of Appalachian diversity is still complicated. Yet it is because Carter is able to tap into the Appalachian value for individuality and the right to individual voice that he comes to re-think and reclaim his geographic identity.

Carter describes feeling both harmony and discord between his Appalachian and queer identities. But by learning to value his right to individuality, he learns to feel at home with himself. It's also how those around him learned to accept his queerness. For example, Carter describes the response he received after coming out to an Appalachian man, who said, "I have absolutely no prob-lem whatsoever with anyone's right to discover who they are and to live ac-cordingly" (79). I find this response fascinating because it is, as I see it, just as typically Appalachian as the prejudice, sexism, and racism that are often perceived in us. Maybe not everyone would accept his queer identity so read-ily if they were aware of it, but Carter demonstrates that others might, if they could be brought to listen to and respect his stories. They didn't need to agree with each other or even have the same experiences; all they needed to do was respect each other's right to be who they were.

So let's talk about individualism. This is a cultural value I've noticed that we in the hills seem to be particularly proud and protective of, one with deep roots. We hear a lot about the Scotch-Irish as an immigrant group into Appalachia; lots of us have Scotch-Irish somewhere in the family tree, but even if we don't, it's hard to live in the region long without feeling something of their cultural influence. Part of this has to do with individualism: being self-sufficient and independent is a deeply held social value, one that has long lived in an uneasy balance with what Warren Hofstra (2012) describes as "the ever-present au-thority of community and the need to live-together" (xvii). In other words, we want to be ourselves and live independently, but we also need to be able to live independently *together*. The result is a complicated culture, the influences of which I don't think we're often consciously aware—especially not if we're among the privileged. And even if we're not, we can find ourselves deeply con-fused about how to define our identities when our communities both enrich us and reject us, as Carter Sickels so beautifully explained.

I'm not asking us to reject our individuality, only to look at how it can expand rather than contract our value for each other's rights. For example, West Virginia's Supreme Court recently ruled that antigay violence does not constitute a hate crime (Stern 2017). It's a verdict that refuses to acknowledge or respect difference. Yet almost concurrently, the city council of Wheeling, West Virginia, unanimously passed a nondiscrimination ordinance to protect LGBTQ+ rights (Berry 2016). Hundreds of people turned out in support of the ordinance, and many who commented on the issue explained their support in individualistic, even religious terms: people have the right to be themselves, and people who oppose LGBTQ+ rights have forgotten that they don't have the right to judge, a right that belongs only to God. In other words, your right to hate does not outdo another person's right to be who they are. This certainly doesn't constitute an embrace of difference (which, personally, is what I'd like to see), but if simply recognizing and valuing people's right to be themselves is where we can start, then by God, let's *get started*.

What I'm asking us to do is to reconsider our rhetoric and what it allows. I spend a lot of my time thinking and teaching about Appalachian rhetoric— which means that I think about how people learn to value things and how they communicate those values to others. By definition, I think a lot about the values I absorbed growing up Appalachian. For example, I learned that place matters. I learned that where we come from is a big part of who we are, even if we don't directly define ourselves as "Appalachian." I see it in how families stay on the same lands for generations and how they demonstrate their knowledge about those lands in words and actions. I read about it in Appalachian-authored books. I hear about it in the stories told by Appalachian storytellers. I feel it in the music, the dance, the crafts—every old way of thinking or doing things that people hold on to and pass down, even when there is no current, practical benefit in doing so. So imagine my surprise when so many of my fellow Appalachians voted to elect men who want to flatten our mountains and poison our air and water . . . in fact, men who are doing this already. Was I wrong? Do you not care about this land? About the generations before you who lived and bled and loved and died here? Or do you care about them so much that you're ready to speed up the process: to die too, you and the land itself, for us all to go together?

What I mean to say is, I once thought place loyalty was one of the things that made us a culture; that enough of us as individuals shared this value, that it formed a messy cultural conglomeration wherein I could hang part of my definition of what being "Appalachian" even means. But like I said, I'm rethinking lots of things. I still believe many of you feel some kind of place loyalty; I see too much of it to believe I was mistaken. But I'm far less sure that many of you want to be a culture, to be different or distinct from the mainstream. For all the talk I hear about you being proud rednecks, you sure were quick to want to join up with the elite. In a postelection interview, Tennessean Trae Crowder

(2016) said: "If you would've polled rednecks three years ago and asked 'What do you think of Donald Trump?' I promise you the consensus would've been 'He's a smug, full of shit Yankee who thinks he's better than everybody else and needs his ass whipped, goddamnit.'" What changed?

Here's what it looks like to me. When a rich, white, entitled, East Coast, urban elite, who thinks he's better than everybody else, told you that he was one of you, you decided that must mean you're better than everybody else, too. Maybe you have been all this time. When he told you all the problems you had were because of people who looked different and sounded different and worshiped different and loved different . . . you so desperately wanted to believe it was true. Underneath that facade of redneck pride you wanted, all along, to be part of the rich urban white boys' club you've been seeming to reject, and he made you believe that you could be. All this time, you've been scared that when that rich white man looks at you, all he'll see is another queer. Maybe if you supported him, you could prove to him that you weren't so queer, after all.

I'm going to be brutally honest here. (You like that, right? When someone tells it like it is?) I think your vote was about fear. Fear of people who are different, but most of all fear of being different yourselves. You wanted to be just like all those elites you've spent all this time talking down. It's funny, all my life you've been telling me that you'uns ain't scared of nothing. All my life I felt ashamed of my fears, because I thought we were different, that showing fear wasn't *who we were*. Like a fool, I believed you. You probably even believed yourselves. And we were all wrong.

The reality is that in a democracy, we can only be individual to a certain degree. Because when you cast a vote, you're not making a decision that affects only you. When your insecurity affects the decisions you make, it's a problem for all of us. Think about the impulse I mentioned at the beginning, the compulsion (that I know damn well some of you feel) to assert yourselves by embracing the stereotype and being as redneck as you can. It's an impulse I understand, and it's one I've felt, too. If asked, you'd probably say it has something to do with individuality—letting yourself be whoever the hell you are, elitist bullshit about propriety be damned. Got it. But what do you think happens to the gender-queer kid in high school who decides fuck your redneck gender standards, he/she/they are going to be whoever the hell he/she/they are. Or the trans kid who knows from experience that the bodies people are born in aren't necessarily the same thing as who they are, the kid who just wants, needs, to be who they are. What do you think happens, then? Maybe you know. Or maybe you don't because the queer kids and the trans kids in your school—and they are there—know not to even try, because internal misery might be slightly better than the alternatives of being out in a rural high school. What I'm trying to say is that the queer kid who wants to be himself/herself/themself is probably feeling the same damn way you do when you decide the hell with whatever the world thinks, you're going to paint your pickup truck camo and fly a Confederate flag (even though you quite possibly live in a Union state). Except, crucially, around here it's ok to go all camo and Confederacy, especially for men. It makes you a man, don't it? A real don't-give-a-shit redneck. It doesn't make you a target. (Any idea what real courage is? Try being the person whose identity makes them a target.) You just don't talk about all that camo for what it is: your drag, your "attempts to compel belief in others" (Richardson 2008) that you are what you're purporting to be . . . in this case, what the people around you agree is a "real man." Not such an individual after all.

I speak about these things as someone who is not, from an Appalachian perspective, a "real woman." Let me tell you something about myself. I'm a female in my thirties. I don't have kids, though I do the best I can to nurture any children whose lives come within my orbit. I'm not married. Never have been. I've never even dated. I'm what you might call nonsexual. Most days, I'm okay with how I am. Most days, it seems like my culture isn't.

We go out to see my great-aunt Nova pretty often, who at ninety is the family matriarch. It's not uncommon that people come in and out while we're there, cousins and cousin-of-cousins and their kids and other distant relations whose kinship to me I'm aware of but couldn't actually articulate. I've gotten to where I like to be doing something with my hands while we sit and visit, so I've taken to crocheting while we're there. I remember one time, I was working on a baby blanket for a friend's upcoming delivery. Of course, it's impossible to sit and crochet without being asked by all and sundry what I'm working on. When I told them, one relative after another asked, "When you gonna start making blankets for some kids of your own?" It's not the first time I've gotten a similar question from family and neighbors, and I seriously doubt it'll be the last. I get asked it at festivals and reunions, often from people who actually know the answer . . . but still make a point of asking. I remember when my cousin's daughter, around eight at the time, assured me that *she* would be married by the time she got to my age. I told my students about that once. They knew I wasn't married, and when I told them what Emmy had said, there was a collective gasp and chorus of "oooh." They knew that although she hadn't meant to be cruel, what she had said was something insulting. To a normal woman, anyway.

So, from an Appalachian perspective, I'm queer. Being a nonsexual, unmarried, and childless woman is queer. I recognize that I'm privileged in my queerness: mine is the kind of queer that results in awkward (and occasionally mean-spirited) conversations and not (so far) violence. Yet I also know that in some contexts, who I am can be, and has been, used to silence me. ("Who cares what she thinks? If she was worth any account, someone would've married her by now.") For others who transcend what we've decided are boundaries of gender and sexuality, the penalties can be much harsher. Regardless, up to now I haven't made my own queer status a thing. I haven't chosen to talk much, particularly with my students, about the fact that my culture considers me abnormal, even when we discuss issues of gender and sexuality. As with many things, I'm rethinking this.

I'm thinking more and more about our need to share our stories, because I still believe that stories matter. But it's not enough just to tell our stories; we need to be able to listen to other people's. Carter was able to find acceptance among others and within himself because he was finally able to share his stories with others who were willing to listen. I remember debating with a man who made homophobic and racist remarks, yet refused to see those remarks as important or potentially damaging to others. "I know I'm a good man," he said. "It doesn't matter to me what you say." Because he fit our culture's norm, because it told him that what he was—straight, white, Christian (at least in name), and a self-proclaimed redneck—was *good*, he assumed the right to judge others and not listen to their differing perspectives. He didn't need to critically examine himself. And he could probably get by believing that, especially if he never moved from the community he was born in. He might never understand what an embarrassment he is to me or much of the rest of the country, especially now that he has a president he's convinced himself he identifies with. Listen: you can be as redneck as you want. I'm not trying to say you shouldn't be. I'm just saying that you've got no right to judge who else is queer or not (or more particularly, whether being queer is a bad thing) based on your own identity. Because if anything, despite what you've been led to believe, in the rest of the world being a redneck by definition makes you as queer as anyone can be.

Maybe I'm being unfair to you. Maybe I'm wrong about your motivations, or maybe I'm being too harsh. I've been so angry since the 2016 election and the hate crimes that erupted in its wake, some of them very near where I live. I'm worried that I'm starting to dehumanize you, which is pretty much what I fear you've been doing to those you consider "other." I don't want to do that. Stories are the best ways I know to make people real, to make them human. So tell me yours. What does the world look like from where you stand? I can't promise I'll agree with you at the end of it, any more than you could promise to be swayed by me. I can't promise that if I see you making decisions based on prejudice or untruths, I won't say so. All I can say is that I'm willing to try my best to see things from your perspective before I make up my mind, because that's exactly what I want you to do for me. I promise to try to remember that we're all human and deserve respect, because that's exactly what I want you to do, too.

I also want you to tell your stories for your own sake. Beyond the listeners, stories matter for the people who tell them. I'm getting a good bit off my chest here that I didn't even know I carried around before writing it. I'm seeing how I'm just as capable of dehumanizing as anyone. We all need to do better. So if there are any teachers reading this, especially Appalachian ones, I'm begging you, get those kids to telling their own stories and writing their own letters. Teach them to listen to each other's stories. When too many people seem to be telling the same stories, find ones that are very different and ask your students to listen to those. Ask them to think about, tell, and read stories about what they are led to believe is normal and what isn't. Ask them to find as many "normals" in their lives and communities as they can. Then ask them to find the ways they don't fit. Don't let them assume that not fitting in is a bad thing. Ask them to think critically about ways that not fitting can be good, that can make them *individuals*.

This might sound easy, but it ain't gonna be. There's another Appalachian cultural pressure I recognize about privacy, isolation, toward "not airing the dirty laundry." And too often difference—queerness—gets folded in with the dirty laundry. It will take time, care, and lots of voices before our kids start to understand that it doesn't have to be this way. But it's an understanding we need to move toward if we want to survive in the world, because our decisions don't affect us alone. It's not enough to be satisfied with the status quo, with things being "just how they are." Not if we want our children to have a chance to grow up whole and free.

I suppose what I had hoped back around election time was that when the chips were down, Appalachian peoples would use their own experience of cultural and identity queerness, by which I mean we'd recognize the ways that we get stigmatized, too, and unite with the oppressed rather than joining in with the oppressors. That was a naive hope, I know. Difference has long been used successfully to prevent that exact scenario. For example, since the conceptualization of race as a factor in early American society, the poorest whites have consistently fought against rather than joining forces with the poor or marginalized of other races. White Appalachians, as a whole, did exactly that in November 2016. It shows that despite what you might tell yourselves, you're just as weak and persuadable as anyone, ready to kick other people under the bus when led to believe you're somehow better or more deserving than they are. I had hoped that we as a whole had gotten enough education and experience to see something of the ways our identities can be used to play us, to keep us and other people at each other's throats and help the people in power stay in power. We haven't. Maybe I overestimated our recognition of just how queer we are in the wider world. I don't think it's a coincidence that the people who showed the most commonality and understanding with Carter are the ones who have, because of their pro-environment, prohealth, anti–coal industry stance, been forced to become outsiders—queers—in their own communities. To a degree, they must have known how this felt before; as Carter points out, many Appalachians encounter negative perceptions about their homes and cultures in the mainstream United States. I think, though, this understanding of our "otherness" can feel distant to those of us who stay within the region, particularly if our local communities are fairly homogeneous and particularly if we fit the norms of those communities anyway. The people Carter describes had otherness forced on them in a far more immediate way. Just as he had. But it seems that more Appalachians than not chose to side with the 1 percent, the mainstream status quo, and to reject their own queerness. To that I say, you might try to forget your queerness. *But the people you're siding with won't.*

Maybe you'll come across this letter in a classroom someday. Maybe you'll find my voice angry and off-putting. (Would you, though, if a man wrote it? Think about that.) Or maybe you'll never read this. But sometimes, some things just feel like they need saying, whether or not anyone listens. Sometimes, we can only put our best intentions forward and hope.

So here's my proposal. Embrace the queer. And I don't just mean the people that you decide are queer. I mean embrace the queerness in all of us. Look for it in your own life, celebrate it in others. When every one of us tells our stories, it's easy to see that there's queerness right below the surface. No two people are the same, no two lives are the same, and there is no normal. We need to accept this, because, my fellow Appalachians, the reality is this: we're here, we're all a little queer, and we most of us ain't a-goin' nowhere. Get used to it. Or better yet, realize that it's who you are, too. And realize that we can be different, can embrace difference, and still be, truly, stronger together.

Give my love to the family,

Amanda

BIBLIOGRAPHY

"The Appalachian Region." n.d. *Appalachian Regional Commission*. https://www.arc.gov /appalachian_region/TheAppalachianRegion.asp. Accessed August 10, 2014.

Berry, Alec. 2016, November 30. "Wheeling Residents Turn Out to Voice Support for LGBT Ordinance." *Intelligencer/Wheeling News-Register*. http://www .theintelligencer.net/news/top-headlines/2016/11/wheeling-residents-turn-out-to -voice-support-for-lgbt-ordinance/.

Bordo, Susan. 2016, July 20. "How to Try a Witch in the 21st Century." *Huffington Post*. http://www.huffingtonpost.com/susan-bordo-/how-to-try-a-witch-in-the_b _11074178.html. Accessed March 14, 2017.

Carpentier, Megan. 2016, October 18. "Why Do People Dislike Hillary Clinton? The Story Goes Far Back." *The Guardian*. https://www.theguardian.com/us-news/2016 /oct/18/hillary-clinton-why-hate-unlikeable-us-election. Accessed March 14, 2017.

Dixon, Elise. 2017, May 11. "Teaching Queerly: Beginning from Desire and Non-Normativity." *Inside Teaching MSU*. http://insideteaching.grad.msu.edu/teaching -queerly-beginning-from-desire-and-non-normativity/. Accessed May 12, 2017.

Hofstra, Warren R. 2012. Introduction. In *Ulster to America: The Scots-Irish Migration Experience, 1680–1830*, edited by Warren R. Hofstra, xi–xxvii. Knoxville: University of Tennessee Press.

Kinsella, Thomas, trans. 1969. *The Táin*. Oxford: Oxford University Press.

Poe, Jim. 2015, November 15. "A Look at Appalachian Culture and History in *The Hunger Games*." *Times West Virginian*. http://www.timeswv.com/news/a-look-at -appalachian-culture-and-history-in-the-hunger/article_2a9f14a6-8b7c-11e5-ad77 -1fe4f69156e0.html. Accessed November 17, 2015.

Richardson, Diane. 2008. "Conceptualizing Gender." In *Introducing Gender and Women's Studies*, edited by Diane Richardson and Victoria Robinson, 3–19. New York: Palgrave Macmillan.

Roper, Emily A., and Katherine M. Polasek. 2014. "Gender, Sport and Popular Culture." In *Gender and Pop Culture*, edited by Adrienne Trier-Bieniek and Patricia Leavy, 151–74. Rotterdam: Sense Publishers.

Sickels, Carter. 2015. "Bittersweet: On Transitioning and Finding Home." In *Walk Till the Dogs Get Mean: Meditations on the Forbidden from Contemporary Appalachia*, edited by Adrian Blevins and Karen Salyer McElmurray, 73–79. Athens: Ohio University Press.

Snyder, Todd. 2014. *The Rhetoric of Appalachian Identity*. Jefferson, NC: McFarland.

Stern, Mark Joseph. 2017, May 10. "West Virginia Supreme Court Rules Anti-Gay Assaults Are Not Hate Crimes." *Slate*. http://www.slate.com/blogs/outward /2017/05/10/west_virginia_supreme_court_rules_anti_gay_assaults_are_not _hate_crimes.html. Accessed May 10, 2017.

"Trae Crowder on How Rednecks Were Taken in by a Carpetbagger like Trump." 2015, November 16. *Youtube*. https://www.youtube.com/watch?v=6DvNzdj529M. Accessed May 10, 2017.

Whited, Lana. 2012. "Review: The Hunger Games." *Journal of Appalachian Studies* 18, no. 1, 326–31.

CHAPTER 2

Challenging Dominant Christianity's Queerphobic Rhetoric

Justin Ray Dutton

The identities of "Appalachian" and "Christian" often ring as synonymous in many popular imaginings within and beyond the region. Although such a generality performs a great disservice to the (a)religious and (a)spiritual diversity of central and rural Appalachia, it also paints an accurate portrait of how a certain dominant form of Christianity exerts power and influence over the region. This dominance is not limited to the church grounds; the faith exerts holds of varying forces on Appalachian cultures at large. Although many aspects of the religion positively complement values traditionally associated with Appalachia and its people, its life-denying and life-destroying effects include a pervasive queerphobia that panoptically enforces toxic rhetoric and realities.

Although much evidence exists (and I argue) that queerphobia traces its roots to civil and additional extraecclesiastical foundations, praxis connects it with Christianity, perhaps especially in regions such as central and rural Appalachia where few differences divide religion and civic life. For this reason, I structure my explanation of and challenge to queerphobic rhetoric in this region through the framework of Christianity, naming the experienced reality as Appalachian Christian queerphobic rhetoric (ACQR).

This does not indicate that Christianity (or even hegemonic Christianity) and queerphobia share a fundamental connection. Indeed, as I present, the opposite holds true. Neither does it indicate that Appalachia is a Christian region any more than the United States is a Christian nation (regardless of what the voices who claim power try to tell us). I name the pervasive queerphobia of the region as "Christian" for two reasons. First, it reflects the reality of the praxical interconnectedness of the dominant Christian theology of central and rural Appalachia that all people must recognize and challenge. Second, by calling out this praxis and juxtaposing it with the fundamentally loving spirit of the person who inspired the founding of the faith, queer and ally people and groups sympathetic to Christianity can use the religion's power and structures to work against the queerphobia it currently creates and enforces. Christianity, along with values traditionally associated with Appalachia, has the ability to encourage and sustain all people in and of the region in a movement toward deep love and acceptance of queer folk.

I name deep love and acceptance as a goal with the understanding that these words take on different meanings for different people. My use of the phrase calls on us all to ask messy and complicated questions from and within a space of love. It depends on the willingness of all engaged parties to actively work, speak, and write in ways that mitigate power differentials so that mutual conversation can take place. In deep love and acceptance, cisgender and heterosexual folk take the time to continually learn about queer experiences and queer individuals and then act in ways that align with the knowledge gained while becoming educators and bridges for those joining in the journey—every word and action expressed without silencing queer voices and the actions guiding them. In short, deep love and acceptance of queer folk by those who currently use and further ACQR necessitates that members of the latter group (trans, queer, cisgender, heterosexual, and people of countless additional identities alike) make antijudgmental love of *every* person an everyday, instinctual reality of word and deed. For those who positively associate with the "C" in ACQR, deep love and acceptance also mirror the ways Jesus expansively cared for all he encountered as he challenged the comfortable religious and political status quos of his time.

The "R" in ACQR brings to light the power of storytelling. Every person around the world tells stories. Sometimes this takes place through spoken or, as demonstrated through this collection, written words; most often it results through a variety of personal and social cues and interactions. Very few (if any) stories exercise neutral power. Many stories give life, but a similar number deny or destroy life, too often in a literal sense. Stories regarding queer folk and queer identities told by forms of Christianity that hold an understanding of the Bible as it has been interpreted by queerphobic white men and their institutions over the past two thousand years too often belong to this second category, with a major effect taking the form of "don't ask, don't tell" when it comes to queer identities in central and rural Appalachia.

Defying this culturally mandated closeting requires committing to difficult journeys. Part of the reason for this rests in the fact that neither Appalachia nor Christianity have a unique claim to queerphobia. Despite this, ACQR poses far-reaching life-limiting difficulties for mountain natives, citizens, and visitors. Perhaps the most discernible of these realities falls in the category of forced choices, such as the consideration of remaining silent or acting and speaking out at significant personal and communal risk and the consideration of staying or leaving. Of course, as "man"-made categories, the binaries I call forced choices represent false simplifications; additional options are always present, especially when one considers the specifics of any particular circumstance. In this climate, however, more options rarely (if ever) alleviate the toxicity regularly encountered by queer people living in a region dominated by ACQR.

The ineffably widespread reality of ACQR's effects grows in proportion to its pervasive reach. As a regional rhetoric that matches national and international trends and realities, ACQR does not experience pushback from large portions of society. Quite the opposite. Throughout central and rural Appalachia and beyond, it remains acceptable (and often celebrated) to tell stories that denigrate and destroy queer realities and well-being. Rhetoric, the kinds of stories told, constitutes more than words on a page or ephemeral words spoken to general audiences. ACQR exercises real and traceable life-denying and life-destroying consequences for queer folks. Its effects do not stop with our lives. They infect the far reaches of society. For the purposes of a single essay, however, I focus the following discussion on how all people can address and challenge the often religiously justified hate queer individuals live with and under. The longer the incredibly real effects of ACQR remain below the surface of cis/het everyday consciousness, the longer queer bodies remain unspeakable others.

Two major effects of living in identities deemed unspeakable by mainstream society include alienation and displacement. Growing up in central Appalachia, I experienced these realities long before I discovered the words to describe them. I identify null curriculum as a key reason I did not discover the extent of my queerness until after I moved away from my home of origin. Although I continue to find unparalleled freedom in living as my full queer self beyond the generally accepted borders of Appalachia, I cannot and do not want to simply set my identity as Appalachian aside; the mountains call me home. I acted on this in 2017 when, after three years away, I moved back to my hometown to more actively help my family care for my grandfather. Seventeen months later, at the time of this writing, I am piecing together part-time and temporary jobs while searching for a permanent position that will allow me to settle in a city where I find refuge among embracing and loving friends, queer and straight alike.

After my grandfather passed away, I remained and worked in my homeland for over a year, intentionally friendless for fear of the repercussions from the discovery of my queer self, before the opportunity to move manifested. My journey back to the small city I now call home finds its foundation in my human need to know and be known. Respect for my not-yet-affirming mother and concern for my physical, mental, and emotional safety continues to keep me from deeply engaging as my full self with people in my hometown and surrounding areas. All the while, respect for my story and emotional/mental well-being along with respect for my fellow queer people keeps me from hiding in a life that is not my own.

To relate my story directly to ACQR, I am a proud central Appalachian (currently living on the borders of home), quick to challenge stereotypes. This is despite the fact that when I first shared my Appalachian self-naming with my mom she warned me to not tell anyone because "they'll think you're a hillbilly." (I have since converted her to a place of Appalachian pride, at least concerning my sense of self.)

I am not, however, a proud Christian. I am actually not any sort of Christian, unless you add "past" to the noun. I was raised a proud and extremely devout central Appalachian United Methodist. I began considering theodicy (the problem of the very discernible and multifaceted reality of evil in a world created and sustained by an all-loving, all-knowing, all-powerful God) as soon as the analytical thinking aspect of my brain developed. In short, I had a problem with Hell. Although I grasped countless straws from the bale of Christianity in an attempt to find meaning in the faith of my childhood, I have since come to peace as a pantheist agnostic: experiencing divinity in all that exists while actively admitting that I could be wrong.

I also know myself as a prophet, a person who calls individuals and groups to renew their beliefs (especially those inherited from traditions of origin) by recognizing the doubt their certainty often veils. In my academic studies and personal understandings, a prophet is a teacher who meets students—and everyone they encounter—where they are, as they are, and challenges them through continuing engagement to do more and be more to work toward established and evolving goals for common goods. Although the word understandably denotes a religious connotation, I continue to self-name as a prophet in tribute to my background and as a queering challenge to what people (particularly Christians) think they know.

Somewhere between the poles of proud and nonidentity, I am also queer. I prefer this word for the opportunities it offers as part of a communal reclamation of selfhood and as an ambiguous identity marker that tends to resist single easy definitions and assumptions. I do not actively hide my queerness—I will readily claim it if asked in most circumstances—but neither do I lead with it.

Nevertheless, coming out remains a frequent topic in my life story. While I am grateful for the countless positive interactions I experience when sharing my full self, I have shed many tears and lived in many days and months of anxiety with physical, emotional, and mental dis-ease caused by circumstances that ignore, do not celebrate, or actively speak and act against core components of my self. Although I count myself lucky to have a mother and sister who will never abandon, disown, or cease to love me, they also inherited and live in a worldview where queerness is morally wrong and theologically sinful. When I shared with them who I am, we began a long and difficult journey toward becoming whole in full love with total acceptance, a journey that, by all indications and hopes, will continue in love for many years before any actual acceptance comes about.

This provides a snapshot of the reality from which I write. I am a white, Appalachian, non-Christian, queer person surrounded by and sometimes inundated with ACQR. As a student of Christian theologies, I see people doing great works of justice, reconciliation, and compassion in Christ's name. As a queer person from the mountains, I see people following the same savior doing great mental, physical, and emotional damage to people of queer experiences. This must change.

Thus, establishing ACQR as an adequate naming of the ultimately ineffable realities faced by queer mountain folk and describing my own situation in this climate sets the foundation for my proposal: a path toward a new worldview where deep love and acceptance supersedes currently queerphobic Appalachians' words and deeds. This journey involves further exploring some of the effects of ACQR on many central and rural Appalachian queer folk, providing evidence that queerphobia emanates from worldly constructions appropriated and furthered by Christian people rather than from their God's wishes and commands, and sharing a call to action for all Appalachians to listen to queer stories and take common pride in our place to challenge the ACQR that too many people and groups consciously and unconsciously support.

Experiences of Many Queer Folk Who Live with ACQR

Stories have incalculable power, largely because words, actions, personal and cultural traditions, and countless additional manners of relaying stories are never once-and-done. Even when a story moves out of explicit circulation, its effects continue to ripple through humans and our institutions. Stories that lurk below the surface of everyday consciousness pose many threats, as do stories that continue to explicitly circulate. ACQR festers in both realms.

Even beyond the explicit queerphobia too often expressed from Christian pulpits and advertised with picket signs, the nature of dominant Appalachian Christian queerphobia as a hegemonic force reaching beyond the walls of churches and Christian homes and effectually saturating virtually all public, private, and other institutions makes ACQR a life-denying and life-destroying reality for queer folk of the region. This queerphobia does not stop at the doors of even the most secular Appalachian institutions. School systems, colleges, universities, corporations, and additional establishments—including those that advertise and achieve, to varying degrees, queer affirmation, celebration, and empowerment—are not immune from ACQR. From students to colleagues, from boards to donors, from antiquated or ignored policies to the latest technological information systems and beyond, ACQR enjoys and takes advantage of countless points of entry.

In short, throughout the region (mirroring the reality of the United States at large), the persons and experiences of straight and cisgender people define normalcy to the extent that anyone who does not fit into these narrow understandings of sexuality and gender face multiple manifestations of discrimination and hate. Although these manifestations take on infinite forms for individual queer persons and our communities depending on the specific circumstances of any given time, certain patterns can be traced. Alienation and displacement provide broad categories through which I review some of the effects of ACQR on Appalachian queer folk.

Queerphobic-based discrimination takes the form of alienation in my life whenever I am in situations where I do not share my full self with others because of fear for my emotional, mental, or physical safety. These situations encompass the vast majority of the time I spend in my hometown. To avoid this alienation, I, for the foreseeable future, choose displacement. I moved away from the region that continues to live in me so I can engage on more equitable ground with peers, colleagues, acquaintances, and strangers.

But not all queer Appalachians have the desire or privilege to make this or similar choices. For many reasons, a lot of queer Appalachians stay—too often at the price of their social, emotional, mental, and physical well-being. Here I am considering queer people who live in various locations in relation to the closets that cisgender/heteronormative society forces us to experience. While queer Appalachian folk who have the desire, luck, and ability to find themselves in or create circumstances of living honest and authentic lives face countless instances of life-denying and life-destroying explicit and implicit queerphobic rhetoric, I focus the following discussion on those who, like myself, experience

ACQR as a forced alienation. Regardless of the specific manifestations of the alienation, it exercises common effects on us.

The difficulty of spending one's life metaphorically relegated to a space comparable to a structure constructed to hold clothing and other nonliving knickknacks cannot be overstated. It represents a toxic state of being. Living in the toxic closet requires remaining silent regarding a major aspect of one's selfhood. One author's words (written in the introduction to the story of a mother lamenting the suicide of her gay son) demonstrate this point: "The distance from silence to suicide is not so great" (Miller 1992, 80; Williams 1992, 272). Research substantiates this assertion. A group of four scholars from different universities, for example, found that participants "who recalled, were preoccupied with, or suppressed an important secret [such as hiding their sexual orientation] estimated hills to be steeper, perceived distances to be farther, indicated that physical tasks would require more effort, and were less likely to help others with physical tasks" (Slepian et al. 2012, 619). Yet family, close friends, and other loved ones often encourage or even mandate silence to the detriment of queer individuals. In practice, it often means remaining single throughout one's life or marrying someone with whom the closeted individual shares no romantic and/or sexual feelings—an action that most often has detrimental consequences for all involved.

Silencing individuals and groups does not constitute the only way ACQR uses the tool of silence against us. Null curriculum not only discourages story sharing (and thus serves as a leading cause of queer folk reflecting on their lives before hearing of or meeting other queer people expressing "I thought I was the only one"), it also has the effect of establishing that which is not talked about as something even worse than that which can be discussed (even disparagingly) in polite company. All of this works together, along with many additional factors, to create a toxic environment that offers little solace for queer Appalachian folk seeking to move away from toxic closets.

Although using terms such as *alienation* and *displacement* to describe the effects of ACQR might imply that they tend to manifest in ways that affect only emotional and mental well-being, ACQR reaches far beyond these realms. The number of queer youth without stable and safe shelter serves as just one example of this reality: 20–40 percent of youth experiencing homelessness identify as queer, many in that situation because of their nonaffirming families of origin (Haas et al. 2010, 22). Furthermore, religiously based "discrimination, harassment, violence, and sexual assault [precipitate] negative mental health outcomes" for queer folk (Carmel and Erickson-Schroth 2016, 346; Haas et al.

2010, 22–23, 27; Barton 2011, 76). Conversely, when queer people experience familial and other support—including the recognition of the validity of their identities and orientations—mental health and safe housing improves across the board (Rust 2000, 449; Haas et al. 2010, 26; Carmel and Erickson-Schroth 2016, 346, 348).

Individual support alone will not bring about long-lasting and meaningful change for the betterment of queer people. When preachers routinely state "that gay people are an abomination, sinners, unnatural and that sodomites were struck down by a wrathful and vengeful god" (Barton 2011, 85) and when these same preachers and their unquestioning flocks hold public office and additional positions of civic power, institutional discrimination becomes and remains the norm. Under institutional discrimination, laws and policies, mental and physical health inequities, instances of bullying and hate crimes, and more challenges join forces to further enforce the ACQR that creates this reality in the first place. All of this contributes to a culture where, as one queer individual put it,

> Sometimes when I see these religious bumper stickers, I feel the way I think a Jew might feel, seeing a swastika displayed on somebody's car. There goes somebody who thinks that I'm less than a full human being, that I can be deprived of my rights. Now granted, these people are not going around collecting us up and putting us in concentration camps and sentencing us to death by hundreds of thousands, but still, these are people who think we are less human, that we have less in the way of rights than they have. Because of that they are a danger in a great number of ways and we are harmed by that. And it's not just symbolic harm, we are truly materially harmed. (Barton 2011, 82)

This must change. All Appalachian people—especially those who identify as Christian—must work to challenge ACQR. (For us non-Christians, plenty more AQR needs challenging and dismantlement.) Queer folk must not, cannot, and should not experience the brunt of the burden of challenging ACQR. Allies (at all levels of tolerance, acceptance, celebration, and empowerment) have much work to do. Even though the focus of this continual striving is the betterment of life and circumstances for queer Appalachians, we will not be the only group benefiting from the suppression of rhetoric that pollutes the air we share.

Mountain folk who find belonging with the (often unconsciously under-stood) labels of cisgender and heterosexual might feel that the stories of their queer peers have little to no influence on their lives. But the rhetoric used, the stories told, by individuals and collectives have importance for all people within a place. Although straight and cisgender Appalachians will never feel the effects of ACQR to the extent that queer and perceived-queer people experience, we are all connected through a variety of commonalities. Given the negative effects of ACQR, cisgender and straight mountain people must pay attention to the way they approach their queer siblings and the language they use toward and about us to move from a life-denying situation of ACQR to a life-giving Appalachian Christian queer-affirming rhetoric.

Although the focus of my argument centers on changing dominant Christian rhetoric, all queer-affirming Appalachian folks can (and must) join in the conversations and actions. Directly challenging dominant Christian beliefs, practices, and institutions is important, but that does not embody all that must take place. ACQR expands far beyond the walls of Christian homes and churches and poisons the mountain air to the point that toxic closets often become and remain preferable over the toxic air.

Specifically, Appalachian people must recognize and challenge ACQR in public and civic life, false and misleading statistics and claims, health care and management inequities, judgments of appropriate conversation topics, and overall attitudes of normalcy. As long as the loudest public voices and the institutions they create and support routinely exercise the power to shun individuals and families who affirm queer identities, the air remains toxic. As long as harmful (and ineffective!) attempts are made to "cure" queer people of attractions and/or genders that do not conform to established norms, the air remains toxic. As long as queer mountain people do not have the right to access adept and affirming mental and physical health care, the air remains toxic. As long as heterosexual and cisgender persons are denied the opportunity to continually engage with their queer neighbors as their full, out selves, the air remains toxic. As long as queer mountain folk know all too well the sentiment expressed by one lesbian woman: "you think about killing yourself cause you're so strange" (Black and Rhorer 2001, 18), the air remains toxic.

Changing Rhetoric: Acceptable or Heretical?

Since the crux of my argument explicitly recognizes the role of currently dominant Christianity in creating and sustaining the queerphobic rhetoric that permeates central and rural Appalachia, I would write irresponsibly if I did not establish Christian precedents for challenging and changing doctrine and dogma within the faith. Indeed, changes such as the one called for in this essay have continually taken place throughout Christian (and human) history.

To put challenges to Appalachian *Christian* queerphobic rhetoric into context, audiences must understand that queerphobia and the Christian way do not share an inextricable foundation. Many forms of Christian religion inarguably perpetuate queerphobia—including the dominant form of the faith in Appalachia—and thus many people in the United States justifiably blame Christianity for the queerphobia that plagues society. Yet at the foundation, this approach is misguided. In truth, the queerphobia encountered in contemporary churches results more from modern social and cultural developments than intense theological, ecclesiastical, and exegetical (the process of deeply reading and studying the Bible) reflection. Queerphobia actually has nothing to do with the Gospel of Christ.

Perhaps the most telling evidence for the fact that Christian faiths do not ontologically damn queer people rests in the reality that not all Christians, not even all evangelical Christians, condemn queerness. Even more, not only does Christianity *not* require its adherents to know queer people as sinners (or as people who [regularly] engage in sinful practices), it *does* require an association with the person and actions of Jesus, a first-century Jewish man who treated all persons, particularly those on the margins of societal norms, without judgment and with benevolence.

Although numerous stories from the four canonical Gospels come together to form this understanding of the Christian savior, accounts such as John's narrative of the Samaritan woman at Jacob's well (John 4), Matthew and Mark's telling of Jesus "eating with the sinners and tax collectors" (Mark 2:16, see also Matthew 9), and John's report of Jesus preventing the stoning of a woman caught in the first-century understanding of adultery (John 8) provide a few examples of the countless canonical indications that the person known as God incarnate loved *all* folks and spurned human judgments of others. When followers of Jesus do not follow his way of nonjudgment and compassion, they fail in the Christian call to make God's love available to all.

Teachings that do not align with this biblical portrait of Jesus might have a long tradition in Christian history, but they are not inherent to the Way. Rather, when faced with queerness—a reality that did not match the cultural and perhaps individual experience of many white European men leading medieval churches—ecclesiastical leaders took the materials and knowledge they had at hand to form a condemnation of that which was different from their own experiences. Even the language employed by Christians for the past two hundred years to describe queer persons (sodomite, invert, homosexual, etc.) originated with political and clinical considerations—considerations that nonetheless used biblical allusions—rather than those of deep-seated theological, ecclesiastical, and exegetical reflections on living in relationship with the Christian God. In other words, the tension between Christian and queer identities espoused by the dominant form of contemporary Appalachian Christianity has a foundation not in an (impossible) a priori reading of the Bible but in the ever-unfolding and refolding narrative known as church history—a history that takes place in conversation and relation with the history of innumerable political, cultural, and other constructed, demographically organized human groupings. Christian and church history requires Christians to continually review and reform so as to live the way of Jesus rather than the way of the world.

Thus, affirming queer folk does not require Christians to set aside their faith identity, pick and choose from the teachings of the Bible, or completely reject their churches' traditions. To the contrary, affirming all people in their individual identities, including gender experiences and sexual attractions, is at the core of the Christian message conveyed through the Bible and upheld by many churches. Although Scripture does indeed contain verses that in recent centuries have been interpreted against "homosexuality," the Christian sacred text includes no reference to the queer life as it is experienced and understood today. (This does not deny the reality of queer individuals and experiences two thousand years ago. People queer in orientation and gender most certainly existed. But cultural, geographical, and additional forms of evolution mean that queer people experience themselves and are experienced by others in virtually incomparable manners over such a long span of time. In the context of this essay, speaking of Jesus's queer contemporaries in the [post]modern sense of the term, while helpful at times, would create anachronistic understandings.) In short, focusing an entire worldview on any one verse or group of verses from different parts of the biblical text or traditional teachings requires ignoring the broad story of salvation enacted through the person, message, and legacy of Jesus Christ.

Appalachian people—queer-celebrating, queerphobic, and others anywhere on the spectrums of attitudes and judgments regarding queer persons—must consider anew the lessons concerning queerness propagated by ACQR. This is not the first time Christian faiths have been reconsidered in light of new information. Roman Catholics, for example, dealt with the inevitability of evolving faith at the Second Vatican Council in the twentieth century as they committed to *aggiornamento*, "bringing up to date." It is time to continue the natural and necessary process of aggiornamento to bring the dominant mountain faith that so heavily influences all areas of Appalachian culture up to date with the lived experiences of queer mountain folk.

The men whose voices have been preserved as foundational to the structure and development of Christian faith agree. Less than four centuries after the initial growth and establishment of Christianity, for example, St. Augustine wrote that the bishops and church councils of his time had the authority to contest the conclusions reached by those who held such power in earlier times when lived experiences prompted the advent of new knowledge and understandings (Robinson 2015, 64–65). The dominant form of Protestant Christianity in contemporary Appalachia traces its roots to Martin Luther in the sixteenth century and the countless other protesters who challenged the Church/state hegemony of their time.

This faith that celebrates the priesthood of all believers has not remained static for the past five hundred years. Perhaps the most recent major example of evolving doctrine arises from the case of divorce. Today's "closeted" queer family members bear a striking resemblance to yesterday's "closeted" married family members who withstood matrimonial hurt and even sometimes various manifestations of domestic violence to not violate Christian teachings against divorce.

Before exploring this connection further, I must share a disclaimer: judgments regarding divorce and judgments regarding queer people vary greatly, and comparing the two bears a great risk of overidentification. Nevertheless, I present a very brief history of changing theological attitudes regarding divorce to bring to light the reality that theological understandings continually change in response to shifting social and cultural realities.

Divorce as a practice was condemned throughout much of church history, up through the previous century. But the procedure became an acceptable method of moving out of unhealthy and unhelpful relations at the same time more and more individuals were granted the ability and tapped into the courage to leave life-denying and life-destroying marriages. Today, church officials and structures that continue to decry divorce are preaching to an audience that is no longer listening, their ears closed because they know and love at least one divorced person. In retrospect, many Christians have decided that the Bible's teachings on divorce are not as unequivocally negative as Christian tradition had made them out to be. All of this has the effect of many churches now consenting to a reality they had unambiguously denounced for hundreds of years. Despite the supposed threat divorce posed to all families as well as the church, Christians and their institutions, including marriage, have survived.

Just as church teachings on divorce became outdated as more and more people left their closets of matrimonial hurt, queerphobic churches are facing an increasingly obsolete theology as more and more queer folk have contact with less toxic air and gain the ability and courage to come out of their closets of secrecy and fear. In the face of the lived realities of so many queer people, mountain churches cannot survive while propagating the assumption that cis/heteronormativity is the only way natural to humans.

The death knell of ACQR has only begun. Queerphobic churches do not face the imminent choice of changing their rhetoric or closing their doors and the people who support and further ACQR will continue to usurp and exercise power in public and civic life, using their religious liberty as justification for unjustifiable words and actions. In this reality, all concerned Appalachian folk must join in a challenge to ACQR guided by queer Appalachian folk.

While Christian-identifying folk must do the majority of the work to challenge ACQR within the realms of Christian churches, societies, institutions, doctrines, and dogmas, all people have roles available to them. Even those who find their faith/nonfaith/antifaith belongings in realities far removed from (dominant Appalachian) Christianity regularly encounter ACQR, and it thus influences lives, often without the conscious awareness of the affected persons. The high levels of queerphobic rhetoric in our contemporary world and its existence apart from Appalachia and Christianity further demonstrate the point that all audiences live in and have the proclivity to express (unconscious) bias. In the journey to challenge this on individual and institutional levels, the Appalachian traditions of sense of place and storytelling provide excellent points of departure.

A Call to Action

Sense of place aids in the strive toward deep love and acceptance of queer folk, especially insofar as it represents the conscious or unconscious recognition and celebration of a variety of evolving cultural and geographic markers that come together to characterize central and rural Appalachia as a distinctive, though not unique, region of the United States. As a social process, place continually embodies social conflict that works as a crucial aspect of creating change for more just and equitable realities. To fully engage with the conflict of a place, however, people and/or groups must discover and tap into the ability and willingness to engage with a variety of others unlike themselves who also occupy and contribute to the place. In so doing, agents of change enter into and influence a continuing history that began well before their own lifetimes and will continue into the future.

This volume represents a challenge to the current dominance of ACQR by providing a platform for a few unspeakable and often silenced others to tell parts of our stories related to this place we know as Appalachia. Countless additional mountain queer folk share vital stories of place and identity through diverse media. But storysharing alone cannot sustain change. It requires receivers: storylisteners.

Too often, straight and cisgender people and institutions thrust the burden of changing minds onto queer shoulders. But queer birth does not come with such a birthright. Nonqueer readers, who must not speak as primary sources on queer mountain realities, must listen, using all sorts of information-gathering to learn from queer Appalachians. Learn from the stories of your queer colleagues, your queer neighbors, your queer students. Learn from the stories shared. And learn from the stories not shared. Do not limit yourself to the stories shared by those with the privilege and power to make our stories known formally. Observe diligently. Continually work to set aside your assumptions. Pay attention.

When you pay attention, you will learn. And learning changes minds: fearing and hating an abstract and unidentified other often comes with ease compared with holding and expressing those same feelings toward an actual person, particularly a person one knows well. There is an assumed naturalness of cisgender identity, heterosexual orientation, and the limited methods of fully living as gendered and sexual persons considered acceptable. It fades in the context of lived realities of everyday experiences of folk, queer and straight alike, whose natural states of living and acting in the world differ from the historically prescribed status quo established by white, cisgender, straight, male hegemony and held in place by the power the people of these identities continue to usurp and exercise over our region, our country, and our world.

Changing minds through interactions with real people being their full human selves is compelling, especially in Appalachia, where sense of place plays a strong role in individual interactions and society at large. Here, individuals tend to experience deep ties with each other and "think about personalities more readily than abstractions" (Jones 1994, 87). One author's description of queer activism in the South provides an excellent model for the same activism in the mountains:

> A common refrain heard from southern lesbian and gay activists is that they work "behind the scene." True to the common stereotype of the South as backward, southern lesbians and gays approach activism not through the confrontational politics of mass protest but rather through personal and cultural negotiations from behind. Rather than being in your face, southern lesbian and gay activists can be viewed as being "in your behind." After all, being a pain in the ass can be just as effective at accomplishing change as being in one's face. A key difference between

these two approaches is that being in someone's ass assumes a certain level of intimacy between the parties involved that is not usually associated with being in someone's face. (Brasell 2001, 164)

Likewise, "confrontation politics have not always worked in the mountains" (Jones 1994, 81), a reality due largely to personalism's influence, where mountain folk tend to evade circumstances that seem to require isolating others.

As mountain queer invisibility becomes mountain queer visibility, many cisgender and heterosexual people can no longer ignore queer identity; they are faced with the reality that "ignoring isn't the same as ignorance, you have to work at [ignoring]" (Atwood 1986, 56), particularly once you truly pay attention to and learn from the experiences of others.

Although telling one's story of being queer and Appalachian represents an important aspect of naming and claiming one's place, the responsibility of overcoming ACQR and entering a state of deep love and acceptance for neighbors and selves, as noted, does not fall on the shoulders of queer folk—Christian or otherwise. All Appalachian folk (always in conversation and interactions with queer rhetoric so as to mitigate the common dynamic of one group attempting to help but actually continuing to silence another) must work for change. Unconscious bias exists—even among queer folk, perhaps especially those of us from or living in largely queerphobic environments. Storylistening can (and should) challenge all of us. Consider the following challenge, an integration of a Facebook post and a statement I formulated in response to my experience in United Methodist, Southern Baptist, and Roman Catholic Appalachian congregations:

> The dominant Christian tradition of Central and rural Appalachia tells us that identifying with and acting on queer life experiences makes us sinners. Many churches and other Christian institutions proclaim that "choosing" queer identities puts us in a state of sin, living against the dictates of the "B-I-B-L-E," as I once witnessed the preacher of my United Methodist church of origin proclaim from the pulpit.
>
> But do you know what is even more wrong? Do you know what is even more sinful?
>
> It is even more wrong that dominant Christian beliefs and dominant Christian actions are causing queer humans to keep secrets that cause us physical pain in addition to the mental, spiritual, and emotional burdens we carry.
>
> It is even more wrong that the judgement placed on queer people causes queer youth to attempt suicide at a rate over four and a half times

higher than straight youth (Kann et al. 2016, 20)—a statistic that goes up an additional 8.4 times for youth who come from highly rejecting families (Ryan et al. 2009, 346, 349).

It is even more wrong that ACRQ influences the fact that a study of youth ages 15 to 21 found that over 25 percent of transgender folks report at least one suicide attempt stemming from negative associations of being transgender (Grossman and D'Augelli 2010, 532).

In light of all of this, perhaps the Christianity that dominates Central and rural Appalachia is wrong. Perhaps this tradition has lost its way in proclaiming the sinfulness of humans who find themselves born into certain categories.

It is time for all who encounter ACQR to assess the life-denying and life-destroying traditions that infiltrate our culture. We must ask ourselves: are we making it easier for our fellow humans—particularly our youth—to experience bullying, murder, and an entire range of negative circumstances than to experience the true fulfillment of an integrated life? Individually, we must each ask: do *my* words and *my* actions affirm life for *all* humans? Or do my words and my actions build walls and spell early death—physical, spiritual, mental, or emotional—for those I love?

Let me make this more concrete. To establish the point in writing for a broad audience, I use my own name below. But as you read, replace my personal noun and pronouns with that of a queer person you know or have personally encountered. For the straight and cisgender among you, after you do that, read it again and place your own name and pronouns in the narrative. Place your self-understanding outside of the hegemonic norm.

- Justin Ray does not deserve adept and affirming physical and mental health care.

- Justin Ray should be denied access to a roof over his head because he is (or is perceived as) queer.

- Justin Ray cannot be allowed to continue to exist because his very existence keeps me from practicing my religion.

- Justin Ray's boss and/or HR department should be able to fire him because he dates men.

- Justin Ray's boss and/or HR department should be able to fire him because his gender does not match the gender on his birth certificate.

- Justin Ray is not fit to raise children.

- Justin Ray should be and present as straight and cisgender if he really wants to get a job.

- When Justin Ray is physically attacked because his attackers view him as queer, they should not face the more severe consequences of hate crime legislation.

- Justin Ray should not be allowed to visit the love of his life in life-threatening or end-of-life circumstances.

- Justin Ray should not have access to the assets acquired throughout a shared life upon the death or incapacitation of his partner.

- If Justin Ray needs to use the bathroom in public, he should just hold it and go home.

- If Justin Ray gets married, that's the same thing as letting people marry animals.

- Justin Ray is incapable of understanding the realities of normalcy.

- In my day, we would have shot Justin Ray in the street.

We cannot and we will not accept this reality. (Dutton 2016)

Many of us are ready to come out of the closets we are forced into by dominant Appalachian Christian ideologies. We are ready to breathe the fresh mountain air, and we are ready to celebrate life and life abundant with our fellow humans.

Unfortunately, not all of us make it out of the closet alive. The currently dominant ACQR creates a reality where the Justin Rays of the world face the realities determined (by external sources of hate) unlivable by the Matthew Shepards, the Lexi Lopez-Brandies, the Tyler Clementis, the Leelah Alcorns, the Mike Penners/Christine Danielses, the Lili Ilse Elveneses, the Children-404s, and ineffable additional names that we all must say.

Despite this reality, some of us find (or are granted) the strength to stay alive.

And sometimes, *we all* have the strength to challenge ACQR. This challenging looks different depending on the current levels of individual resilience or community support at any given time. Whether our challenge to the hegemony takes the form of getting out of bed and being able to make the choice to live another day or being present on the front lines for justice, we must continually engage in such challenges for ourselves and for each other.

I'll start with the challenging, specifically speaking to readers who still (again, very justifiably) believe that Christianity is hopelessly queerphobic.

Read for yourself the passages from the Hebrew and Christian Bibles that you have been told speak against homosexuality. Put them in conversation with the rest of the text. I'll give you some hints:

1. Jesus *never* even mentions sexual orientation.

2. Jesus *regularly* celebrates and empowers women, eunuchs, and others whom society shunned for reasons of gender difference.

3. Ezekiel 16:49 explicitly states that the sin of Sodom was inhospitality—no part of the biblical text mentions homosexuality. Even the New Testament reference to the destruction of Sodom and Gomorrah (Jude 7), while mentioning "sexual immorality and perversion," remains broad: gang rape—which the author of Genesis does recount—fits that category much easier than the loving, committed, same-gender relationships of today.

4. Leviticus 18 is sandwiched between passages that speak of the sacrifice of animals to God and what should be done when a man has sex with his female slave. There is also a verse indicating that readers should not wear clothing made of two different materials.

   a. If you know someone who insists that "man shall not lie with man," perhaps you should suggest that they go home and change clothes (actually, they would probably need to go to a fabric store and then go home and *make* some new clothes).

   b. They should also stop by the slavery market to buy a human to exploit and rape.

   c. Or else they could simply stop damning individuals based on an ancient law code that has no bearing on contemporary life.

5. Paul wrote the letter to the Romans. 2 Peter 3:15–16 reminds readers that sometimes people twist Paul's words, "as they do the other scriptures."

6. Nobody really even knows what the Greek word translated in antiqueer ways in 1 Corinthians and 1 Timothy even means (Newheiser 2015, 127–28). Paul might have made it up!

The variety of Christian beliefs—even within individual denominations and congregations, including evangelical forms of the faith—now and throughout history demonstrates that perhaps Paul was not the only one to make up interpretations. Perhaps those hundreds of people who formed the currently dominant Appalachian Christian tradition brought cultural and individual ideas and biases into that which we have inherited. Indeed, could they have done otherwise?

Let us now bring our own queer histories and experiences as queer individuals to the table of our culture. Let us now challenge judgment against and harm to those whose voices are routinely and systematically silenced.

Concluding Thoughts

Everyone has roles to play in the quest to transform our beloved Appalachia into a place of deep love and acceptance for queer humans. As queer people create and discover spaces where we can be our full selves without insurmountable risk to our physical, emotional, mental, and spiritual well-beings, we have opportunities to share our life stories with others and thus perform actions that work toward the diminishment of queerphobia by replacing an often impersonal label with familiar faces—a replacement that makes queerphobia an increasingly difficult stance to maintain.

But the task does not belong solely to queer folks. Currently queerphobic people and, perhaps especially, folks who do not take explicit stands of supporting their queer human siblings have the *obligation* to find and take opportunities to storylisten and deeply learn from the experiences of individuals unlike themselves. If one identifies as Christian, the additional opportunity of reevaluating inherited theology in light of the increasingly visible and knowable experiences of queer people arises. Theology, like any other "-ology," does not represent a static, once-and-done knowledge. It must continually re-form in response to evolutions and innovations that shed new light on its historically and currently traditional teachings

Insofar as Appalachian culture continues to follow ACQR's denigration of queer people, it will continue to endorse and further fear-based hate. As long as straight and cisgender persons, institutions, and other human groupings remain silent and do not act against life-denying and life-destroying norms, they endorse and further the toxic air. Central and rural Appalachia and the people who call it home offer much to take pride in. Let us work to add deep love and acceptance of queer folk to the list of central Appalachia offerings to allow this place to follow the claim of the North Carolina state slogan: a better place to be.

BIBLIOGRAPHY

Atwood, Margaret. 1986. *The Handmaid's Tale*. Boston: Houghton Mifflin Harcourt.

Barton, Bernadette. 2011. "1CROSS + 3NAILS = 4GVN: Compulsory Christianity and Homosexuality in the Bible Belt Panopticon." *Feminist Formulations* 23, no. 1, 70–93.

Black, Kate, and Marc A. Rhorer. 2001. "Out in the Mountains: Exploring Lesbian and Gay Lives." In *Out in the South*, edited by Carlos L. Dews and Carolyn Leste Law, 16–25. Philadelphia: Temple University Press.

Brasell, R. Bruce. 2001. "Greetings from Out Here: Southern Lesbians and Gays Bear Witness to the Public Secret." In *Out in the South*, edited by Carlos L. Dews and Carolyn Leste Law, 159–72. Philadelphia: Temple University Press.

Carmel, Tamar C., and Laura Erickson-Schroth. 2016. "Mental Health and the Transgender Population." *Psychiatric Annals* 46 no. 6, 346–49.

Dutton, Justin Ray. 2016, September 19. "Public Witness Statement." Presentation, Wake Forest University School of Divinity MIN 790A, Prophetic Ministry: Public Witness, Protest Arts, and Preaching, Winston-Salem, NC.

Grossman, Arnold H., and Anthony R. D'Augelli. 2007. "Transgender Youth and Life-Threatening Behaviors." *Suicide and Life-Threatening Behavior* 37, no. 5, 527–37.

Haas, Ann P., Mickey Eliason, Vickie M. Mays, Robin M. Mathy, Susan D. Cochran, Anthony R. D'Augelli, Morton M. Silverman, Prudence W. Fisher, Tonda Hughes, Margaret Rosario, Stephen T. Russell, Effie Malley, Jerry Reed, David A. Litts, Ellen Haller, Randall L. Sell, Gary Remafedi, Judith Bradford, Annette L. Beautrais, Gregory K. Brown, Gary M. Diamond, Mark S. Friedman, Robert Garofalo, Mason S. Turner, Amber Hollibaugh, and Paula J. Clayton. 2010. "Suicide and Suicide Risk in Lesbian, Gay, Bisexual, and Transgender Populations: Review and Recommendations." *Journal of Homosexuality* 58, no. 1, 10–51.

Jones, Loyal. 1994. *Appalachian Values*. Ashland, KY: Jesse Stuart Foundation.

Kann, Laura, Emily O'Malley Olsen, Tim McManus, William A. Harris, Shari L. Shanklin, Katherine H. Flint, Barbara Queen, Richard Lowry, David Chyen, Lisa Whittle, Jemekia Thornton, Connie Lim, Yoshimi Yamakawa, Nancy Brener, and Stephanie Zaza. 2016. "Sexual Identity, Sex of Sexual Contacts, and Health-Related Behaviors among Students in Grades 9–12—United States and Selected Sites, 2015." *Centers for Disease Control and Prevention Morbidity and Mortality Weekly Report, Surveillance Summaries* 65, no. 9.

Miller, B. Jaye. 1992. "From Silence to Suicide: Measuring a Mother's Loss." In *Homophobia: How We All Pay the Price*, edited by Warren J. Blumenfeld, 79–94. Boston: Beacon Press.

Newheiser, David. 2015. "Sexuality and Christian Tradition." *Journal of Religious Ethics* 43, no. 1, 122–45.

Robinson, Geoffrey. 2015. *2015 Synod, the Crucial Questions: Divorce and Homosexuality*. Hindmarsh, Australia: ATF Press.

Rust, Paula C. 2000. "Neutralizing the Political Threat of the Marginal Woman: Lesbians' Beliefs about Bisexual Women." In *Bisexuality in the United States: A Social Science Reader*, edited by Paula C. Rodríguez Rust, 449–97. New York: Columbia University Press.

Ryan, Caitlin, David Huebner, Rafael M. Diaz, and Jorge Sanchez. 2009. "Family Rejection as a Predictor of Negative Health Outcomes in White and Latino Lesbian, Gay, and Bisexual Young Adults." *Pediatrics* 123, no. 1, 346–52.

Slepian, Michael L., Negin R. Toosi, E. J. Masicampo, and Nalini Ambady. 2012. "The Physical Burdens of Secrecy." *Journal of Experimental Psychology: General* 141, no. 4, 619–24.

Williams, Walter L. 1992. "Benefits for Nonhomophobic Societies: An Anthropological Perspective." In *Homophobia: How We All Pay the Price*, edited by Warren J. Blumenfeld, 258–74. Boston: Beacon Press.

PART II

Queer Diaspora: Existence and Erasure in Appalachia

CHAPTER 3

A Drowning in the Foothills

Adam Denney

Vignette: Lake Cumberland

With a shoreline that stretches for more than twelve hundred miles, Lake Cumberland is one of the largest reservoirs for the Cumberland River. The lake was formed by the creation of Wolf Creek Dam in Russell County, Kentucky. The project was authorized by two acts of Congress—the Flood Control Act of 1938 and the Rivers and Harbors Act of 1946—and carried out by the Tennessee Valley Authority and the US Army Corp of Engineers. Heavy rainfall began to inundate the region in 1951, and by 1952 the lake was fully incorporated. The sole purpose of the Wolf Creek Dam Project was to provide flood control and produce hydroelectric power for the surrounding areas. The dam is located on karst terrain, which provided engineers with a unique challenge as large caverns, sinkholes, and underground channels created difficulties that have carried over to the present day (Applegate and Miller 2009). The ecological, geographical, and anthropogenic collide in the histories of Lake Cumberland. As plans for the inundation of the region were announced, the families who had understood the intimacies of the area were forced to reconcile and find home elsewhere.

The histories of those who relocated during the flooding of the river bottoms are preserved in newspaper archives, government documents, a few published titles, and a tradition of oral storytelling unique to Appalachia. In Norma Cole's *The Final Tide* (1990), the story is told through the narration of fourteen-year-old tomboy Geneva Hawe, who in 1948 had to uproot and relocate her life during the completion of the dam. As Geneva's family prepares to leave, Granny Hawe, who lives down the valley, sits with a shotgun in her lap and dares any government man to try and take her from her front porch. No matter how much the family urged, the stubborn granny would not budge. Her resistance became known through her acts of rebellion. In one scene, she enlists Geneva's help to smash and hide her husband's tombstone so he wouldn't be dug up and relocated with the rest of the cemetery. Granny Hawe eventually leaves her home behind and goes with her family as she learns, along with Geneva, that home is something you carry with you even when it becomes denied to you.

The personage of Granny Hawe—defiant, stubborn, resourceful, and protective—is common among the oral histories of those who reflect on the narrative of Lake Cumberland. It seemed there was a Granny Hawe in almost every holler to be vacated. Among brilliant storytellers, the histories of Lake Cumberland became fused somewhere between truths and tall tales. The fabrications develop as stories are told, shared, and passed on. In a community of storytellers, most locals love the opportunity to tell a few good tales. As the tourist industry came to fruition in the 1980s and 1990s, the stories regarding the flooding of the river bottoms, and Lake Cumberland in general, became more supernatural, mythological, and even macabre. I grew up behind the counter of gas stations. I would often hear the tall tales fly toward any out-of-town guest as they were filling up before a long weekend, soaking in the stories with every accented word. There were talks about catfish the size of small trailers, depths that reached to two hundred feet, haunted Civil War battlegrounds along the shoreline, and the specters that remain from those who never left the river bottoms, either by circumstance or free will. Whereas newspaper articles and government documents recorded during this time were often void of human emotions, the stories that the locals express, whether true or false, express a humanity that refuses to be forgotten. By the act of storytelling, these stories resist the active process of erasure and survive through the narration as they are retold.

A Drowning in the Foothills

A mythology ravels and unravels. It is knowledge, a science of life open only to those who have no training in it. It is a living science in which begets itself and makes away with itself.

—Louis Aragon (*Paris Peasant*, 1926)

Act One: Understanding

———

The Chorus

The aquatic simulacrums of the river bottoms I imagined as a child—the decomposing churches, cemeteries, farms, and schoolhouses—are more than necromantic renderings curated by an impressionable mind. They have provided a unique way for me to express and understand my experiences of growing up as a rural queer in the Bible Belt. Acting as more than an analogy, the mythos of Lake Cumberland gives reference toward a feeling. Feelings have a way of resurfacing as we reflect on our journey. They reach out from the depths of the past and into our presence as they become located through storytelling. Stories have magic; they illuminate our potential to manifest psychic bonds between person, space, and place. Stories are felt in the flesh; they entice goose bumps, acts of rage, sparks of laughter, or floods of tears; they live ferociously through us and are acted out on us. As I depart from the folklore of those who stayed for the flooding, I seek to explore a sensation of drowning, both at and for home, that rural queers know too well. We are experts at holding our breath, and sometimes this act is not about giving up but is about resistance and survival.

Queerness haunts my hometown. It is something that borders on the in-betweens of in/visibility. It is loud but not heard. It is sensed but not seen. Queerness is something that happens outside the borders of home, school, community, and the church as others' versions of queerness become ingrained in the social, cultural, and legal fabric of our daily lives. When the promise of home (comfort, connection, genealogy, space, and place) is denied, home becomes a mythology in and of itself; home is scattered with truths and lies, a nostalgic longing for something that is unknown yet strangely familiar. Diasporic feelings of home in Appalachia are not unique to queer experiences. As a region where poverty is rampant, ecological resources are privatized, education is divested, and where white supremacy and xenophobia are rampant, the effects take a toll on the body of Appalachia. As both neoliberal and alt-right players control the remotes, the Appalachian body, both human and nonhuman, becomes a toxic reservoir composed of waste and neglect orchestrated via the insatiable appetite for reproducing a depressed and dependent Appalachian. Seen as a justifiable mean with an eminent end in sight, the iron fists of a new postmodernity clutch the region as more mountaintops are removed, more land is fracked, and more people migrate away.

This essay seeks to unravel the hidden cartographies of queer experiences that have been mapped along Lake Cumberland. As I have weaved together stories from queer persons who came of age in this region, my goal is to provide a way we can creatively engage with the active nature of self-awareness and place-making in the Bible Belt through the communal act of storytelling. These stories are woven in a spiritual fashion that beckons toward a call-and-response. As we tell our stories, we actively participate in preserving our experiences. We survive through our stories, for they outlast us all. As a writer,

I intend to address what I needed to hear as a child during the times I did not think I would surface. As we speak our truths we give part of ourselves to others, and my hope is that in the fragments that follow, the parts we give may be exactly what you needed to hear.

Act Two: Foundations

It is necessary to dry up a section of a river valley by diverting the river's natural path during the construction of a dam. Paths are cleared through the rocks with explosives, creating new passageways for the water to flow. A cofferdam or a temporary dam is put in place to block water flow from the construction site (Hydro Tasmania n.d.).

I am a specter like the ones before me.

Fragments

I often wonder about my queer ancestors. We never talk about them. Their stories are withheld and drained from the very possibility of being. They were drowned in the shallow tubs of the pulpit cloaked under the guise of salvation and grace. As specters, we traced out a world that did not belong to us. We obsessed over whether they could see us. The speculation became a prison. We became masons and carpenters constructing a protective fortress we could never finish. The limestone that we had used was full of cracks and joints . . . it was just a matter of time before it would become too weathered and, like cavities, toxins would begin to leech in. We were vulnerable.

> *I had known since elementary school. I always felt different. I wasn't like the others, and everyone could see that. Most of the time I spent alone, physically and emotionally. I became comfortable alone because there was safety in being left alone.*

We didn't ask for it. We were told queers did not exist here; if they tried, it didn't work. The lesson? Don't try it. We began to listen. It cultivated within us, putrefying in small chambers. And from it we made our catacombs into labyrinths. Sometimes the walls would crumble so badly we became exposed; we were trapped in those eerie moments of difference, discomfort, and guilt. It would hit us like a ton of bricks, orienting us toward the opening of the caverns where our spirits lie dormant. In silence, we waited. We dare not budge, for the truth could get you killed. One explosion is all it took. However, the tide was destined to come early—it had already been foreseen.

> *I was told from a young age to act right, don't speak that way, don't get overly excited, basically don't do anything that came naturally to me. I remember my father telling me he would beat the sissy faggot right out of me one time when he caught me playing in my older sister's makeup, and he tried. I couldn't have been more than eight years old. No matter what I did, I was always a sissy to him and he couldn't stand the sight of me.*

Characters were created. We put on costumes and donned our masks; we disguised our voices. The choreography had been rehearsed. We were tasked to stay on beat. If you slipped, they would notice. We listened and observed. And if mimicry didn't work, we brewed another batch of invisibility. Some of our codes of conduct became lethal. We held others accountable when they were not careful. We estranged ourselves from each other. We were denied community as we sought to define a space that was impossible, a place that couldn't become, a path that was forbidden. Inhale. Wait. Don't move.

> *Honey, in those days we didn't have what you have now. Y'all have technology, we didn't. I never had any words to describe myself. No one talked of lesbians or dykes. Hell, quare meant you were strange, and I guess there were always code words for people like us. I wasn't privy. Anyway, how are you supposed to know who you are when you haven't got the words?*

Stability was a mirage. We became cognizant of where we placed our feet, cautious of the sinkholes that dipped among the valleys. Once more, our caverns had collapsed beneath us, and we were left to bear witness to the aftermath. We were told about the pits of fire waiting below. We became weary of the dripstones that formed around us—inside us—as if they were coordinating the long passageway of the damned. The Bible Belt had a way of finding itself twisted around your neck, pulled tighter by the churches, the schools, the leaders. Some of us didn't make it. We were immersed in a spiritual warfare that raged from the inside out. Deliver us from evil, we read, among a few Scriptures, in one good book. And all the while Jesus wept.

> *The guilt became unbearable. Tight knots would form in my stomach, and my throat would tense up like I was choking. I was so angry and afraid. I*

just wanted forgiveness and someone to say it was going to be okay. That was a bad time.

We found ourselves at odds with the social and cultural geographies for which we were present. The pressure to not be read as queer tangled with our spiritual plea to not *be queer*, created a burden within us that was no less than unbearable. Denied authenticity, we contracted a new self that was unknown. We lived within our own temporalities inclusive to an uncomfortable present, shaped by the queer missteps of the past, while being unable to conjure an image of a future for which we could be home, happy, and queer. We concealed ourselves as others sought to erase us. Make no mistake: erasure is an act of violence. We traced a place unto a world that was not our own. We operated in brightened shadows, a place between the blurred lines of the hidden and the magnified.

I had a dream the other night. It was the same dream I had the night before, and the night before, and the night before. The one I had told you about. I was lying along the shoals, draped in lace dyed in indigo. I could feel it approaching, but I just kept looking beyond the horizon.

She chuckles and we sit in silence as she sips her coffee and smokes the last of her cigarette. I can divine the past in her worn and wrinkled eyes.

Act Three: Inundation

———

In late August, crews of men with saws, big log trucks, and gasoline to set fires. Steam-driven earth-moving machines swarmed over the mountains that circled their river bottom. They cut every tree that might be in the future lake bed. They hauled off the big logs, piled up the brush, and burned piles of it night and day. The air was smoky and hazy from the fires, and the barren hillsides looked naked and ugly.

—Cole (1990)

Follow the stream to the swallow hole; that place where the water disappears.

Anticipation

Home is where you go to feel at peace. It is not home if you don't experience those feelings. I just happened to be born and raised in a small town, a bloodline that refused to see me, and a school district I couldn't even graduate from. It wasn't home. So, no, I don't really go back.

When home does not present itself as a place of harbor and refuge, we understand it differently. Home becomes transitional; it manifests between the cracks of psychic potential and real-world consequences. It can play out like a nostalgic quest for place and space, both known and unheard. Home, as we desire, becomes solidified when we are able to feel at ease. However, ease is woven with the knowledge of danger. Comfort is fragile; it can rupture at any moment. Fissures linger in the peripheries, threatening us, coercing us to wager our security, stability, and safety. For them, home is vulgarly mapped among narrow lines based on imaginations of origin, network, and residence. Our bodies are at stake, yet our bodies hold the key to survival. We found home within the body; yet learning to carry home within is a path that is hard to take. Sometimes we got by without being noticed. We held our breath. And then it would hit us, like the strike of a hidden snake coiled among dead leaves. The smell of rotting apples.

> As soon as I walked into school, they would start to scream, "Fag! Queer! Hide your ass! Hold your dick." There would be so many of them, screaming, laughing. I would turn to any adult around. They looked at me. "Don't you hear them?," I would scream. They'd pretend they didn't hear it. I became so angry.

We are poised as antithetical to our surroundings. They cast us as unnatural and we became hardened. We began to breathe slower, shallower, with longer pauses in between. Public spaces were not made for us here. We became masters of awareness. We avoided the places that made us vulnerable: bathrooms, locker rooms, sporting events, fairs, schools, church, home, et cetera, et cetera. The burdens always seemed to cling the tightest throughout the night. We prayed, yet nothing happened. "Dear God, deliver me from this." Again, "Lord, please do not abandon me." AGAIN, "I know not what I do." We retreated further inside. We sought help from a god that wasn't our own. It told us we had brought this pain on ourselves. Safety was a luxury. We weren't safe from ourselves. We continued to build, but it was never enough. We felt the tide come closer, and once again we held our breath.

> The staff was far worse than the students. My principal said that when I get made fun of, it was my own fault. Isn't that some shit. Not if, but when. He knew what was going on. For him, I deserved it.

The faces of those who could have helped yet remained passive bystanders still burn in our minds. Teachers. Preachers. Coaches. Principals. Parents.

Stranded, with no resources and no examples, we waited. We inhaled and held on even longer. We closed our eyes and kept on. We went on. Grinding our teeth and clenching our fists, we put our trust in distance. Even that trust was shattered. It came with the inevitable shove. Limestone tastes like copper. We were fragile, not because of our queerness but because of what our queerness provoked in others. Brokenhearted, we grieved for what we thought we would never know. We longed for an intimacy we couldn't fathom, an intimacy we couldn't imagine was possible.

> *And one day I just told him, thinking he would say it back. He began to look at me with disgust, and it crushed me. I tried to play it off as a joke, he pretended to buy it. When I got home, I went straight to bed and just cried. I became so nervous I got sick. I just knew what tomorrow would be, and I didn't want to face it.*

Revelations. As the curtain is pulled, we are revealed. Naked for them to gaze. We begin to hold our breath before the tide hits. Everything begins to spin as the rain pours down from our eyes. The blood of our clenched fist is our sacrifice. Another shove. It was bedevilment, they would say. And then came the gasps, the ones that began filling your lungs. It burned holes in our head. It was spontaneous. It shook us. It required us to respond. We were present.

> *My parents saw me for the first time at fourteen. I had snuck out of my house to meet a guy who was twenty-one. He told me he didn't know if he wanted to fuck me or beat me up. I didn't care. I wanted to feel loved. The police picked me up, laughed at me, and took me home to my parents in my black dress and running mascara. My parents shaved my head and sent me away to a crisis house.*

As time passed, our wounds turned to scars, and they created a pictograph of cautionary tales. The surface water boiled while the depths began to freeze. Chemicals begin to combine in synchronized battles. We were consumed. The bubbles began to form. They hissed, and it was hypnotic. We knew we had overstayed our welcome. The barren terrain was transformed as the cofferdams were destroyed. The water rushed in, and it was greeted with a smile. This moment was known before it happened. The dead began to rise as the waves interred their unmarked graves. The rapture was conducted through an act of necromancy.

I just took a handful of pills, downed two bottles of cheap brut, and got in the tub. It was that easy. I was fine. Content. Happy. I was so relaxed until my phone rang. And just like that I became aware of my surroundings, my body, and my breath. I panicked. I didn't want to do it. I gagged myself, threw up the pills, and lay naked on the cold bathroom floor for what seemed like days. That phone call saved my life.

As we held our breath, we were changed. There was a roaring in our souls and the impact of the flood swept us off our feet. We had refused to give in. Our deep inhalations had become our resistance. We had been denied the means to build a home for ourselves, so we crafted new tools. We found others like us; we clung to them and held them close. We were aware, perhaps for the first time, how deafening our silence had been. We began to make declarations. We demanded to be seen. We resurfaced from the very tides that sought to destroy us. We were transformed.

Curtain Call: A Reprieve

WATER COVERS BURNSIDE WEEKS AHEAD OF TIME
Unusually heavy rains and melting snow over the entire watershed during the last few weeks revised the engineers "schedule" in one sweeping stroke. Water behind Wolf Creek Dam rose more than 25 feet in the last few days. Water Now 117 Feet Deep . . . Faith In Future Is High. (Reister 1951)

Do not be afraid. Jump. There is nothing left to lose.

Transformation

A moment came when we understood that as specters we were free to haunt in such a way that we transcended our boundaries; we became poltergeists, determined to create ripples in the spaces that were once denied to us. We stood. Firmly. We fought back. Mighty. We were seen, and the speculation didn't matter. We did not retreat. We armed ourselves with an arsenal of our own making, our own crafting. We decided to wake up, dry off, and go out. We longed to face what was waiting because we knew we could handle whatever it was. We joined hands. We made love. We spoke up. We were louder, bolder, and we pitied those who stood in our way.

I couldn't tell anyone I was trans, my mom made me promise. At school I would sneak and wear makeup. My God, the teachers hated it. They would take my makeup, send me to the office, and take away any privileges they could. But it didn't matter. There was always more makeup and I had few privileges anyway.

We took back what was ours. We appropriated their weapons to use against them. We become forces of mass destruction. Our disruptions were like tremors. When once the tides had been against us, we learned to navigate its flows. Poseidon was within us. Instead of being silenced, we began to laugh. Louder. Like waves, crashing down. We made them look. Our bodies became our shields and swords. They trembled as we came before them even when they stood like Goliath among us. We refused to be anything but authentic and that authenticity became our bedrock. Our trident.

I came home once to pamphlets for a conversion camp. At first I was pissed. Then I convinced myself that I was going to go and my job was to bring out the holy queer in all of 'em. I'd shut it down. I think that may have been why my parents didn't send me; they knew I was stubborn enough to do it.

Again they tried their tired tricks. We used our magic. They grew weaker. We opened our doors so those who were tired of fighting could find refuge among us. We gave bread to our enemies as they began to lift their veils. We began to own our visibility and make no apologies for it. We refused to compromise with hatred because it wasn't in our nature. We learned that pride may not be so sinful after all. We were neither abashed nor ashamed. We were hopeful. We harnessed the power that came from lifting each other. It fed us. We are unstoppable and no dam walls could hold us back.

We were so tired of seeing all those racist and Confederate flags lining our streets. It became a constant slap in the face, like a pathetic attempt at intimidation. To bad for them, we don't scare easy. So we put up rainbow flags! They called the city to have us take them down. It's our middle finger, high and mighty.

We reconciled. Our queerness became honored. We danced, and it was like thunder. We sought out the strength of others, and we listened. We cast new narratives that became transcendental. We found new ways to speak defiance in tongues. We laid roots and we channeled the storms. We shared as we survived. We engulfed our enemies, and they sank inside us. We forced them to see their reflection for the first time. They were face to face. Three points make a plane. Our echoes collided.

I was eighteen when I went to my first queer bar. We drove two hours and stayed in a dump, but I didn't care. From the moment I walked in, something came over me and almost brought me to tears. I saw all these people, some that looked like me, many that didn't, and some people I couldn't even describe. It felt like home. It was a sanctuary, and I saw Jesus in drag. I'm sure some people will never understand that. That doesn't matter. We did.

We no longer hid from our reflections, and we basked in our glory. And as we gazed, we knew it wouldn't be easy. But we were born courageous. We had found our power, and they didn't know what to do with us. Their campaigns grew weaker.

They had made us into false idols by the power of their condemnation. The light reflected from the beauty of our skin and blinded them. They were no longer lost. The lights were part of our transformation, and they took a knee by our feet. We became holy. We were touched. We gave thanks and we prayed.

I remember being terrified on the way to the crisis house. It's true, but I ended up loving it. At that crisis house, for the first time in my life, an adult looked at me and told me I was beautiful, that I was okay, that I was perfect just as I was.

We made a home for ourselves, on our own terms, in our own visions and from our own bodies. We used the remnants of our past to form a foundation. We plucked four strands from our future and used them for posts. Before we laid down to rest we wove a roof from the glory of our being, our presence, and our lives. We grew. We were humbled. And from this—our rib—we engineered an immaculate bridge that towered over the limestone structures of our past; we know walls never work. The tides crash. You can hear them. The tides rise. You can feel them. Inhale. Exhale. Hold. Repeat.

One day, someone hurled a "fag!" my way. This time I decided to just look at them and smile. Laughing, I asked if they had anything more original. Fag had been used up. I turned to walk away and I felt their power come right into me. That felt so good. Eventually I didn't hear it anymore. Not that it stopped (it didn't). It just didn't affect me the same anymore.

The road ahead is long, and together we begin to travel. We are not few but many, and our tales shall be heard over the raging tides. We take the hands of who we were and hold them tight. We were always holding them even when we did not know it. Perhaps it was that grip that kept us going as we continued to make place and find home for ourselves, within ourselves. The waters were turbulent, but we stood our ground. We were always standing. We faced our fears as we smiled, as we laughed. Our laughs split the tides in half, and we called out to those who had been lost among the depths. They walked to us. They greeted us with love, and we welcomed them with open arms as we placed them in our skies. Their radiance burned so brightly the heavens became envious of their beauty. It revived us. We raised a resistance that could no longer be ignored. We are here. We are home. For we are Appalachian even when we leave.

BIBLIOGRAPHY

Applegate, Kris, and Jarenda Miller. 2009. *Around Lake Cumberland*. Charleston, SC: Arcadia Publishing.

Cole, Norma. 1990. *The Final Tide*. New York: Margaret K. McElderry Books.

Hydro Tasmania. n.d. "How to Build a Dam." *APLIUT*. http://www.apliut.com/pages /aideenseignement/swapshop_Nimes07/desparbes_howtobuildadam.pdf. Accessed October 31, 2018.

Reister, Joe. 1951, February 14. "Water Covers Burnside Weeks ahead of Time." *Courier-Journal* (Louisville, KY).

CHAPTER 4

A Pedagogy of the Flesh: Deconstructing the "Quare" Appalachian Archetype

Matthew Thomas-Reid with Michael Jeffries and Logan Land

Introduction: He's a Queer One, All Right

Queer [kwir] and Queer [kwar]

Down in the holler, I am a boy who is good to his momma: an eccentric who listens to classical music and brings a delicacy to every potluck. Being a boy good to his momma, I come from a tradition of the queer [phonetically *kwar*] in Appalachia. There is a rich history of the queer [kwar] in my community, from my lifelong bachelor great uncle to my father's "rebel younger brother," who died under unknown circumstances at the height of the AIDS crisis. Schooled in the southern Appalachian Brushy Mountains of North Carolina, queer [kwar] identity narratives abounded while queer [kwir] identities were marginal, simply too explicit to name in anything louder than a whisper.

One noted usage of this word spelled phonetically as *quare* can be found in E. Patrick Johnson's " 'Quare' Studies, or (Almost) Everything I Know about Queer Studies I Learned from My Grandmother" (2007). I note at this point that although Johnson uses the spelling and pronunciation *quare* to consider an intersection between queer identities and racial identities, I take a slightly different viewpoint from my own narrative history, suggesting that there is a cultural distinction between the two pronunciations [kwir] and [kwar] that are specific to the rural southern Appalachian region that deserves critical phenomenological interrogation. I draw a distinction between his usage and mine by continuing to write the word as it would have been written (queer) and indicating the phonetic distinction in brackets [kwar]. In fact, I distinctly remember as a ten-year-old hearing my father explain to my mother that queer [kwar] and queer [kwir] were spelled the same way, but that pronouncing it queer [kwar] made it okay. He seemed to be suggesting that from a dialect perspective, queer [kwar] had an entirely different lineage and meaning and was distinctively regional: a linguistic artifact unique to Appalachia.

Queer [kwir], in my usage—whether as a noun, adjective, or verb—is meant to be diametrically opposed to queer [kwar] through an explicit connection to marginal gender and sexual identities. I want to clearly conceptualize queer theory here in a way, as David Halperin (2003) writes, "to call attention to everything that is perverse about the project of theorizing sexual desire and sexual pleasure" (340). I take my cue from the troubling idea that even today in the academic sphere there is a tendency to "tame" the word *queer*, to eliminate its connection to the flesh, to the carnal, to the sexual: "While some may seek to tame queer . . . eliminating the queers association with (homo)sexuality—such a move is problematic as it 'dematerialize[s] any possibility of queerness itself' because homosexuality is a piece of the queers 'definitional center' . . . Such a move ignores the role of sexual orientation in queerness" (Greteman and Wojcikiewicz 2014, 568). These authors and Halperin make the argument that queerness in its very definition has an association with the flesh. The flesh, or sensual attraction, while being a critical component in human relationships, is often removed from identity in favor of less explicit attributes. The taming that Greteman refers to is the way "queer" in theoretical parlance often reduces the word *queer* to making things strange, different, or wonky, allowing the concept to have the carnality stripped from it. In a parallel way, queer [kwar] in Appalachian parlance seemed to be used to tame the more carnal aspects of queerness [kwir].

Where I grew up, in the foothills of the southern Appalachians, it was okay to be queer [kwar], the Appalachian dialectical equivalent of strange, unusual, or even colorful. My uncle would serve beautifully prepared French meals out of antique crystal serving dishes to rave reviews by the ladies of the church as long as his quare identity kept him beautifully isolated from immoral sins of the flesh implicit (to me) in his innocuous identity as the eccentric bachelor. As a boy in church, I hid behind my queerness [kwar], dressed in my Sunday best and singing solos punctuated by "amens" from the ladies on the front pew. I listened intently to the preacher delivering the words of Paul from his well-worn King James Bible: "For the flesh lusteth against the Spirit, and the Spirit against the flesh: and these are contrary the one to the other" (Gal. 5:17). The writers of the King James Bible capitalized *Spirit*, while *flesh* is uncapitalized, suggesting the supremacy of the Spirit over the flesh. My lesson was clear: I could never be defined by my flesh, the carnal embodied force that left me breathless every time I saw the deacon's son shirtless during a church volleyball game. The "spirit" of my identity was caught up in a non-flesh performance; my queerness [kwar] was acceptable in spirit as long as it was separated from the queerness [kwir] of the flesh. It was even okay to be queer [kwar] in school; developing identities like the drama weirdo, the choir geek, or the chess nerd, I could be written off with the phrase "he's just a little bit differnt [sic]."

The problematic nature of the acceptance of the queer [kwar] in Appalachian identities in and out of classrooms and the rejection of the explicit nature of the queer [kwir] in virtually all spaces is clear to me in reflection; the disconnect is predicated on the separation of the Spirit and flesh. If we consider flesh described as "a basic term describing the phenomenon of perceiving and of being the object of perception, of reciprocal tactile contact . . . carnality expressed as texture," we might imagine the development of Appalachian queer [kwar] identities as an attempt to suppress a fully realized enfleshed queer [kwir] identity (O'Loughlin 1997, 27). In the context of Appalachia, queer [kwar] archetypes develop homonormative identities compatible with heteronormative Appalachian culture.

These themes resonate with me now in a pedagogical context as I have spent the past thirty years in Appalachian classrooms as a student, teacher, and now professor of education witnessing the evolution of these queer [kwir] and queer [kwar] archetypes. I stand in the middle, so to speak: a bridge from a generation of queer [kwir] Appalachians who hide behind the queer [kwar] and a new generation of queer [kwir] Appalachians who have a whole new language available to define them. I reflect on Appalachian classrooms, where the boy who is good to his momma excels in the arts and becomes the sweet submissive pleaser in a performance allowing no fully embodied identity. The separation of the spirit and the flesh denies academic voice: "The flesh is the body inasmuch as it is the visible seer, the audible hearer, the tangible touch" (Merleau-Ponty 1968, 274). We might think of the classic drama club dilemma: there is the unspoken fact that queer youth often gravitate to theater, but how many school drama programs are doing queer theater? The bodily expression of Queerness [kwir] is denied in favor of the innocuous queer [kwar] archetype of the artsy kid. Narratives of the flesh and opportunities for queer [kwir] embodiment for and by queer youth are missing in K–12 schools, and the only available identities are that of the queer [kwar].

The Spirit and the Flesh

I choose to provide a space for queer student narrative, using a blend of personal and shared student narrative in a queer phenomenological approach described by Sara Ahmed (2006) in her work "Orientations: Toward a Queer Phenomenology" as considering the "importance of lived experience, the intentionality of consciousness, the significance of nearness or what is ready to hand, and the role of repeated and habitual actions in shaping bodies and worlds" (544). This approach is relevant because phenomenology accepts that meaning is correlational and not purely object oriented (Sokolowski 2000, 4). Furthermore, queer phenomenology allows us to challenge accepted truths if there are perspectives with a different correlation to truth (Ahmed 2006, 564). Developing narratives from my family's history, my personal narrative, and narratives of current students, I seek to examine new correlations between individuals and queer Appalachian identity. This work has the potential to shift understanding of how Appalachian queer [kwir] identities are constructed through language and ways language is used to strip individuals of queer [kwir] identities.

I develop three distinct sets of narratives, the first taken from my memories of two uncles and the second a personal narrative of my experiences. For the third, I invite two students to share their stories. These three sets provide examples from Appalachia's past, present, and future. Then I suggest a vision for a pedagogy that disrupts these queer [kwar] archetypes by allowing the flesh to be communicated through explicitly embodied queer [kwir] narratives—it isn't just okay to be different, it must be explicitly okay to be queer. There is more than the academic at stake; in our classrooms right now queer bodies are starving themselves, cutting themselves, and drugging themselves. I advocate for a pedagogy in Appalachia that embraces the narratives of the flesh, the voices of fully formed queer [kwir] identities liberated from the queer [kwar] constructs that favor cultural safety by promoting queer [kwir] folk in Appalachia as sexless curiosities. Finally, I conclude that the space of language can make explicit a multiplicity of queer identities which ought to be seen as never ending and is made real in the exploration and reinvention of words that can express the queer [kwir].

In the pages that follow, I develop a temporal triangulation of the queer [kwir] and the queer [kwar] as developed in three epochs: the flesh longed and lost, the flesh found, and the flesh fragmented. My goal is to draw on narratives from the near past and present to see the evolution and continuation of Appalachian queer [kwir] and queer [kwar] identities. In this effort, I will resist this temporality as a modernist reading of progress. It would be too convenient to buy into the trope of progress and end in a positive manner, pointing out just how far "we" have come. On the contrary, I end on a distinctly queer [kwir] and almost negative note with "the flesh fragmented" by denying the tidy stasis of a positive narrative of progress and not reaching what Jose Muñoz (2009) calls a "queer futurity" (10). Rather than couch this as a study about protecting the future and creating a world of harmony, I seek to remember that the queer [kwir], kept open, will continue to trouble, through language and embodiment, "the queer . . . signif[ies] actions . . . [and] can be thought of as a verb (Britzman 1995, 153). In this way of thinking, a modernist narrative where the next generation of queer [kwir] teachers make the world better for queer students would risk retreating to the queer [kwar]: the spirit separate from the flesh. Along with the interplay of queer phenomenological analysis, I look to Robert Heasley's (2005) novel approach to queering typologies in straight masculinities as a framework for unseating our current typologies of queerness [kwir]. Heasley writes: "many straight men experience and demonstrate 'queer masculinity,' defined here as ways of being masculine outside hetero-normative constructions of masculinity that disrupt, or have the potential to disrupt, traditional images of the hegemonic heterosexual masculine" (2005, 310). What if there is a new set of queer [kwar] typologies that need to be considered, set in the context of working forward and backward in the landscape of nonnormative gender and sexuality in Appalachian narratives? How might triangulating narratives from different epochs in Appalachia help us begin to think about these? Although this chapter's aim is perhaps not the clear and distinct formulation of a new set of typologies, it certainly makes the case that new orientations to old words are necessary to better understand the myriad identities found within Appalachia, somewhere in the nexus of the spirit and the flesh, the queer [kwir] and the queer [kwar].

The Flesh Longed and Lost

The fabric of possibilities that closes the exterior visible in upon the seeing body maintains between them a certain divergence (écart). But this divergence is not a void, it is filled precisely by the flesh as the place of emergence of a vision, a passivity that bears an activity—and so also the divergence between the exterior visible and the body which forms the upholstering (capitonnage) of the world.

—Merleau-Ponty (1968, 272)

Charlie [He/Him/His]

My Uncle Charlie was always queer [kwar], as far back as I can remember. He kept a weed whacker in the kitchen and a fifteen-year-old bar of Neufchâtel cheese in his refrigerator. He was many things: a southern bachelor gentleman in the vein of Tennessee Williams, a boy who was good to his mother, a cultured eccentric, and a grumpy old man. Uncle Charlie was many things to many people, but to my mother's family he was just uncle Charlie and not in need of any other descriptor, as his identity was something known to all but veiled in terms that reduced his identity to a queer [kwar] archetype. To this day, people and actions are still described in my mother's family as being "very uncle Charlie." To return to the quote by Maurice Merleau-Ponty, there was no "emergence of vision" of Charlie's flesh because it remained deeply disconnected from the spirit.

While his later years are fairly easy to recount, his childhood and early adulthood are only really understood in small snippets of family lore drawn together over the rather straightforward facts about his life. He never married, and this short statement was all that was ever spoken about his queer identity—everything else was simply queer [kwar], odd, unusual, and eccentric. His life seemed fairly simple: he served in the navy as a switchboard operator in World War II, left the military, and repurposed his skill as a switchboard operator for Duke Power for nearly forty years, then retired to lead a quiet life with his church and spend time with myriad nieces, nephews, grandnieces, and grandnephews. I am drawn back to Merleau-Ponty when he writes, "I see you in flesh and bone; you are there. I cannot know what you are thinking, but I can suppose it, guess at it from your facial expressions, your gestures, and your words—in short from a series of bodily appearances of which I am only the witness" (1964, 114). I can then only recount what I witness, and this is completely wrapped in in the queerer [kwar] aspects of Charlie's being.

He was also a boy who was good to his mother. When his father passed away, his mother, called Mamma Sharpe by the family, came to live with him, and his social life essentially became bridge games with her and her friends. They lived together until she passed away, and her nightgown hung in "her room" until the day Charlie passed away. This momma's boy persona was never lost on my mother, who in my early adulthood constantly worried that she might become my Mamma Sharpe, thus stultifying a more fully realized identity.

He was a cultured eccentric who collected opera records and candlewick crystal. After his mother died, his house, filled with curiosities and tchotchkes, became the family gathering spot for my mother's family. Charlie took his place as family patriarch, though he never had any children of his own. My summers as a child at his house were filled with antiques stores, opera records, and *Masterpiece Theatre* on PBS. He was wise, funny, and quite the mentor for someone like me who also did not fit the mold of the Appalachian male.

But Charlie inhabited another queer [kwar] identity: he was a grumpy old man. You see, the danger with queerness [kwar] in Charlie's case was turning him into something to be admired, a saintly man who followed the principles of his church and was good to his family. My father threw this at me years later when I came out to him, asking why I couldn't just "be like Charlie" and take my place as the family's lovable eccentric queer [kwar] (read: sexless) uncle.

As far as I can guess, Charlie possibly had a fleeting queer [kwir] identity as a young man, but he made a choice early on to "try really hard to be good," as referenced in a letter to his mother just after World War II. My mother tells me he once spoke of being in love as a young man, but the conversation never went any further than that. The only definitive proof that Charlie was queer at all was my mother discovering a few 1950s-era muscle magazines in his closet in her youth.

Other than these little fragments, Charlie's life was clearly quare, rather than queer; even the amusing story of him teaching my mother how to walk in high heels reeks of the quare—the off-kilter, strange, and even oddly amusing, but never quite queer [kwir]. Maybe the clearest example of this was a comment he made to me when we were at an antiques store when I was ten: I suggested that a naked statue was pornographic, and Charlie responded, "Does it turn you on? Because as long as it doesn't turn you on it is art, not pornography." As long as he denied the flesh being aroused, his "orientation" toward the world, to use Ahmed's (2006, 557) phrasing, could continue to be queer [kwar], not queer [kwir].

I often try to picture what it might have been like if Charlie had grown up in New York or California, understanding "that body-subjects are always, in an important sense, 'place construed' " (O'Loughlin 1997, 27). I cannot help but imagine that Charlie chose aspects of identity that could identity his difference, but never cross over into the queer [kwir] because of the specificities of the Appalachian landscape that created a straight space in particular ways: "Spaces are oriented around the straight body, which allows that body to extend into space . . . Repetitive performances of hegemonic asymmetrical gender identities and heterosexual desires congeal over time to produce the appearance that the street is normally a heterosexual space . . . Spaces become straight" (Ahmed 2006, 563). Queer [kwir] bodies in Appalachia in the era of

Uncle Charlie had a way of addressing their wonkiness without directly disrupting the straightness of their space.

Ricky [He/Him/His]

As a spectator of the gestures and utterances of the other's body before me, I consider the totality of signs thus given, the totality of facial expressions this body presents to me, as the occasion for a kind of decoding. Behind the body whose gestures and characteristic utterances I witness, I project, so to speak, what I myself feel of my own body. No matter whether it is a question of an actual association of ideas or, instead, a judgement whereby I interpret the appearances, I transfer to the other the intimate experience I have of my own body.

—Merleau-Ponty (1964, 115)

Because Ricky's identity is only reconstructed through narrative, language both queer [kwir] and queer [kwar] become of paramount importance. His life and death are a record of memory, garnered in fragments and retold as a bit of a queer historiography. I offer a narrative that fills in the gaps between these fragments and highlights the queer [kwir] and queer [kwar] aspects of his life as I knew it. To reference the quote by Merleau-Ponty, there was always something unspoken between him and me, something that simply could not be uttered between a twelve-year-old gay boy and his gay uncle, "for the cult of the child permits no shrines to the queerness of boys and girls, since queerness, for contemporary culture at large . . . is understood as bringing children and childhood to an end" (Greteman and Wojcikiewicz 2014, 563). There is a constructed straightness in the mentor–mentee relationship between the adolescent and the adult: a straight uncle could talk frankly with his straight nephew about sex, puberty, and relationships. A queer [kwir] correlate in this scenario simply does not exist because of Greteman's point about the cult of the child; Ricky was viewed as an entity to be protected from, not a resource for a boy entering an adolescence he was entirely unprepared for. In this sense, there is no space for queer [kwir] adolescence because queerness [queerness] simply ends childhood in the construct of the "cult of the child."

Ricky was the youngest of six siblings, born in an impoverished environment to a mother who was at the time estranged from his father, both of them much older. Ricky was firmly a Generation X child with siblings ranging from the GI generation to Baby Boomers. Given the fact that he was significantly younger than his siblings, Ricky was raised much like an only child, with his older siblings more like aunts and uncles swooping in from time to time with advice about his future. These childhood years were described in retrospect by his older brothers and sisters as a time that he was "babied" and "spoiled rotten." The identifiers "spoiled," "babied," and "coddled" coalesce around the queer [kwar] identity "momma's boy." Being a momma's boy in Appalachia contains many of the same identifiers that might be used elsewhere, but with a few cultural specifics tied up in the notion of masculine duty. Ricky never worked in the field priming tobacco like his brothers did; his youth was spent learning to play piano and reading books when many of his siblings never rose above functional illiteracy. As a momma's boy, Ricky seemed to shun the practical world that his siblings inhabited in favor of impractical things of beauty and culture; music, art, and literature became his passions. His mother, my grandmother Annie, seemed to allow this exploration, but many years later seemed to lament indulging her youngest son. My mother distinctly remembers Grandma Annie warning her that "you can love a child too much."

I had never really reflected on this admonition, but now I see it as a powerful connector to this notion of the queer [kwar]: boys in Appalachia were to be detached, wild, masculine, and naturally gravitating toward the male-dominated sectors of the culture. Perhaps my grandmother saw this same attachment to the feminine in me, the same queer [kwar] connections that existed between her and Ricky.

Ricky's years after high school graduation (top of his class, I'm told) are somewhat more difficult to trace. According to the family, he was accepted at Juilliard to study piano, but was discouraged from attending due to finances and the lack of any practical application. My father often spoke of trying to talk Ricky into going to law school, only to become exasperated when Ricky refused. During the 1980s, in Ricky's twenties, he disappeared from our lives for some time, living, I was told, in Charlotte, North Carolina. He gained work as a pianist for the upscale City Club for some time, as it was recounted to me.

As best I can guess, he lived as openly queer [kwir] during this period in his life. Years later, I met people in the gay community of Charlotte who remembered him vaguely; one man remembers playing with him occasionally as a part of an informal gay tennis club, another recalls him playing piano at a house party. At some point he met a young man from Sweden, but nobody associated with Ricky knows this young man's name. The nature of their relationship (or whether they even had a relationship) is unclear. What I do know is that apparently Ricky contracted HIV from this young man.

I can put together Ricky's next few years through vague memory; I was a preteen witnessing events I had no context for. I was only able to give meaning to these fragments of events in retrospect. Ricky moved back in with Grandma at the trailer park and back into my life. I got to know him during this declining period of his life, and these interactions formed a huge part of my early identity. My earliest memory of this time was being chastised by my grandmother for playing dress-up with her jewelry and having Ricky come to my defense. He argued that I had as much right as my female cousins to play with the jewelry, and I remember this being a bone of contention between him and my grandmother.

I would come over to the trailer, and he would make me cups of herbal tea with honey and lemon, and he would share pictures of famous artists and talk about how the impressionists differed from the expressionists, how the artists used color and composition to develop meaning in a painting. He would play the piano and let me sing along; he played everything from Peter, Paul, and Mary to musical theater standards, and I remember feeling so much more comfortable with him than with my other aunts and uncles—there was a softness, an approachability, a sparkle of intellect and culture in a world that lacked both.

These interactions did not come without reproach from other family members. I remember hushed-voiced conversations between my parents, aunts, and uncles whenever I spent time with Ricky. In particular, I remember a strange visitor from Sweden, Gudren, who played the piano and told stories of her home country while other family members looked on awkwardly. I remember my grandmother crying very hard that night, and in retrospect I think that was when she realized Gudren's son had a relationship with Ricky, and Ricky had contracted HIV.

The memories became fractured after that: a hospital trip here, a hushed argument there, and everyone in my family slowly isolating Ricky. After developing what I know to be AIDS-related dementia, Ricky was committed to a state mental facility, where he spent his last months before he died; the family told everyone he had a brain tumor.

My memory of his funeral included seeing my father smoking the only cigarette I ever saw him smoke, my grandmother breaking down in the first pew of the church, and my uncle quoting verses from Romans to my mother while explaining to her that Ricky was in Hell. He had succumbed to the sins of the flesh; the queer [kwar] had become queer [kwir] despite the family's best efforts to hide it, and the family silenced any further dialogue about it. That same year, my grandmother told me tearfully in her car on the way to the supermarket that Ricky was gay, and I had better be especially careful that I not make the same choices, otherwise I would share his fate.

The Flesh Found

Every historical object is a fetish.

—Merleau-Ponty (1968, 275)

Matthew [He/Him/His]

As a child, my father called me queer [kwar] all the time. It never felt malicious; it was always accompanied by a slow head shake and a wry smile. Typically, it was after I said or did something that departed from what he thought I should have done. At first, I really did not understand what made my behaviors queer [kwar], but because these actions seemed to garner more laughs and smiles than admonishments, I began to fashion my early identity on this queerness [kwar]. I also had Ricky and Charlie as models for me at an early age, and, as the quote by Merleau-Ponty illustrates, I learned to fetishize the historical models of the queer [kwar] I had been presented with. As Deborah Britzman (1993) points out, "But the 'queer,' like the 'theory,' in Queer Theory does not depend on the identity of the theorist or the one who engages with it. Rather the queer in Queer Theory anticipates the precariousness of the signified" (6). In this case, there is a certain precariousness with how I read the significations of the queer [kwir] and the queer [kwar] in the lives of Charlie and Ricky and embodied those attributes that I could see, even if some aspects of the signified were hidden from view.

In reflection, clothes were probably among the earliest manifestations of the queer [kwar] for me. Although there was some gender bending involved (I was rather obsessed with wearing girls' swimsuits to the pool when I was around ten years old) generally the clothing choices deemed queer [kwar] by my father and others around me were not quite so overtly queer (kwir). I remember making a Native American costume out of some old cloth scraps and deer antlers just for fun, and my father deemed this action queer [kwar]. I loved dressing up and being theatrical, and my parents seemed to tolerate this behavior as long as it wasn't too public. I remember a Halloween party at the local mountain music dance hall that we frequented (I was an avid clogger), where I wanted to dress as the phantom of the opera. My father was absolutely adamant that the costume was too flamboyant for the venue, making the point that he knew I was queer [kwar], but that I shouldn't go too far. He always couched these admonishments by saying he was trying to protect me from ridicule, but it was easy to read on his face that I was a little more different than he was comfortable with.

For some reason, this difference was something I became comfortable with. I discovered by middle school that as long as I fashioned an identity for myself and played to it, folks would not put other labels on me. I used words that I heard on *Masterpiece Theatre* and made references to theater, art, and opera while my peers were more interested in Garth Brooks and *The Simpsons*.

In a sense, my early queer [kwar] identity was in many ways self-perpetuating; I played to the odd, the different, the slightly off-center, as it came easily to me and set me apart just enough to develop a fledgling adolescent identity around it. Being queer [kwar] had the double advantage of allowing me to not have to navigate the complicated world of normal and not come across as queer [kwir]. I am not sure when I first heard this harsher, more abrasive pronunciation of the word; something about it felt abhorrent but fearfully familiar.

My first clear recollection of hearing the word *queer* (kwir) came on the fifth-grade school playground; we played a rudimentary version of football where the only object was to dogpile the person with the ball, referred to as the "queer" (kwir). While the game "smear the queer" was the subject of great schoolyard fun for most of the boys, it was a source of anxiety for me, as I was not terribly athletically inclined. More often than not, I was the one unfortunate enough to be tossed the ball at the last moment and then dogpiled; the lesson that the queer (kwir) was to be rhetorically and physically punished was clear, and I began to develop a real understanding of the risk of physical danger for queerness [kwir]. I spent years wondering if this phenomenon was something specific to my school or region, only to discover that after reading Lisa Loutzenheiser's 1996 article "How Schools Play 'Smear the Queer'" that the practice was common as far from Appalachia as liberal (by comparison) northern California (59).

On further reflection, perhaps the most interesting part about queerness [kwar] was that I cultivated it; certainly my middle school years saw bullying because of my difference, but by high school I had achieved a certain status as an eccentric. In fact, from the moment I learned the word *eccentric* in the seventh grade, I sort of clung to it as a moniker. It was my earliest linguistic identification with the queer [kwar], and I had managed to fashion a respected identity with it. I was in every school musical and the show choir, I was captain of the chess club and voted most intellectual; I managed to create an identity around this notion of the funny, artsy, smart, weird, lovable eccentric. The problem, of course, was that there was one more adjective that described me during this time: sexless.

Certainly, I had a few girlfriends; I was drawn to the smart, funny, awkward, and generally religiously conservative girls who I secretly knew were not going to want anything sexual beyond a kiss or two. But beyond the occasional light public displays of affection in these few fleeting relationships, there was little outwardly sexual about me; I tended to wear old-mannish ill-fitting clothes, made goofy jokes, and was far more Paul Lynde than Paul Newman. More than one friend in high school simply described me as "asexual."

On the inside, however, was a fairly typical hormonal boy who knew he liked boys. At age thirteen, around 1992, I watched an episode of Maury Povich's show where a group of teenagers were interviewed about their sexuality, and I finally had words for what I was feeling. One boy, close to my age, spoke about being bisexual, and several others identified as gay. *Gay* was a word that seemed the closest to describing me, and I distinctly remember uttering the words to myself: "I am gay." It was another five years before I spoke these words aloud to another person, but I had this self-defining language of "gay" as a part of my hidden identity for all of those years.

Being gay in my high school in the 1990s simply wasn't an option I was willing to accept. The identity still had connotations of extreme femininity and passivity, and that was not how I projected my queer [kwar] identity to the world. People described me as artsy, eccentric, perhaps even dramatic, but this queerness [kwar] was a nonsexual, nonexplicit way to cover the truth of my feelings. Like many of my generation, however, college became a space not so much for self-discovery but for self-redefinition; I had embraced the queer [kwar] parts of my identity as the artsy, hippie, bohemian, but by age eighteen I was developing the empowerment to begin folding in my previously hidden sexuality as a piece of who I was. I was the gay bohemian, the artsy eccentric who would, to borrow the words of a college friend, "announce his sexuality with a handshake."

This outward identification received the typical homophobic pushback and a slightly subtler criticism: people began to suggest that my being gay should be treated as simply a minor part of my personality and that I put too much emphasis on it. My cousin told me at age twenty that "You are all about being gay, you act like that is all that you are, when it is just one part of you." Others would comment that I had to "push my gayness in their face." The reality to me was that this was a critical part of who I was, and a holistic identity had to include my sexuality, the same way it does with straight people. This is echoed in the words of a young trans man who explained that the culture he was coming from was "very much *not* interested in approval from straight people," which was, he explained, "the main way in which [the radical queer culture he was coming from] seemed to differ from mainstream gay and lesbian culture" (Blackburn 2014, 5).

What I realized in retrospect was that I was finally developing an identity as queer (kwir). Queer [kwir] was a fully formed state of being that took into account the "wonky" of the queer [kwar] yet also understood the "slant of queer [kwir] desire" that is a critical part of me as a fully embodied subject (Ahmed 2006, 562). This is where the queer [kwir] / queer [kwar] dichotomy became significant to me: queer [kwar] seeks to strip the subject of their embodiment, to separate the spirit from the flesh. At stake here is something in the essence of the nature of the phenomenon of "queer [kwir]." In a sense, this began my acknowledgment that queerness [kwir], to borrow the adjectives of David Halperin (2003), is graphic, carnal, enduringly sexual, and always becoming (343). This realization was critical in helping me begin to discover the radical potential for the very notion of queer [kwir].

In returning to the notion of identification and typology in my narrative, I reflect on Heasley's words that "the "sensitive" (translation: "sissy") young boy in films such as *Stand By Me* is portrayed as needing the protection and guidance of an older, heteronormative masculine boy (Heasley 2005, 311). Where does this place the somewhat masculine-reading boy seeking the guidance of sissies? Clearly this was my experience, yet the lessons I learned never made me identify or even present as sissy, at least not in traditionally accepted uses of the word. In fact, my mother still describes my presentation growing up as "all boy," and when asked if she knew something was different about me, she points out that my rather geeky penchant for arranging my toy soldiers into Greek phalanx formations was more noteworthy than any sense of nonnormative gender presentation. Gender presentation did not seem to be a component to my queer [kwar] identity, as it did with my uncles. The suppression of the flesh seemed not as manifest in my identity as the suppression of the spirit, and both become increasingly muddled in the experiences of my two students, as we will see in the remaining sections.

The Flesh Fragmented

In short, when it metamorphoses the structures of the visible world and makes itself a gaze of the mind, intuitus mentis—this is always in virtue of the same fundamental phenomenon of reversibility which sustains both the mute perception and the speech and which manifests itself by an almost carnal existence of the idea, as well as by a sublimation of the flesh. In a sense, if we were to make completely explicit the architectonics of the human body, its ontological framework, and how it sees itself and hears itself, we would see that the structure of its mute world is such that all the possibilities of language are already given in it.

—Merleau-Ponty (1968, 155)

Like many queer [kwir] educators, I have made a choice to be what Maughn Rollins-Gregory (2004) calls the "queer teacher as native informant" to my students (59). As a high school teacher and later as a college professor, I wanted to normalize queerness [kwir] by my openness and, in an almost patriarchal way, be a guide and mentor to "my little queer babies" (Blackburn 2014, 6). These goals are problematic in the same distinct way: somehow, we are still working in a linear fashion to move toward some great noble goal, this "general characteristic of modernism . . . that we will get 'there' someday" (Greteman and Wojcikiewicz 2014, 562). In the first instance, I cannot make normal that which is by definition not normal, or it then ceases to be; if the queer [kwir] can remain abnormal in the classroom, then a native informant perspective can work not as a normalizer but as a disturber, with a pedagogy of interruption, to use the words of Gert Biesta (2010) from his book *Good Education in an Age of Measurement: Ethics, Politics, Democracy.*

The second instance, being a queer [kwir] mentor and guide, brings us to this final section, where I have begun to discover that in queerness [kwir] mentor–mentee relationships become wonky, fluidic, and blurred, much like any other binary notion viewed through the lens of queerness [kwir]. To say that my understanding of the queer [kwir] is being constantly queered [kwir] by my students is an understatement. With this in mind, it makes more sense to construct this part of the chapter in collaboration with them, as the themes and ideas presented are not so much about them as authored by them. I am re-minded by them constantly that "Students are often among the first to respond to changing terminology either by adopting them themselves when finding words to better describe who they are or by advocating for organizational name changes. Often less constrained by bureaucratic processes and institutional resistance that more departmental-level changes, student organizations can quickly adapt to ensure inclusion and comfort" (Jourian 2015, 21). It was in fact at their behest that we started the Gay and Progressive Pedagogy (GAPP) student organization at our university. Through the conversations in this stu-dent-driven club, many of the themes and ideas for this paper originated.

Logan [They/Them/Theirs]

When considering Logan's narrative, it is worth remembering many of us in Appalachia grew up hearing about "sins of the flesh" from the pulpit, but it is also worth remembering that for just as many of us, Christianity made up a part of our queer [kwar] identities. Make no mistake, Christianity is by far the most prevalent religion in the southern Appalachians, but this does not mean that the level of devotion to the faith doesn't vary greatly. Many learn early on that an almost extreme Christian identity functions as an aspect of the queer [kwar]. In Logan's case, Christianity has always been linked to their queer [kwar] and queer [kwir] identity—it has both been an enabler and a point of shame at different points in their life. For twelve years, they went to a conservative, private Presbyterian school that taught "hellfire and brimstone" sermons every Wednesday "as if we weren't getting enough of that in classes." If anything should have ensured their heterosexuality, it was that place; Logan would have been expelled if there was any hint of them not being straight. On top of that, they continued to go to youth group at their Baptist church, which their family had attended since Logan was an infant. As Logan continued to grow and realize who they were, their friend group at church also did. Logan and their friends soon realized they were all very different; it was never explicitly said that they were all queer [kwir] and that's what bound them all together, they just knew they needed to stick together. Jesseh was polyamorous and genderqueer, Alyssa and Ashlyn were dating each other, and so were Suzy and Jessica. Jesseh soon brought their friend Lily to vacation Bible school the summer before Logan's senior year. The flesh here can no longer be separated from the spirit, but in such radical ways that the spirit seems to work to redefine the flesh, rather than the other way around.

Lily and Logan immediately clicked and, once they finally started dating, youth group was one of the only places they got to see each other. Logan remembers once sitting in a sermon and the pastor said, "And I'm going to say it . . . homosexuals will burn for eternity in Hell." Logan and Lily were actually holding hands in church while the pastor uttered those words; Lily was so shocked that she screamed out loud, "What?!" Logan remembers singing "How He Loves" and changing the pronouns to *she* and thinking about Lily: "*She* is jealous for me, Love's like a hurricane, I am a tree, Bending beneath the weight of *her* wind and mercy." The flesh, in this instance, indicates a longing, but soon this was harder to separate from the spirit, as Logan began a literal reorientation of the flesh.

For Logan, clothes also blurred things between the queer [kwir] and the queer [kwar]; the first time they dressed masculine in public was at youth group one night with Lily. Logan wore a blue button-down shirt, beige jeans that were too long, and brown leather shoes. With their short haircut, Lily holding their hand later at ice cream with other friends, Logan remembers thinking that they could block out the fact that their wide hips made the lower half of the shirt way too tight. After that, Logan began feeling less comfortable in feminine clothes and started shopping regularly in the men's section.

They ditched the push-up bras that had never felt quite right and cut their hair shorter, shorter, and shorter. This physical transformation actually speaks to a shift in perception and identity—Logan was not outwardly becoming what they had inwardly always been, but was becoming through the manifold interactions of the body and perception, "the experience of my flesh as gangue of my perception has taught me that perception does not come to birth just anywhere, that it emerges in the recess of a body" (Merleau-Ponty 1968, 9).

Still, Logan refused to recognize their changing presentation as anything related to a changing gender; they still thought trans people didn't exist. When Logan went to college, they still refused to use people's correct pronouns and just thought those people were confused. Logan began to use the identifier *gay* after a date with a guy their freshman year almost became intimate. This discovery prompted a two-week-long anxiety attack when Logan started thinking for the first time about pronouns and how others saw them. Nothing felt right to them anymore, and they could hardly leave the dorm room to go to classes. Even Logan's genderqueer ex criticized Logan's pronouns, suggesting Logan was co-opting transgender peoples' space.

For the next few months, they were in a state of limbo; they tried wearing makeup, not wearing makeup; shaving, not shaving; shopping for men's clothes, wearing dresses; they allowed themselves time to experiment. They even played for a while with the identity "pan-romantic demisexual" (demisexual people experience sexual attraction only when a stable emotional connection has been established. In a society where the existence of sexuality is a given, with phrases like "everyone has sex" seeming innocuous, asexual people may indeed feel queer themselves, meaning different from the given norm; Jourian 2015, 21). One of the most powerful moments of queerness for me, in learning from and growing with Logan, has been an understanding that there is no such thing as a universality of sexual attraction. The carnal flesh of the queer [qwir] is not bound by a universal understanding of attraction; making such an assumption is to impose a restriction on the queer [kwir] that limits understandings of the flesh that does not include a particular type of sexual intimacy.

For Logan, once they had the nonbinary language to describe their reality, the next semester was all about validation—they found queer hook-ups, friends, professors, and communities that allowed them to exist as they were. They write that they became secure in their queer and nonbinary identity, and this later translated to coming out to more family members and dressing in an even more masculine fashion—chest binders, boxer briefs, and all. For Logan, finding the appropriate language allowed them to queer [kwir] their performance of the flesh. In returning to the notion of typology, Heasley writes, "I propose a typology of straight-queer males—males who disrupt both heterosexuality and hegemonic masculinity—as a contribution to the expansion of the conceptualization of straightness and of masculinity" (2005, 311). Where in this typology is a space for gender identity, I wonder? What of the nonbinary body that seeks masculine gender expression, in Logan's case? If we truly want to expand the notion of masculinity, how do we conceptualize the masculine body in a nongendered context? Parsing out the expression from the identification seems to be a powerful intersection between the queer [kwar] and the queer [kwir] seeing a literal transformation of the flesh, but one that needs no correlation to the spirit.

Michael [He/Him/His]

Michael continued to feel the need to perform a sense of the queer [kwar] even after he acknowledged his explicit queerness [kwir]. Like Logan, Michael found the language to describe himself and found a need to alter his flesh to align with the language, but in a very different way. Michael identified as a gay cisgender male but began to believe that his flesh did not represent the gay male archetype he envisioned. In his narrative, we can see real fragmentation of the queer [kwir] and the queer [kwar]. Even after embracing one queer [kwir] identity, the need to conform to a queer [kwar] notion of the performance of gay led to a queer [kwir] encounter with traditionally feminine eating disorders. In the words of Judith Butler (1990), "The body is not a 'being,' but a variable boundary, a surface whose permeability is politically regulated" (139). The regulations of Michael's body in his story speak to a fragmentation of the flesh, even once queer [kwir] identities are realized. The troubling nature of the political regulation here is that it does not come from a public understanding of gender and gender roles but from a gay community standard of beauty and the enduring and damaging archetype of the gay male Adonis.

Michael writes that apparently everyone knew he was gay before he did. His mother has told him on multiple occasions that she knew both his sister and he were gay the minute they were born. In middle school he was bullied for being gay, even though it was not an identity that he was open about. He knew he was not straight in middle school because he would look at the athletes in his classes and daydream about them, but he tried to convince himself he was bisexual. He kept telling himself that until junior year of high school in an attempt to keep some attachment to language that connected him in some way to the opposite gender. He realized that sexuality plays a huge role in how one is treated, what opportunities are available, and how one interacts with others; he thought being straight was his only chance of being normal and accepted, but he knew he was not so he believed bisexuality would somehow keep him connected to some sense of heteronormativity. He would talk to girls and build close relationships with them but thought about being with guys at the same time. His junior year was when things came to a climax.

Michael was, in his words, "practically dating" a girl named Nicole, but at the same time he was "getting close" with Aaron, a guy he met in orchestra. He felt terrible for leading Nicole on because his "heart was not in it." His use of *heart* here is recognition of the queer [kwar] or a lack of the flesh in his relationship with Nicole. This denial of the flesh literally embodied itself when, one day in orchestra, he looked over at her and started having a panic attack. His body literally betrayed him; he could not breathe, his mind was racing, and he started shaking. The panic attack culminated later when, in front of his mother he broke down and muttered, "I think I'm gay." She did not hear him the first time, so he yelled it and continued to sob. His mom just held him and kept saying how everything was going to be okay and that she will always love him no matter what. Had the story ended there, we would have a heartwarming gay coming-out story, but it is problematic to end there because queer narratives rarely tie together so neatly.

While Michael identifies as a cisgender male, he envisions his gender expression as being somewhat more fluid, and sometimes we can see this manifesting in damaging ways. While suggesting that eating disorders are seen as a more feminine act, he writes about struggling with anorexia and bulimia. In fact, Michael was somewhat frustrated with a reading he encountered in my class where the author ascribed eating disorders as being typically a part of feminine performance (Felman 2001, 98). He troubled this by asking why men like him who starve themselves get overlooked. It's ironic that Michael's struggle with the flesh does not seem to be performing the feminine, but performing a particular gay version of the masculine. The realization of the flesh of the queer [kwir] led to a whole new need to perform to a particular bodily standard.

For sixteen years of his life, he was one of the largest kids in his grade. In the summer before his junior year of high school, he tried going to the gym and eating healthy to "fix" his appearance; when that did not work, he stopped eating altogether. Throughout the year, he lost about one hundred pounds. He shamed himself during this time, believing he was performing the feminine, living the stereotype of a feminine gay man with an eating disorder. He masculinized his language, telling people he was working out and eating healthy rather than disclosing his anorexia, which is seen as a feminine weakness. Even within a realization of his gayness, he fought a new compulsive normativity, that of homonormativity, and crafted his language in such a way that he felt less feminine.

He would almost black out standing up, walking, and playing bassoon. He constantly thought about not eating, what he did eat, how he was going to lose weight, how he looked, and how to go through life. Everyone noticed his dramatic weight loss, teachers asked if he was okay, peers talked behind his back, and his family worried about him. Eventually his parents' fears were confirmed that he had an eating disorder, and they got him counseling for eating disorders, depression, and anxiety.

It seems upon reflection that even after coming out, Michael never really stopped performing the queer [kwar]. Here we can see a problematic morphing of the queer [kwar] to include the flesh in damaging ways. The queer [kwar] Appalachian archetype for Michael never really left; instead of the eccentric sexless curiosity of my youth, Michael's version of the queer [kwar] was of the thin, stylish gay boy. Even after a year of not purging, he struggles with this dysmorphic image, even though he can feel every vertebra in his spine, he can see his ribs, and his hip bones protrude. In returning to Heasley to think of typology, he writes, "we do not have a language or framework for considering the ways straight men can disrupt the dominant paradigm of the straight-masculine nor a language that gives legitimacy to the lived experience" (Heasley 2005, 311). I wonder where this lies for Michael, whose particular and literal suppression of the flesh seems to fit into a queer-masculine that tries to subvert dominant paradigms of male queerness as the weakling or the chubby sissy.

Conclusions: Of Language and Bodies

In preparing texts for this essay, I turned the narratives of my childhood into a crisp, clean story that had a clear beginning, middle, and end; I took the stories of my uncles as a cautionary tale about closets and suppression in Appalachia, and I was ready to speak passionately about a pedagogy that empowers queer [kwir] students to be out, be proud, and be themselves. Then I started listening to the voices of the youth in Appalachia whom I teach, and I heard things that challenged my rather linear read of my experiences. I was experiencing what Merleau-Ponty (1964) called a "lived decentering" (110). I was a cisgender white married man with a very specific and narrowly defined concept of the queer [kwir] based on my experiences and the meaning I had made of it. For me, the queer [kwir] and the queer [kwar] were binaries separated by an acknowledgment of my sexual attraction, and this was oversimplified. Listening to the stories of my students, I realized that in triangulating the queer [kwir] and the queer [kwar] over time illustrates that I risked substituting one narrow definition of queer for another.

One goal here was to point out that the queer [kwar] was a subtle tool of control for the suppression of the queer [kwir]. In fact, as an ongoing project of understanding the queer [kwir], I am concerned about its watering down, "turning it into a generic badge of subversiveness, a more trendy version of liberal" (Halperin 2003, 341). I wanted to suggest that the queer [kwir] was indelibly linked to the gay, lesbian, bisexual, transgender, genderqueer, asexual, intersex, demisexual, and pansexual identities behind those who associate themselves with queer [kwir]. What I learned from Michael, Logan, and other students was that "names, labels, and language communicate a great deal about our knowledge, assumptions, intentions, and interpretations of particular topics and experiences. Practitioners and scholars have an ethical responsibility to cultivate an openness within themselves and campus-wide to shifting and contextually based terminology and to adopt practices that promote individual and community meaning making" (Jourian 2015, 21–22). While I recognize myself as a pretty "radical queer" [kwir], I had to have students explain many of the identities that they gravitate toward. I now know that *gay* and later *queer* were the vocabulary available to me, and I wonder what new identities I might have explored had I been born twenty years later. I have become homonormative, and my students have decentered this understanding for me. I actually find that my self-understanding is morphing as I learn from a new generation's experiences of the queer [kwar] and the queer [kwar]. I grew up in the tail end of an era where there was one unspoken identity, this "love that dare not speak its name," and yet now trans students are drawing unicorns with sliding scales to indicate the fracturing and fluidity of sex, gender, and sexuality (Pan and Moore 2017). Drawing on my narrative, I focused on coming out, and we can see with Michael and Logan that coming out is fraught with complexity. What is it that one "comes out" as? What are the queer [kwir] and quare [kwar] body politics and body violence at play? This queerness [kwir] my students present makes possible a constant "disruption or the violent undoing of meaning, the loss of identity and coherence" that ought really to be a part of the essence of an understanding of queer (Greteman and Wojcikiewicz 2014, 568).

This is certainly not to say that the queer [kwir] and queer [kwar] histories and perspectives written about here are pointless. The historicity of queer

[kwir] and queer [kwar] identities in Appalachia are critical for developing the kinds of dialogue across generations of queer [kwir] students and teachers. Understanding the contexts that shaped the identities of Uncle Charlie, Uncle Ricky, and myself are keys to richer dialogue with youth that are redefining the queer [kwir] and the queer [kwar] in southern Appalachia. A queer activism informed by the queer [kwir] and the queer [kwar] in southern Appalachia might be seen as fighting for the spaces in which students can give voice and body to their queer [kwir] self-identifications. As Judith Butler writes, "I can only say 'I' to the extent that I have first been addressed" (Butler 1993, 18). This queer activism might then seek to first address queer students in southern Appalachia, then work collectively to disrupt, discern, and deconstruct that which might be queer [kwar] and that which might be queer [kwir]. In the flesh and the spirit, there is an interesting postmodern interplay between gender expression, gender identity, and sexuality. Most notably in this study is the idea that the qweerness [kwar] in spirit, or nonnormative gender expression, and queerness [kwir] in flesh, or nonnormative sexuality, vacillate significantly between generations. While my uncles expressed queerness [kwar] openly, they often suppressed queerness [kwir]. I early on learned to express queerness [kwir] openly, but my queerness [kwar] became almost a comfortable quasi-normative, if quirky, facade to hide behind. Logan and Michael, on the other hand, seemed able to find more intricate intersections between the spirit and the flesh, the queer [kwar] and the queer [kwir]. How would Logan have identified in Ricky's era? Would Charlie have identified as asexual, demisexual, or perhaps even trans if he were coming of age today? Would I have lived as a straight-passing man in Charlie's time, Michael an eccentric bachelor? These questions suggest an important interplay that might well suggest new typologies unconsidered in the hills and hollers of Appalachia.

BIBLIOGRAPHY

Ahmed, Sarah. 2006. "Orientations: Toward a Queer Phenomenology." *GLQ: A Journal of Lesbian and Gay Studies* 12, no. 4, 543–73.

Blackburn, Mollie V. 2014. "(Re)Writing One's Self as an Activist across Schools and Sexual and Gender Identities: An Investigation of the Limits of LGBT-Inclusive and Queering Discourses." *Journal of Language and Literacy Education* 10, no. 1, 1–13.

Biesta, G. 2010. A New Logic of Emancipation: The Methodology of Jacques Ranciere . *Educational Theory* 60, no. 1, 39–59.

Britzman, Deborah. 1995. "Is There a Queer Pedagogy? Or, Stop Reading Straight." *Educational Theory* 45, no. 2, 151–65.

Butler, Judith. 1990. *Gender Trouble: Feminism and the Subversion of Identity*. New York: Routledge.

———. 1993. *Bodies that Matter: On the Discursive Limits of Sex*. New York: Routledge.

Felman, J. L. 2001. *Never a Dull Moment: Teaching and the Art of Performance*. New York: Routledge.

Greteman, Adam J., and Steven K. Wojcikiewicz. 2014. "The Problems with the Future: Educational Futurism and the Figural Child." *Journal of Philosophy of Education* 48, no. 4, 559–73.

Halperin, David M. 2003. "The Normalization of Queer Theory." *Journal of Homosexuality* 45, no. 2, 339–43.

Heasley, Robert. 2005. "Queer Masculinities of Straight Men: A Typology." *Men and Masculinities* 7, no. 3, 310–20.

Johnson, E. Patrick. 2007. " 'Quare' Studies, or (Almost) Everything I Know about Queer Studies I Learned from My Grandmother." *Text and Performance Quarterly* 21, no. 1, 1–25.

Jourian, T. J. 2015. "Evolving Nature of Sexual Orientation and Gender Identity." *New Directions for Student Service* 152, 11–23.

Loutzenheiser, Lisa W. 1996. "How Schools Play 'Smear the Queer.' " *Feminist Teacher* 10, no. 2, 59–64.

Merleau-Ponty, Maurice. 1964. *Primacy of Perception*. Evanston, IL: Northwestern University Press.

———. 1968. *The Visible and the Invisible*. Trans. A. Lingis. Evanston, IL: Northwestern University Press.

Muñoz, J. E. 2009. *Cruising Utopia: The Then and There of Queer Theory*. New York: NYU Press.

O'Loughlin, Marjorie. 1997. "Corporeal Subjectivities: Merleau-Ponty, Education and the Postmodern Subject." *Educational Philosophy and Theory* 29, no. 1, 20–31.

Pan, Landyn, and Anna Moore. 2018. "The Gender Unicorn." *Trans Student Educational Resource*. http://www.transstudent.org/gender. Accessed August 28, 2018.

Rollins-Gregory, Maughn. 2004. "Being Out, Speaking Out: Vulnerability and Classroom Inquiry." *Journal of Gay & Lesbian Issues in Education* 2, no. 2, 53–64.

Sokolowski, R. 2000. *Introduction to Phenomenology*. New York: Cambridge University Press.

CHAPTER 5

Pickin' and Grinnin': Quare Hillbillies, Counterrhetorics, and the Recovery of Home

Kimberly Gunter

Momma calls with news from home. Daddy is mad, a fact that is noteworthy by itself. As innocent a soul as ever trod the Earth, he had once advised me, an angsty, angry sixteen-year-old struggling with unspeakable impulses toward Sheila E., to hum a Christmas tune whenever I felt sad. He reasoned, hand to God, "No one can feel sad when they're hummin' 'Frosty the Snowman.' "

Momma's voice whispers into the harvest gold rotary phone on her kitchen counter, beams to the satellites orbiting in space, and finally echoes through my grimy iPhone. She lays out the scene: "Daddy went down to the feed store." His brother, my uncle, James Earl (pseudonyms are used throughout the essay) loaded sacks of corn and oats and Goat Grow into people's pick-ups by day and read Job by night, preparing for his Sunday sermons as a lay minister (and the second coming, too, obviously). "I reckon everything was fine until Romy Womack came in, and just out of nowhere, James Earl started saying all these hateful things about gay people."

I reach across the galley kitchen for my Ina Garten cookbook, trying to measure saffron for couscous. "Who's Romy Womack?" I ask, distracted and clearly missing the point.

"He's nobody. Just a redneck smartass. He's younger than me and dad. Anyway, James Earl starting saying things like 'God made Adam and Eve, he didn't make Adam and Steve.' Daddy got so mad he just turned around and walked out," Mom harrumphed.

"Well, *that* was original. I hope his sermons are better than that. He'll have all of Keatonville asleep by 9:45 ever Sunday mornin'.'"

Jonathan Alexander and Jacqueline Rhodes (2012) stipulate that queer rhetoric must first acknowledge the power-laden, creative discourses of (normative) sexuality and second disrupt such normalizations: "Queer rhetoric . . . relies on (1) a recognition of the . . . ways in which sexuality . . . constitutes a nexus of power, a conduit through which identities are created, categorized, and rendered as subjects . . . and (2) a reworking of those identifications to disrupt and reroute . . . power, particularly discursive power." The first provision relies on realization. The second is more challenging, for it requires intervention.

So the question for me becomes whether my father's response to "the feed store incident" constitutes a rhetorically queer response? My dad certainly recognized the clichéd insults James Earl uttered as homophobic, and he didn't miss the implication that my uncle, whose false bravado was bolstered by an external audience in the sad form of Romy Womack, was talking about me in particular. My uncle's homophobic rhetoric invoked a powerful trinity of southern culture. Playing a kind of hometown Jerry Clower (a southern humorist who had worked as a salesman and a preacher before making his living as an entertainer, which ought to tell you something), James Earl built his ethos in that feed store (1) on a specific incarnation of Christianity, (2) on his own demonstrated if hysterical heterosexuality, and (3) on humor. Moreover, James Earl redoubled these moves. Not only did he quote, if hollowly, biblical history, but he did so as a minister. Not only did he cite the accepted heterosexuality of Adam and Eve; he implicitly invoked his own thirty-year marriage. (Bless Aunt Trish's heart.) Not only did he use humor to make his point, he did so behind a bullying veil of "can't-you-take-a-joke" banter, working to undercut any objection that his listeners might have. Even the physical space surrounding this discourse boosts his ethos. In a world where you can buy a latte at the Co-Op and chicken feed off Amazon, the homespun feed store, a relic of the past, is a place where my uncle truly could have been chewing on a hayseed.

In his quick deduction of this discursive breach, my father, hurt, recognized the hateful rhetorical moves before him, fulfilling Alexander and Rhodes's first criterion, but did his silence and departure constitute a rhetorical disruption of the normalization that was under way? I might have first said no, perhaps wishing my father had instead climbed upon a pallet of Oyster Shell and Chicken Starter, pulled out the P-FLAG constitution, and recited it aloud, preferably in the voice of Paul Robeson. But in hindsight and in a world where deciding whether to go to a family reunion is no simple deliberation, I can't help but wonder about the sonority of his silence. For the easiest of all of my grandmother's children, a man who smiles even in the sepia-toned baby pictures taken by carnival photographers, anger has always been an emotion of last resort. When my uncle began his homophobic litany, be it thoughtless or calculated, he as rhetor attempted to hail his listeners into rhetorical being as coconspirators, not unlike his Sunday calls for little lambs to join him at the altar and accept Jesus as their Lord and savior. Rejecting that hailing into homophobic discursiveness, simply by turning on his bootheel and walking out, my father's silence spoke loudly in a place where saying farewells can take as long as the dinner conversation from which you just pushed yourself back. There was an embodied rhetoric on my father's part that strikes me as powerful, given a whole host of facts—everything from their mother lying in the ground at Blue Hills Cemetery to Daddy's poststroke anomic aphasia to the specter of me floating above that dusty room.

———————

Leaving the 1993 March on Washington for Lesbian, Gay, and Bi Equal Rights and Liberation, I trudged up Capitol Hill, trailing behind my mom who trailed behind my friend Rosie. Refugees from across the South, we were now a bonded trio. The last few days had included buying Lambda Rising postcards of Bill Clinton and Al Gore's heads Photoshopped on embracing men's bodies; dancing to RuPaul in his star-spangled sequins; cheering Urvashi Vaid's admonitions; participating in the Dyke March with its chants of "We want Hillary!" as we passed the White House; walking among panels of the AIDS Quilt; talking with gay soldiers and gay pacifists; and Rosie swooning as she spoke with Dominican nuns about women's health. As we looked over our shoulders back down to the National Mall, on our way to Rosie's hotel room to retrieve our Disappear Fear tickets, already in a kind of afterglow, I mused, "Can't we all just stay? Let's just all get jobs and stay here, all one million of us."

Just then, a different trio overtook us, clearly "family," three women wearing the Pride gear available on ever street corner. One woman, with hitched lip, amid the others' giggles, snarled at us, "Go home, country dykes!"

———————

In their incisive article, Alexander and Rhodes (2012) argue against the false bifurcation of identities, acknowledging, "The binaries of black/white, ethnic/nonethnic, as well as gay/straight and female/male, must be challenged." They urge us to remember that "[José] Muñoz and [David] Wallace insist that we think multiply about subjectivity, that we understand how the experiences of sexuality, race, ethnicity, and gender complicate one another, and how rhetorical practices might have to shift to articulate and intervene in particular representations and debates about sexual experience and identity." Ultimately, though, Alexander and Rhodes insist, "A focus on queer rhetorical practice . . . seeks to catch those moments in which a self-conscious intervention is made in discourses of normalized, and normalizing, sexuality."

I extend Alexander and Rhodes in at least one way and perhaps revise their work in another. The acronym itself reveals the impulse of many LGBTQIA scholars and activists to be inclusive. Thus, expanding Alexander and Rhodes's list of binaries in need of challenging to include urban/rural or country/metropolitan or blue collar/white collar or North/South seems reasonable to the point of mundanity. Adding place and class to the list of lenses through which we might apply queer rhetorical analysis, though, allows us to unpack complex instances of discourse that is both antiqueer and anti-Appalachian, for instance, those "Paddle faster. I hear banjos" T-shirts and bumper stickers that litter roadside gift shops throughout Appalachia. (The lasting cultural impact of *Deliverance* remains unquestionable.)

The success of that inclusive impulse in LGBTQ history, activism, and scholarship is, however, ultimately questionable. Jill Todd Weiss (2003) argues that biphobia and transphobia within "the" LGBT community have resulted from the mainstream gay and lesbian movement's use of "gender appropriateness and accommodationism" as strategies to convince a straight public that "gays and lesbians are 'just like you' " (49); Chong-suk Han (2008) has examined the "primacy of White masculinity within the gay [male] community" (19). The list continues, filled with writers and scholars who examine the marginalization of members of subaltern groups within the larger subaltern LGBTQ+ community, the doubly and triply minoritized.

The understanding of this scholarship is deepened when we situate it within the larger schema of work done on homonormativity. More than fifteen years ago, Lisa Duggan (2003) described a "new homonormativity that does not challenge heterosexist institutions and values, but rather upholds, sustains, and seeks inclusion within them" (50) (in the examples above, with inclusion in binary and naturalized notions of gender and in racism, the fact that the 1993 March notably excluded trans folk from its stipulated focus supports Duggan's point). Michael Warner's (1999) extrapolation of "palatable gays" suggests that the strategies of many mainstream LGBT organizations are not so far-flung from those of the 1950s homophile movement that found neatly dressed young men in jackets and ties and women in skirts and modest dresses holding placards reading "No society can be great without all of its citizens" and simply "Opportunity" (Royles 2016), and Susan Stryker (2008) eloquently argues that, "A decade before *homonormative* became a critically chic term elsewhere . . . transgender praxis and critique required an articulation of the concept" (149).

It's no surprise, then, that Alexander and Rhodes (2012) urge us to recognize the false binaries of subjective existence. While the success of gestures toward "inclusion" and "diversity" within LGBTQ theorization, activism, and communities is debatable, the liberatory and intellectual need to do so has been well documented. Alexander and Rhodes, though, then proceed to "focus primarily on the queernesses of . . . practices, even as we call for additional work on how such queernesses intersect multiple identity positions and practices," and this decision is problematic. Largely abandoning their focus on race and gender to prioritize queerness risks reinstantiating the normativity of queerness itself (that is, its genderedness, its whiteness, its middle-classness). Admittedly, setting aside (even temporarily) considerations of race or place or gender or class, on one hand, may sometimes need to be done—we cannot talk about every possible subject position every time we talk about queerness, just as we cannot talk about queerness every time we talk about race or class or location. On the other hand, whenever we do set aside a given subjectivity, we risk furthering queerness's too frequent instantiation as a monolith, its too frequent failure of self-reflexivity, and the alienation of the folk who call themselves that.

Years later, having driven through the Mississippi Delta in an un-air-conditioned, sky-blue Bronco, thinking about crossroads and humming Robert Johnson because a Lucinda Williams tape had gotten stuck in the cassette deck, I stepped down from the Ford and into a hug from Rosie and the oven that is New Orleans in August. Better than the heat box that was Rosie's apartment, we were off to Hansen's for a Sno-Blitz and then a walk around the French Quarter, when one of God's emissaries, sounding more north Georgia than Louisiana, held his New Testament in the air and proclaimed to Rosie, "Jesus loves you."

"No, he doesn't. Jesus doesn't love *me*," Rosie replied.

A series of "Oh yes, sister" and "Nope, I don't think so" volleyed back and forth, and I thought about all Rosie had given up to call herself *lesbian* or *gay* or *dyke*, or *feminist* for that matter. Her mother would have prayed for her every Wednesday night and twice on Sundays in her Woodbury, Tennessee, Church of Christ, peppering prayers with damnation and longing. But the *Will and Grace* crowd did not accept Rosie either. What are we to do when we risk everything—the blood and dirt of home—only to come out from that which is not us and into that which can seem equally foreign?

I suppose I am a country dyke—I have drawn water from the well, priming the pump and hoping the blue-tailed skinks didn't come scuttling out of its recesses; sitting at my grandmother's knee, I have broken up runner beans from the garden in the morning and eaten them along with a plate of ham hocks in the evening. I know that it's too cold in east Tennessee's Appalachian mountains for water moccasins but that some, ignorant and fearful, kill any water snake they see. But for years now, I've thought off and on about that slur, *country dyke*, and it seems to me that the phrase was uttered then not as a fact but as an allegation, not unlike *queer* has been used. I've wondered about all the exiles we face, from without and within. And one thing I know: when the promise of queerness is truncated by its own stasis, by its own homonormativity, if now dressed up in Kenneth Cole loafers and retro Members Only jackets and Lavett & Chin pomade, the Appalachian queer refugee may be leaving one home without the promise of another.

―――――――――

Only one panel attending to gay subjects was on the program of that year's Pedagogy of the Oppressed conference. The single panel, a "roundtable," consisted of three speakers: one who canceled due to illness, one who simply didn't show up, and me. The moderator decided that audience members should introduce themselves. After all, we had time.

During these introductions, the fact that the semi-circle of attendees was divided into two demographic camps became clear. To my right sat nine or so women in their late forties and older, all white, all who self-identified as lesbians, and some of whom were living on womyn's land in the rural Southeast. The other six or seven attendees to my left were younger, maybe in their mid-twenties, about half of whom were men. I talked through my ideas, largely a queered deconstruction of gay and lesbian identity and then the postulation that deconstructed identities might feasibly be more liberatory in composition classrooms because they are less likely to run the risk of tokenizing or homogenizing gay students. Admittedly, there was nothing groundbreaking here.

It had not escaped my attention that only half the voices laughed and nodded when I had hoped, whereas an awfully loud silence permeated the other side of the room. One side of the room engaged, the other was leaden; it was clear that those demographic divides were also ideological, and I was not surprised that during Q&A not everyone was pleased. However, I was not prepared for the vehemence of the objections.

"I have one foot out the door," one woman began. If she were to stay in the room, she continued, she simply had to express her outrage. I had used high-flown jargon, she complained; while she considered herself educated and well read, she didn't understand a word I was saying. Bound more by propriety (I'm embarrassed to say) than anything else, I meekly offered that I was using terminology purposefully to situate myself in a lineage of ideas which I wanted to invoke and affiliate with; that, in a way, all discourse is jargon; that *womyn's land*, for instance, is jargon. Gasping, a woman nearby picked up the complainant's cause. Ultimately, she concluded, all that theory stuff was just "male" and, in the end, "bullshit." Facing unadulterated fury, I didn't dare offer my normal "Well-not-having-a-theory-IS-a-theory" spiel.

The split in the room concretized when, after about half an hour of critique, one of the young women on the left side of the semi-circle protested. She was tired of feeling as if she had to "dumb down" her work. We were, she complained, at an academic conference. The moderator, in alignment with the contingent of older women and offended by this younger lesbian's comment (though she had certainly taken no offense to the earlier accusation of "bullshit"), asked her not to use "language like that," the younger woman remaining silent thereafter.

One of the young men, who had expressed his interest in queer theory in his introduction, began to draw out my ideas about how he might apply Judith Butler when constructing classroom activities. As he and I talked about queer theory's possible pedagogical uses, grumbling began to grow louder, finally miring our exchange. After a brief silence that felt a bit like the quiet that might have preceded a shoot-out, one of the most vocal critics shot: "We're just noticing who's talking now—the men."

―――――――――――

At my father-in-law's memorial service, I retreated to the women's room to press a cool cloth to my forehead. A photographer, a musician, a racecar driver, no man was loved more by his daughter. I'd held Tasha's hand through two years of the horror of watching her beloved Da shrink before our eyes and through two hours of listening to distant relatives and old friends share stories about her childhood with a single dad.

Renewed, I left the restroom only to run into one of the Boston contingent, a sister of an aunt by marriage, I think. "You're Tasha's partner, right?"

Conversation, rehearsed by now, followed. "Yes, twenty years together," smile and nod. Affirm, "Yes, western North Carolina." "Well, actually, we love living there," correct gently. Admit, "Yes, there is poverty," remembering another northeastern relative whose children kept coming South in the summers to repair the homes of impoverished Appalachians. "Tell them there's a poor school teacher who needs an upstairs bathroom," I'd chided Tasha.

"You must really have to watch out for the hillbillies," she offered in all sincerity and innocence and ignorance.

Drawing out the vowels, all on purpose, my voice sounding suspiciously like Andy Griffith to my own ears, I replied, "Oh, no ma'am. It's the professors that I'm careful of."

In her history of the Council of Writing Program Administrators' consultant-evaluator service, Shirley Rose (2013) describes the field's long-standing respect for both scholarly and experiential knowledges. In some ways, she needn't have noted the scholarly, for all too often, the experiential is what needs defending, not just on the pages of academic journals but at the horror that is the academic cocktail party. And during annual reviews. And in faculty meetings, Lord have mercy, the faculty meetings.

The late Native American novelist and scholar Louis Owens, a mentor to my dear friend Jesse Peters, once shared with him, "The problem with academia is that there are too many people in it who have never done anything else." That observation has stuck with me, partly because it has served as a touchstone to remind me of the type of academic I want to be. Because of where and from whom I come, I *have* done other things.

I sit here today, a world away from my grandfather's farm in Woodbury, Tennessee, a parcel of land that seemed to grow limestone and cedar trees better than beans and tobacco. The only person in my family to have graduated from college and one of the few who graduated from high school, today, like most days on the job, I feel yet again, "How do I bridge the space from there to here? How to contend with the constant liminality?" I keep threatening to get a T-shirt printed to document my reality. It might read, "Just another blue-collar, redneck lesbian with a Ph.D. teaching queer theory on a Catholic campus." And in Connecticut, my god, Connecticut!

A displaced Appalachian and a wandering queer, I waffle between two rhetorical strategies. The first, puffery, is one of which I'm none too proud. It's addictive because it's effective, but it does leave a country girl feeling right dirty at the end of the day. The Federal Trade Commission, Marc Fetscherin and Mark Toncar (2009) tell us, "defines puffery as a 'term frequently used to denote the exaggerations reasonably to be expected of a seller as to the degree of quality of his product, the truth or falsity of which cannot be precisely determined' " (147). And it is puffery to which I turn so often, to amuse New York relatives or win over hiring committees. Here, puffery is not so much amplifying my southernness or referencing my Appalachianness. Instead, it is a kind of fetch and step, putting on a show of southern jive seen as authentic to those who are not that, because, bless 'em, they have watched too many hours of *The Beverly Hillbillies* or *Gomer Pyle U.S.M.C.* When I was a student in a language seminar at Illinois cotaught by Dennis Baron and Paul Prior, one of those fellows shared with us an anecdote, that an East Coast mafioso had begun to mimic the speech of actors from *The Godfather* after they saw the movie, the fake leaping from the looking glass to influence the original. I have no idea whether that story is true. But it ought to be because the rhetorical strategy would be effective, because, right or wrong, it will play on an audience's internalized tropes. If I'm parking on a dark street in Tribeca, just trying to get to Bubby's for a slice of sour cherry pie and, after I've fed the meter, Big Pussy walks up to me and says, "Hey, dis is Tony's block. You owe me twenty," I'm handing over that bill because the scenario fits into a clichéd and stereotyped and ignorant but functioning schema. Similarly, when I'm looking to charm or sell or calm my introverted nerves at a New York Christmas party, I might well describe my former assistant Louise's shouted admonition, "Get behind me, Devil!" every time she felt tempted to gossip or lie. Alternatively, I might throw over my shoulder as an excuse for leaving the party at my chair's house that I need to get to my Sisters of Sappho meeting, explaining that I'm leading the discussion on the fiction of Gertrude Stein.

Puffing up these identities allows them to intrude into yet not threaten the discursive hierarchy of the moment, thus hardly qualifying them as queer rhetoric in Alexander and Rhodes's terms and, on some level, ultimately increasing the shame of being the Other in the room, even as the rhetorical device allows for temporary influence through self-effacing placation. Self-imposed puffery wins laughs and "friends" but at a cost—primarily the cost of performative agency. Trading one aped performance for another, all for an audience from which one feels alienated, soon the inherited nature of all discourse becomes all too clear, and it matters little that Butler would console us by saying that we are all "impersonating an ideal that nobody actually inhabits" (Kotz 1991, 85). Stopping short of agentive subversion, puffery makes all discourse seem replicative performance. It's like watching *Hee Haw* with a friend from Scarsdale and Archie Campbell suddenly not seeming so funny anymore.

More interventionist (and, incidentally, more spine-straightening) is the rhetorical act of disidentification. Too often, as queer, as Appalachian, we find ourselves "standing under a sign to which one does and does not belong"

(Butler 1993, 231). To the extent, then, that queerness is homo- *or* metronormative or that Appalachianness is straight, it becomes necessary to disidentify with one or both. José Muñoz (1999) writes, "Disidentification scrambles and reconstructs the encoded message of a cultural text in a fashion that both exposes the encoded message's universalizing and exclusionary machinations and recircuits its workings to account for, include, and empower minority identities and identifications. Thus, disidentification is a step further than cracking open the code of the majority; it proceeds to use this code as raw material for representing a disempowered politics or positionality that has been rendered unthinkable by the dominant culture" (31). More effective than an exaggerated Foghorn Leghorn imitation, then, when my northeastern family (condescendingly?) coos, "Oh, I like your accent," is to say, "Thanks, I like yours, too," and it's more effective to respond to "country dyke" with, "Girl, your clit don't care if I'm from Knoxville or not."

"Who doesn't know what a weed eater is?" I gently chide a former professor *cum* friend *cum* girlfriend *cum* friend *cum* girlfriend. . . .

"I don't, you fucking redneck!"

My composition student, discussing her semester topic of racist and homophobic bias on the part of British soccer fans, described how Swindon Town fans began, stadium-wide, to chant "Town full of faggots!" to distract Brighton's players. "And, you know," she stammered to our class, "that's hate speech, because I don't think anyone is going to stand up and say, 'Hi, I'm a . . . you know, *that* word' or 'I'm gay.' "

Half a beat, and I interject, "Well, I will. I'm gay."

"I'm sorry, Dr. Gunter, but I'm scared to take your class." It seems to be the day for tearful graduate students.

"For heaven's sake, why?" I'm pushing a box of tissues across my desk.

"Well, I *want* to take your class, and *please* don't tell her I said this, but Dr. Shites Roses says that Rhetoric and Composition isn't a real field and she's pressuring me not to take your class."

As queer and Appalachian, as lesbian and southern, I inhabit liminal identities. That liminality gets replicated in my professional life. As a writing program administrator, I am not quite an administrator to Academic Affairs, not quite colleague alone to the writing faculty. The bulk of them nontenure track, I work with faculty inhabiting liminal designations within our university. I have a doctorate in rhetoric and composition, and I work in a liminal discipline, perhaps part of English, perhaps not; perhaps in the social sciences, perhaps the humanities.

My deeply interstitial experience of the world and the world of work has helped make me a better writing teacher, for it has inspired me to stand beside my students through the transmogrifications of subjectivity that only they can initiate and, more important, do so with empathy. I teach students who are themselves bridging transitions. Any student in the process of earning a degree moves from one social site, one identity, to another, and we see particular incarnations of that process in writing classrooms. Basic writers who work to bridge home languages and academic discourses; timid writers who come to their voices; graduate students who move from novice to professional; acclimatizing first-year students, leaving test-taking pedagogies behind and now plunged into the sea of no single answer in my writing classrooms—we all do exhausting, frightening, high-stakes work. I read Audre Lorde to them, remind them that she advises that we can learn to work when we are afraid just as we learned to work when we are tired. Lorde, my colleagues, and especially my students have convinced me that as absolutely unnerving as all this liminality can be, freedom and agency are to be found in this shifting space.

The intersectionality described by Karma Chávez (2012), that is, "the interlocking nature of race, class, gender, sexuality, ability and nation" (21), is an ethical, interventionist, practical strategy, in- and outside the composition class. Intersectionality allows for us to meet in ways that matter to omnipresent first-year composition goals and outcomes like "Students will demonstrate critical thinking" or "Students will contribute to ongoing scholarly conversations." It also allows us to combat everything from fake news to the myopia of selfie culture and to work toward counterrhetorics and counterpublics by using intersectionality and alterity as tools "to understand operations of culture, identity and power" (Chávez 2012, 22).

Intersectionality and the more specific rhetorical strategy of reminding ourselves to consider alterity within and outside any audience, even a subaltern one that is itself marginalized within the majoritarian sphere, work to achieve some of the early, still unfulfilled promise of queer studies. First, intersectionality cracks open concepts and identities that have been naturalized to appear singular. Intersectionality allows us, for example, to consider the odd political positions and potential alliances that Michigan Womyn's Music Festival organizers undertook in 2000 when they began to stipulate that only "womyn-born-womyn" could attend the festival. If Simone de Beauvoir is right that no one is born a woman, then females sure as hell aren't born "womyn," a political position that no one is assigned at birth. Putting that aside, the insistence on a naturalized, acultural biology leads to specious results. Presumably women like Phyllis Schlafly and Ann Coulter would be more welcome at the now-defunct Michigan festival than would Kate Bornstein or Leslie Feinberg. In an even more bizarro world, the Michigan festival organizers could be put into political alliance with North Carolina's "bathroom bill" supporters, who infamously demanded in 2016 that people had to use public restrooms that are designated for their gender assigned at birth. Intersectionality (here, considering not just cis but trans women) requires moving beyond myopic navel-gazing in its denaturalization of monolithic categories and party lines, requiring that we see lesbians as more than Ellen and Portia, Appalachians as more than Jethro and Jed. In its refusal of a sole core of identity, intersectionality helps prevent the expansion of oppression of those already oppressed.

Second, in its insistence that identity is not "static" but is "negotiated with other people, cultures, spaces, and values" (Chávez 2012, 22)—put another way, in its insistence that the enculturated audience plays a role in the discursive creation of subjects—intersectionality facilitates the very coalition-building that queer activism has advocated. Nedra Reynolds (1993) argues that ethos spawns from "the individual agent as well as the location or position from which that person speaks or writes" (326), and Sara L. McKinnon (2012) writes more specifically, "The nature of audiencing . . . means that the possibility to be seen as a subject with a public, political voice is contingent upon the audience who receives the subject . . . and the acknowledged intersubjectivity between the speaker and the audience" (192). If part of what discursive agents need—what queer subjects, what Appalachian activists, what student writers need—is "the power to name oneself and determine the conditions under which that name is used" (Butler 1993, 227), how horrific is the violence that robs agents of that power? Freedom lies in abandoning what Maria Lugones (2003) has labeled "purity logics" and bringing to rhetorics of sexuality, place, race, and class an intersectionality that is "concerned with shifting webs of relationships rather that singular articulations of identity" (Woods 2012, 79).

Risking being labeled revisionist, I return to Audre Lorde, who refused to ignore or hierarchize her identities of woman, Black, lesbian, warrior, mother, and poet. Lorde (1984) detailed decades ago how "racism, sexism, and homophobia are inseparable" (110), foretelling the coming of queer and intersectional politics. Advocating an "interdependency," Lorde argues, "Difference must be not merely tolerated, but seen as a fund of necessary polarities between which our creativity can spark like a dialectic" (111). If, as Chávez (2012) warns, "singularity [is] always already a fiction, and a tool designed to uphold power imbalances" (25), focusing too exclusively or too frequently on single subjectivities, themselves too often reduced to monoliths, oversimplifies our analyses of subjectivity, agency, and culture. Instead, focusing on alliance and coalition enables visions such as that of the Highlander Research and Education Center, a grassroots organizing and education nonprofit in east Tennessee that, through systemic meta-critique, builds its mission around mutually informative campaigns for causes such as migrant justice, decriminalization of youth, workers' rights, and environmental sustainability.

Not only-queer then, not only-Appalachian, not only-compositionist but, improbably, always all of those and more. When we refuse to e-race ourselves to be gay or desexualize ourselves to be Appalachian and all the other ways that we rob ourselves of our ourselves and each other, we take back performativity and, yes, performance, too, using what Muñoz might call our hybrid selves to enable counterrhetorics, counterpublics, and counterworld-making.

Alone in a North Carolina Cracker Barrel, I text Tasha. "How far away are you?" I follow up, more desperate, "At some point, I started feeling alienated" and, an afterthought, "I ordered you a sweet tea."

Alienation is a constant negotiation for some Appalachian queers, including me. When strains of "Uncloudy Day" ("Oh, they tell me of a home far beyond the skies. / Oh, they tell me of a home far away") crackled from my grandmother, bent over a stove, I dreamed of faraway lands, too, cities where anonymity might protect me from the damnation of home, if not from Jesus. Is there a tribe?, I wondered. . . .

It's a struggle, writing this essay. It feels a bit like watching one's own surgery. I bounce a rubber ball off the wall of my office and stare at the Mason jar on the corner of my desk. It has been washed clean of the sticky residue of the last batch of sweet pickles that my grandmother ever put up. (She fed us, even after she was long gone.)

The day that we auctioned off my grandparents' farm, I took that jar and went from spot to spot, digging up clumps of dirt and packing them inside, tight. If I could, I would sew the dirt from that jar into the seams of my clothing. It would feel just right in the cuff of my blazer as I deliver tomorrow's guest lecture on Foucault.

BIBLIOGRAPHY

Alexander, Jonathan, and Jacqueline Rhodes. 2012, January 16. "Queer Rhetoric and the Pleasures of the Archive." *Enculturation* no. 13. enculturation.net/files /QueerRhetoric/queerarchive/Home.html. Accessed March 23, 2019.

Butler, Judith. 1993. *Bodies That Matter: On the Discursive Limits of Sex*. London: Routledge.

Chávez, Karma R. 2012. "Doing Intersectionality: Power, Privilege, and Identities in Political Activist Communities." In *Identity Research and Communication: Intercultural Reflections and Future Directions*, edited by Nilanjana Bardhan and Mark P. Orbe, 21–32. Lanham, MD: Lexington Books.

Duggan, Lisa. 2003. *The Twilight of Equality? Neoliberalism, Cultural Politics, and the Attack on Democracy*. Boston: Beacon.

Fetscherin, Marc, and Mark Toncar. 2009. "Visual Puffery in Advertising." *International Journal of Market Research* 51, no. 2, 147–48.

Han, Chong-suk. 2008. "No Fats, Femmes, or Asians: The Utility of Critical Race Theory in Examining the Role of Gay Stock Stories in the Marginalization of Gay Asian Men." *Contemporary Justice Review* 11, no. 1, 11–22.

Kotz, Liz. 1991, November. "The Body You Want: An Interview with Judith Butler." *Artforum*, 82–89.

Lorde, Audre. 1984. "The Master's Tools Will Never Destroy the Master's House." In *Sister Outsider*, 110–13. New York: Crossing Press.

Lugones, Maria. 2003. *Peregrinajes/Pilgrimages: Theorizing Coalition against Multiple Oppressions*. Lanham, MD: Rowman & Littlefield.

McKinnon, Sara L. 2012. "Essentialism, Intersectionality, and Recognition: A Feminist Rhetorical Approach to Audience." In *Standing in the Intersection: Feminist Voices, Feminist Practices in Communication Studies*, edited by Karma R. Chávez and Cindy L. Griffin, 189–210. Albany: SUNY Press.

Muñoz, José Esteban. 1999. *Disidentifications: Queers of Color and the Performance of Politics*. Minneapolis: University of Minnesota Press.

Reynolds, Nedra. 1993. "Ethos as Location: New Sites for Understanding Discursive Authority." *Rhetoric Review* 11, no. 2, 325–38.

Rose, Shirley K. 2013. "What Is a Writing Program History?" In *A Rhetoric for Writing Program Administrators*, edited by Rita Malenczyk, 239–51. Fort Collins, CO: Parlor Press.

Royles, Dan. 2016. "Civil Rights (LGBT)." In *The Encyclopedia of Greater Philadelphia*. philadelphiaencyclopedia.org/archive/civil-rights-lgbt/. Accessed March 23, 2019.

Stryker, Susan. 2008. "Transgender History, Homonormativity, and Disciplinarity." *Radical History Review* no. 100, 145–57.

Warner, Michael. 1999. *The Trouble with Normal*. Cambridge, MA: Harvard University Press.

Weiss, Jillian Todd. 2003. "GL vs. BT: The Archeology of Biphobia and Transphobia within the U.S. Gay and Lesbian Community." *Journal of Bisexuality* 3, no. 3/4, 26–55.

Woods, Carly S. 2012. "(Im)mobile Metaphors: Toward an Intersectional Rhetorical History." In *Standing in the Intersection: Feminist Voices, Feminist Practices in Communication Studies*, edited by Karma R. Chávez and Cindy L. Griffin, 78–96. Albany: SUNY Press.

PART III

Both/And: Intersectional Understandings of Appalachian Queers

CHAPTER 6

The Crik Is Crooked: Appalachia as Movable Queer Space

Lydia McDermott

Its land is "strange" and its people are "peculiar"—in speeches in the 1870s and the politics of 2016. . . . Again and again Appalachia is relegated to the past tense: "out of time" and out of step with any contemporary present, much less a progressive future.

—Engelhardt (2017, 5)

Judith (Jack) Halberstam delineates queerness along the axes of time and space in her 2005 book, *In a Queer Time and Place: Transgender Bodies, Subcultural Lives*, projecting from queer lived experiences and media productions to an opening of the time-space continuum that allows me to suggest that Appalachia is a queer movable space. I sense hackles rising for good reasons, but let me spin this yarn for now and we will see what to make of it by the end (if ends can exist in a ruptured sense of time and space). Halberstam suggests that "A 'queer adjustment' in the way we think about time, in fact, requires and produces new conceptions of space" (2005, 6). I argue that Appalachia already maps onto queer time and space in the popular imagination, neither fitting into a defined space nor ever seeming to exist in the present or future tense (Engelhardt 2017, 5). In this chapter, I attempt to adjust my conceptions of Appalachian space queerly and, in so doing, adjust time, a reversal of the causal relationship Halberstam suggests. The form of this chapter will echo[1] this queer adjustment of time and space.

First, I must figure queer time and space as they relate to Appalachia. Halberstam explains her extrapolation of queer time and space: " 'Queer time' is a term for those specific modes of temporality that emerge within postmodernism once one leaves the temporal frames of bourgeois reproduction and family, longevity, risk/safety, and inheritance. 'Queer space' refers to the place-making practices within postmodernism in which queer people engage and it also describes the new understandings of space enabled by the production of queer counterpublics" (Halberstam 2005, 6). Already I am stretching. Can Appalachia exist in queer time and space? First, we must allow the possibility that queer lives are everywhere, in the hollers of Appalachia as well as the boroughs of New York City. Furthermore, I must show that in Appalachia, queers are creating counterpublics, which they are and which I explore again in a later section (Garringer 2017; Mann 2003; Taylor 2011). Furthermore, as an imagined space—the geographic/physical contours of Appalachia as always in flux given differing definitions of the space as poor, rural, mountainous, culturally isolated, and more—Appalachia and its people are already represented as "queer" in the sense of "peculiar." I suggest a further linkage with "queer" in terms of nonnormative sexuality and kinship. In regard to time-keeping, Appalachia is already understood as subversive, being imagined as totally outside bourgeois nuclear family structures that revolve around the reproduction of 2.5 children, and with a seeming disregard for individual longevity, suggested in stereotypical practices of addiction and poor health, in favor of familial lines. I suggest a queer and postmodern turn in our understanding of Appalachia, which too often has been represented as static, as Engelhardt points out in the epigraph. I seek to reread this "out of step"–ness as queer, as rhetorical, and as postmodern, which I in turn read as sophistic and mêtic, to which I turn in the next section.

I must interrupt myself: I am wary of too much extrapolation at the risk of lived queer and Appalachian experiences, so my foray here includes a pastiche of personal and retold queer experiences that resonate in Appalachian ground, but I am foraying in this way specifically to suggest a broader queering of rhetoric encompassing Appalachia.

I explore multiple senses of queerness in Appalachia: queer as "an outcome of strange temporalities, imaginative life schedules, and eccentric economic practices" (Halberstam 2005, 1); queer as disturbing ground in a process of disorientation (Ahmed 2006b); queer as bodily understanding and sexual practice. I ask: if *queer* can be deployed as a verb of dis-orientation and dis-identification, can Appalachia also move and subvert?

———————

Earliest definitions of Appalachia were based on the natural features of the region— vegetation, climate, and physiography—and were part of the process of "discovery" undertaken by European explorers in the sixteenth century whose goal was to define, delimit, name, understand, and thus process "new" lands in the name of various European monarchs.

—McCann (1998, 89)

While Appalachian identity is a regional identity, it is also a cultural identity, rooted in the place of the Appalachian Mountains, but not necessarily restricted to this place alone.

—Webb-Sunderhaus (2016, 16)

View from the Porch

I remember when the neighborhood went downhill: when the house around the corner suddenly erupted with children, dirty and barely clothed, no adults in sight. The hillbillies had moved in, said Grandma, Big Red.[2] My grandmother had been less distressed when a black family moved in down the street.[3] At that time I did not understand "hillbilly" to mean anything other than a slur against white families that did not live up to Big Red's standards. I did not know what hills they came from, or if they actually came from anywhere other than our small city in the Rust Belt. I knew they sounded vaguely "southern": said "warsh" instead of "wash," "crik" instead of "creek," and pin and pen sounded like the same word, "pin." But some of my own family members also sounded this way. Grandma herself called us "y'unz" when she called us into the house.[4] The family around the corner were poor, but so were many of my own family members. I played outside with my cousins and friends and got filthy, just like those children. The family around the corner seemed to extend beyond the boundaries of the middle-class nuclear family of American prime time, but my family lived in a duplex occupied by my nuclear family, my grandmother and her sister, and my aunt and cousin, as well as a stray boyfriend of my grandmother's. As a child, I could not quite identify the difference Big Red seemed to home in on with this family, perhaps because it wasn't so much a difference from us but an echo of our potential difference. I had never set foot in Appalachia, as far as I knew, and "hillbilly" was just a generic insult applied to poor white people, just as West Virginia was the go-to state for insults in Ohio.

When I look now at the Appalachian Regional Commission's map of the central Appalachian region, I find that although our small Ohio city lies just outside the map's boundary of Appalachia, Grandma grew up deep in the hills of Pennsylvania, an area not even on the fluctuating outskirts of Appalachian cartography but central to Appalachia. Many rural families from West Virginia and other Appalachian states followed the "hillbilly highway" to the Rust Belt, and although West Virginia was used as a stand-in for Appalachia in Ohio, my grandmother's rural Pennsylvanian family would fall into this same category of migration (Zelenko 1990).

The Hillbilly as Mêtic

Migration as a theme connects Appalachian lives and queer lives, even when they do not already overlap as queer Appalachian lives. I'd like to connect the queer Appalachian rhetoric I engage here to a tradition of traveling, shifting rhetoric: mêtic rhetoric as defined by Jay Dolmage, Michelle Ballif, and myself in various writings.[5] Mêtic/Mêtis can be understood as relating to the trope of the hillbilly and to the space of Appalachia in a number of ways. Mêtic as a noun refers to a person and suggests an outsider—someone not from the polis (city); Mêtis as goddess represents a connection to the maternal, to the feminine, and to the adaptable, curved, and crooked body; Mêtis as an attribute or facility—a cunning, shifting, embodied, artisanal intelligence—further links to "dis-ability" or to bodily difference as generative (Dolmage 2014). Classical sophists were also often mêtics in the first sense of the word—travelers from outside of Athens, selling their rhetorical expertise. Mêtis is also closely associated with sophistic rhetoric in its reliance on "cunning" and the possibility of making the weaker argument/body the stronger. I suggest that mêtis echoes Halberstam's notions of queer time and space as well as Sara Ahmed's sense of queer as a productive dis-/re-orientation. I release Mêtis to echo[6] in the mountains of Appalachia.

As trope, the hillbilly is always an outsider, like the mêtic. Like the mêtic sophists, the logic represented as Appalachian relies on a nonlinear orality, rather than a linear argumentative discourse, often accompanied by a banjo or fiddle. In the public imagination, Appalachia has an unhealthy kinship determined by extended familial ties or clans, accusations of incest as particular to the area and culture, subsequent accusations of abhorrent motherhood, and a physical manifestation of disability as a result (ABC News Productions 2009). We can probably all hear the famous "Dueling Banjoes" echoing in our ears at the mention of these "tellable stories"—stories that adhere easily to preconceived narratives about a culture (Creadick 2017; Webb-Sunderhaus 2016). The 1972 film *Deliverance* represents a touchstone of Appalachia in the US cultural imagination and illustrates some of the ways that mêtis can apply to the figure of the hillbilly. The banjo-playing boy in the film is represented as mentally inferior and physically weak following the premise that he is the product of unhealthy kinship and desire.[7] The boy functions as a common disability trope—"a sign of social ill" because of his presumed incestual conception (Creadick 2017, 73; Dolmage 2014, 36). This premise of monstrous kinship and desire plays out later in a male-on-male rape scene that through synecdoche has become linked to the disabled yet musically gifted boy and the "Dueling Banjoes" (Creadick 2017, 72): "the evidence of the film and the hit song suggests that his is a mystical difference, in which he is both lesser-than and greater-than these men from the city" (Creadick 2017, 67). This mystical association is another common disability trope of overcoming or of the "super-crip" that we often see functioning in representations of autism, where a disability is made up for by a special gift or even a super power (Dolmage 2014, 35). Furthermore, the film presents mountain people as aligned with nature as opposed to civilization: "If the logic of the novel/film is man *versus* nature, the 'hillbillies' are aligned with nature, and nature, or too much nature, has mutated boys and men into something Other" (Creadick 2017, 73). Like many marginalized rhetorics and experiences, Appalachia has become distilled to a connection with nature, or a kind of precivilization. It is also attached to a non-normate sense of kinship, and to disabled bodies, and thus to mêtis. Mêtis can be, as Dolmage suggests, a representation of rhetoric as "an extraordinary body" (Dolmage 2009, 5). So let us make Appalachia also an extraordinary body of rhetoric.

Perhaps my grandmother, Big Red, is such a body, entwined with her sister in a kinship of caregiving premised on disability.

If orientation is a matter of how we reside in space, then sexual orientation might also be a matter of residence, of how we inhabit spaces, and who or what we inhabit spaces with.

—Ahmed (2006a, 543)

Mêtis *values bodily difference as generative of meaning.*

—Dolmage (2006, 122)

Rather we would consider sophistry as mêtis, a sophistic quality that eludes Platonic hunters. Mêtis is a knowing, doing, making not in regards to Truth (either certain or

probable), but in regards to a "transient, shifting, disconcerting and ambiguous" sit-
uation such as our postmodern condition (Detienne and Vernant 3).

—Ballif (1998, 53)

Downstairs

Come in off the porch, now, y'uns, and into Big Red's house.

Aunt Dorothy, sometimes Dot, most likely will be in sitting on her favorite chair and ottoman in the living room, until late in the 1980s, at which point you might find her in the back bedroom, because she is bedridden, having suffered many falls in her lifetime. We'll assume she's in the living room. Big Red might be in the kitchen making something bland for dinner, or perhaps she is watching football on her large television that functions as a piece of furniture, as they did back then, and cussing at the players on the screen.

Pan out to catch the sisters' relationship.

Grandma always told me that Dorothy was the pretty one in the family, but she's never been "quite right." From my current vantage point, I do not accept her various diagnoses—mental retardation and schizophrenia. I see the effects, though. Dorothy has never functioned on her own. She needs my grandmother, and I think my grandmother needs her to need her. Dorothy chants repetitive slogans and requests in her corner most of the time, but she also sometimes has "fits" that can turn violent. Big Red is and always has been, as far as I can tell, her sister's keeper.

Robert, my grandfather, left Big Red a long time ago, so long ago that I don't remember him, but they never officially divorced. Grandma was just abandoned in this small, dying city caked in rust, after moving away from her family home in the hills of western Pennsylvania. They are two older women living in a large turn-of-the-century duplex, dependent on each other in ways that our culture does not like to acknowledge.

Can two older women living their entire lives together as sisters be considered to be living a queer life? If we throw in the extended family also cared for by this matriarch, what then? I cannot define my grandmother's identity and desires.

Possibly also in this half of the house are my aunt (Big Red's daughter) and her son. They lived there for a time after their house suffered fire damage. Earlier in my life, a time I don't remember, Grandma's mother, L'il Mom, also lived there and cooed over me and Shane (my cousin). My mom tells me L'il

Mom used to wear men's underwear on her head while cleaning house. That detail has no critical significance, it just pleases me. My grandmother's ex-boyfriend, Delford, is living in the basement (possibly, depending on the time period). My aunt always calls him a "hillbilly" with extreme derision. He did have the speech patterns of the family around the corner, but mainly his sin was that he drank a lot of whiskey on the front porch and embarrassed my aunt.

Let me move away from this house a minute, to another problem in this play of hillbilly and queer stereotype threat starring me and my best friend, whom I'll call Jeremy. We are misfits in the neighborhood for a variety of reasons. I wear my cousin Shane's hand-me-downs and have the same bowl haircut, so I get mistaken for a boy often, plus my best friend is a boy. Jeremy has it harder than I do, though. Jeremy has ADHD at a time when it was not as frequently diagnosed and when there were fewer good medications. He changed schools all the time. He breaks things without noticing he's doing it. He is not welcome in many kids' homes. 'Course, I got grounded often from my neighbor Carrie's supposedly because Big Red's dog barked too loudly. It wasn't just Jeremy's disability that made him unwelcome. He was effeminate; he read as queer to the neighborhood, whereas even though I was often mistaken for a boy, once people knew I was a girl, I fit neatly into a tomboy identity. Jeremy and I spent lots of time together. We played dress-up. We played with his dollhouse and my Barbies. We played wizards together. One Halloween, I dressed as Doc the Dwarf and he dressed as Snow White.

Jeremy was a scapegoat, too. He was two years younger than my cousin and two years older than me, so we often all played together in my yard. Whenever Shane got into trouble, Grandma liked to blame Jeremy as a bad influence. Though Shane is the one who eventually dropped out of high school, who narrowly escaped juvenile detention several times, Jeremy was the one who seemed queer, "not quite right." Later in middle school and high school, Jeremy was often beaten up for being a sissy. He made it through, though he became addicted to various substances, and is now living with HIV in a more urban area. And yes, he is queer.

While Appalachia is seen by other parts of the country as conservative (and it often is), single parenting is common among men and women because of unmarried mothers or divorce. However, family support and family structures remain bulwarks of culture, and prospective teachers are not only aware of the support (or lack of support) that families can provide, but also of the ways in which families interact, often with multiple generations in one household.

—Swartz (2003, 65)

It is for this reason that disorientation can move around: it involves not only bodies becoming objects, but also the disorientation in how objects are gathered to create ground, or to clear a space on the ground (the field).

—Ahmed (2006b, 160)

Repetition—the very repetition that is the famous mechanism of the "performative," through which meaning is stabilized and destabilized—here turns out to be a mechanism that produces the reverse effect.

—Cavarero (2005, 160)

Crooked: Echo as Dis-orienteer

Dolmage connects the facility of mêtis to the Greek god of metallurgy, Hephaestus, who is visually and textually represented as having crooked feet: "Like a crab, Hephaestus's symbolic movement is not straightforward" (Dolmage 2006, 121). The cunning of mêtis is also crooked, bent, queer: "The word *mêtis* shared an association, from its very first usage, with the idea of a physical curve, with the idea of a body not composed in perfect ratio" (Dolmage 2009, 7). I have elsewhere argued that Echo, the mythological nymph and the rhetorical practice of repetition, can yield a productively disruptive mêtic rhetoric, moving as she does through multiple bodies, imagined and material, and bouncing back to us (McDermott 2016). I further align the process by which an echo/Echo creates a vocalic body—ventriloquism (McDermott 2016)—to Raymie McKerrow's conception of the corporeal as containing both imagined and material bodies: "a conception of the body that is as much metaphorical as real, as much a product of the imagination as it is a product of lived experience . . . a body that houses the fullest range of potentialities available" (McKerrow 1998, 319). I find this conception of embodiment to be crucial for any queer figuring. Queer rhetoric should concern itself with the imagination as much as with the material; without such imagined bodies, we would be doomed to mere repetitive normate materiality. As Judith Butler warns, we cannot merely return to materiality, as if that in itself is not an imagined construct on which gender and sexuality rest (Butler 1993). So let us bend space and time through echoes to become disoriented and reoriented.

A corollary concept to mêtis is *kairos*, which represents an understanding of time that is not chronological (*chronos*), but situational, episodic, occasional, like my Great Aunt Dorothy's fits. Dolmage explains, "*Metis*, then, is the capacity to act in a *kairotic* world" (Dolmage 2006, 121). When my grandmother responded to her sister's fits, knowing when to hold her tight and when to let her go, she was exhibiting mêtis. In this repetitive caregiving, this ebb and flow of dependency, her sense of time and place were queered. This fit connects with a fit from years ago, connects with a fit to come; this reaction, this touch, reverberates with a childhood touch, with a motherly touch. Echoes upon echoes, here in this rust city duplex, there in those hills.

Ahmed tells us, "We might speak also of 'family background' which would refer not just to the past of an individual, but to other kinds of histories, which shape an individual's arrival into the world, and through which the family itself becomes a social given" (Ahmed 2014, 97). So I have begun to speak of family background. In Appalachia, this can be complicated by the closeness of family in one dwelling, by backgrounds of poverty, and by the "tellable narratives" that may resist queer backgrounds and counter publics. Webb-Sunderhaus connects the idea of "tellable narratives" to the performativity that Butler teaches us in her case study of six self-identifying Appalachian students, suggesting that those parts of student identity that do not match the tellable narratives of Appalachia given to the wider culture leave those students disoriented, unable to fit their own experiences into the identity they feel they inhabit. Counterpublics can arise to meet that need—an alternative but coinciding narrative of otherness in Appalachia. This can mean practices of naming, such as Frank X Walker coining the term *Affrilachia*, and the subsequent movement of African American poets from Appalachia of TheAffrilachianPoets.com (Taylor 2011). Or to name queerness in rural settings, a West Virginia–based nonprofit serving LGBTQ youth, STAY (Stay Together Appalachian Youth) has been born, as well as a digital oral history project called "Country Queers" (Garringer 2017, 80). One of the oral histories features Sam from Virginia, who formed a group at Berea College for queer Appalachians that named itself "Fabulachians" (Garringer 2017, 82). Projects and renamings such as these echo Appalachia but subvert dominant narratives of time and space and identity in Appalachia, causing a productive disorientation.

In other words, mêtis is a tacit, nonlinear form of knowledge that appears as needed to help solve a problem when no ready solution is at hand and creative, or even devious, thinking is needed.

—Wilson and Wolford (2017, 22)

I try to use the concept of queer time to make clear how respectability, and notions of the normal on which it depends, may be upheld by a middle-class logic of reproductive temporality. And so, in Western cultures, we chart the emergence of the adult from the dangerous and unruly period of adolescence as a desired process of maturation; and we create longevity as the most desireable future, applaud the pursuit of long life (under any circumstances) and pathologize modes of living that show little to no concern for longevity.

—Halberstam (2005, 4)

The black sheep and other family deviants could even be considered to offer an alternative line of descent: indeed, the family deviant gets easily read as a stranger, or even a foreigner, whose proximity threatens the family line.

—Ahmed (2014, 101)

Yarn-Spinning and Keepin' Time

I understand from family folklore, that back in western Pennsylvania, Grandma's family distilled their own whiskey, and everyone played an instrument. This was told to me by my aunt to explain my father's musical inclinations and perhaps to explain the trend of alcoholism in the family. In my young imagination, this conjured a Prohibition speakeasy with smoky jazz, something urban and glorious. But looking at our family background, it was probably a more rural scene that resonates with many stereotypes about drunkenness and banjoes. Webb-Sunderhaus explores how these common narratives can become "untellable" by those who identify with the region to outsiders because they reinforce stereotypes. In my own mind, I was adjusting the narrative of my family because of the anxiety of stereotype threat. "Schueler whispered and turned bright red as he confided that his family made moonshine. . . . I could see and feel Schueler's discomfort in that moment, and as a fellow Appalachian who has felt the shame of exemplifying stereotypes about Appalachians and moonshine, I wanted him to know I shared that history and would not judge his family or him" (Webb-Sunderhaus 2016, 21). I need to be careful. I need to tread lightly. Already I have called upon stereotypes to understand my personal history: a hillbilly family around the corner with filthy children and no adult supervision, whiskey distilling, musical aptitude. To be honest, when I wrote the word *warsh*, above, I cringed. It is a physical reaction to a stereotype threat. Neighborhood kids complained I was a grammar teacher, telling them not to say *ain't*. I don't want to spend my time here correcting double negatives, correcting doubling identities, and I also do not want to distill people into a single narrative.

My adoptive father (Big Red's eldest), my mother, and I lived in the upstairs apartment of my grandmother's duplex. Even in our small nuclear family, we had queer senses of time and space. Addiction ran through the family in ways that reinforce and trouble popular orientations to Appalachian identity. Alcohol is the common denominator, beginning with the whiskey distillation I never saw, continuing through Delford's whiskey-fueled delusions on the front porch, and trickling through my dad and his siblings, and their children, and so on. But Dad was the black sheep of the family.

Rather than play football, he played French horn. Though he, like other family members, worked at Republic Steel, at Timken Roller Bearing, and as a bricklayer at various points in his life, he also went to college on the GI bill and studied music and philosophy. Something in him always wanted to get out, to migrate away, if not in physical material form, then in imagined corporeal form, through altered time-space experiments in drug use. I've had a hard time coming to terms with my father's blatant disregard for his own health, his longevity. But it does represent a kind of counternarrative that I could choose to read queerly.

Like many family members before him, Dad died young from liver cirrhosis. Whiskey in the veins. This is a familiar narrative not just in my family but in recurring representations of drunken hillbillies. There is a shame in this for me, but what is more troubling (in many senses) is his drug use. As far as I can reconstruct, my dad tried every drug known to humankind. He regularly smoked pot after work, he did eight-balls with friends at parties I was attending, he tripped on acid and couldn't sleep for days. He became a crack addict by the time I was a teenager and we no longer lived in the extended family duplex but in our own ranch-style house. His sense of time was utterly bent, and he would go missing from home for days at a time. His narrative, while adhering to the trope of addict, does not adhere to conservatism or the more recent rise of "hillbilly heroin."

According to Urban Dictionary, oxycodone and other prescription opioids are often called "hillbilly heroin." In recent years, abuse of these drugs has spread to the middle classes and it is now a major public health concern. Hillbilly heroin was not a thing when my dad was alive, or perhaps he would have tried it. His addiction to crack doesn't follow the hillbilly narrative or the upwardly mobile white middle-class narrative our new house represented. Crack maps onto urban slums, criminality, and color. Somehow dad fell into the wrong narrative in his quest to migrate away from the one he was born into.

Returning Down the Hillbilly Highway

For many of us raised in the country, following this normative queer migration narrative rips us from landscapes, communities, and traditions that are as much a part of ourselves as our queerness.

—Garringer (2017, 80)

I have never identified as Appalachian, although I have been drawn to the region's beauty. Like my grandmother, as a younger woman I actively worked against the stereotype threat of Appalachia, careful not to adopt the regionalisms of some of my family members, and I was keenly aware of the prospects of college education. Yet when I started college, I literally moved back down the hillbilly highway and into Appalachian southern Ohio. I accepted the un-Appalachian identity my grandmother and father passed on to me, despite the echoes of hillbilly past in my extended family. In a similar vein, my queerness has always been an invisible boundary-crossing. Attracted to both men and women and having been sexually involved with both, I resisted any labels through my undergraduate career. I hung with an activist group called "The Swarm of Dykes," but never actively identified as a dyke. I lived in Appalachia but distinguished myself from the "townies." I was dis-oriented.

I never engaged with Appalachia as a material region or a culture until I started graduate school in that same location. There, I helped direct the summer institute for the Appalachian Writing Project, and I learned that many of the teachers of the impoverished region could not imagine that there were queer children in their Appalachian classrooms, that there could be queer teachers right there in the room with them. But it was also there, as a teaching assistant, that I met queer Appalachian students.

I taught students from area schools that had been profiled in Jonathon Kozol's *Savage Inequalities*. I showed the film based on that book, *Children in America's Schools*, and some students squirmed at seeing the schools they attended represented as if caught in time, stuck in a past without heat or indoor bathrooms (Hayden 2004). Others squirmed to see their wealthy city high schools shown in comparison. I also showed the ethnographic film *Stranger with a Camera* to illustrate how researchers can incorporate personal information critically. This film is set in Kentucky, not too far away, and interrogates the killing of a filmmaker from Canada, media response to this killing, and the tensions that could have led an Appalachian man to feel a need to defend the image of his home (Barret 2000). By showing these films in a classroom filled primarily with suburban students but sprinkled with students from the mountains, I learned more about my grandmother's heritage. Like my Appalachian students, the dialect would slip out a bit after the viewing, and reactions to stereotypes would be heated, with faces flushed. Some of these students were also queer. Most had migrated to a university in hopes of escaping the stereotypes they were reacting to in the films.

Now, my family life in Washington state seems far removed from Appalachia and queerness. I am married to a man, whom I love, and have three children. We live in a nice house that we do not rent. We look like a pretty typical "American middle-class" family, but this label does not describe our desires, our gender identities, or our regional working-class history accurately. I am untangling my roots to re-tangle them differently. When I came to Athens, Ohio, for college and then for graduate school, my feet sunk in to the Appalachian ground, the hills and hollers that surrounded me. Perhaps Appalachia is genetic, perhaps it travels through bodies and through time; perhaps my feet spread Appalachia all the way to Washington. I can't help but feel the pull of those distant hills when I visit the mountains here, and even more so when I am out in the stark landscape of eastern Washington high desert, so vulnerable and exposed without trees and hills to hold me in. I want to queer my space and my time; I want to hillbilly.

NOTES

1. Echo returns later in the chapter. Listen for her. For more on Echo, echolocation, and sonogram methodology, see McDermott (2016).

2. In the 1980s, West Virginia lost 73,000 people to migration on the so-called hillbilly highway, which led primarily to more urban areas of Ohio and Pennsylvania (Zelenko 1990, 55).
3. This is not to exclude black experience from Appalachian experience or vice versa (hooks 1989; Taylor 2011). Rather, it is to highlight my grandmother's ranked prejudices and assumptions regarding fixed identities.
4. A variant of "y'inz," associated with Pittsburgh, also a regional dialect of the central Appalachian area, featuring pronunciations such as "warsh," and the pin-pen confusion. My mother-in-law says we live in "Warshington" now.
5. See Dolmage (2014), Ballif (2000), and McDermott (2016) for more thorough explorations of mêtis. Mêtis, the goddess that represents the intellectual quality of mêtis, was swallowed by her lover, Zeus, when she was pregnant with Athena. Athena was subsequently born from the brow of Zeus.
6. Echo is a queer little nymph, having been cursed to abandon her body and merely repeat the words of others in a never-ending loop of desire. *Nymphë* in ancient Greek not only refers to such a minor nature goddess like Echo but also to the clitoris (McDermott 2016).
7. For more on the productive possibilities of the maternal imagination, see McDermott (2015).

BIBLIOGRAPHY

ABC News Productions. 2009. *A Hidden America: Children of the Mountains*. New York: Films Media Group. Video. https://fod.infobase.com/PortalPlaylists.aspx?wID= 103018&xtid=52813.
Ahmed, Sara. 2006a. "Orientations: Toward a Queer Phenomenology." *GLQ: A Journal of Lesbian and Gay Studies* 12, no. 4, 543–74.
———. 2006b. *Queer Phenomenology: Orientations, Objects, Others*. Durham, NC: Duke University Press.
———. 2014. "Mixed Orientations." *Subjectivity* 7, no. 1, 92–109.
Ballif, Michelle. 1998. "Writing the Third-Sophistic Cyborg: Periphrasis on an [In]tense Rhetoric." *Rhetoric Society Quarterly* 28, no. 4, 51–72.
———. 2000. *Seduction, Sophistry, and the Woman with the Rhetorical Figure*. Carbondale: Southern Illinois University Press.
Barret, Elizabeth. 2000. *Stranger with a Camera*. Whitesburg, KY: Appalshop. DVD.
Butler, Judith. 1993. *Bodies That Matter: On the Discursive Limits of Sex*. New York: Routledge.
Cavarero, Adriana. 2005. *For More than One Voice: Toward a Philosophy of Vocal Expression*. Trans. Paul A. Kottman. Stanford, CA: Stanford University Press.
Creadick, Anna. 2017. "Banjo Boy: Masculinity, Disability, and Difference in *Deliverance*." *Southern Cultures* 23, no. 1, 63–78.
Dolmage, Jay. 2006. " 'Breathe upon Us an Even Flame': Hephaestus, History, and the Body of Rhetoric." *Rhetoric Review* 25, no. 2, 119–40.
———. 2009. "Metis, *Mêtis, Mestiza*, Medusa: Rhetorical Bodies across Rhetorical Traditions." *Rhetoric Review* 28, no. 1, 1–28.
———. 2014. *Disability Rhetoric*. Syracuse, NY: Syracuse University Press.

Engelhardt, Elizabeth S. D. 2017. "Trying to Get Appalachia Less Wrong: A Modest Approach." *Southern Cultures* 23, no. 1, 4–9.

Garringer, Rachel. 2017. " 'Well, We're Fabulous and We're Appalachians, So We're Fabulachians': Country Queers in Central Appalachia." *Southern Cultures* 23, no. 1, 79–91.

Halberstam, Judith. 2005. *In a Queer Time and Place: Transgender Bodies, Subcultural Lives*. New York: New York University Press.

Hayden, Jeffrey. 1996. *Children in America's Schools with Bill Moyers*. Columbia, SC: South Carolina ETV. DVD.

hooks, bell. 1989. *Talking Back: Thinking Feminist, Thinking Black*. Cambridge, MA: South End Press.

Kozol, Jonathan. 1991. *Savage Inequalities: Children in America's Schools*. New York: Random House.

Mann, Jeff. 2003. "Appalachian Subculture." *Gay & Lesbian Review Worldwide* 10, no. 5, 19.

McCann, Eugene J. 1998. "Mapping Appalachia: Toward a Critical Understanding." *Journal of Appalachian Studies* 4, no. 1, 87–113.

McDermott, Lydia M. 2015. "Birthing Rhetorical Monsters: How Mary Shelley Infuses *Mêtis* with the Maternal in Her 1831 Introduction to *Frankenstein*." *Rhetoric Review* 34, no. 1, 1–18.

———. 2016. *Liminal Bodies, Reproductive Health, and Feminist Rhetoric: Searching the Negative Spaces in Histories of Rhetoric*. Lanham, MD: Lexington Books.

McKerrow, Raymie E. 1998. "Corporeality and Cultural Rhetoric: A Site for Rhetoric's Future." *Southern Communication Journal* 63, no. 4, 315–28.

Swartz, Patti Capel. 2003. "It's Elementary in Appalachia: Helping Prospective Teachers and Their Students Understand Sexuality and Gender." *Journal of Gay and Lesbian Issues in Education* 1, no. 1, 51–71.

Taylor, Kathryn Trauth. 2011, 21 June. "Naming Affrilachia: Toward Rhetorical Ecologies of Identity Performance in Appalachia." *Enculturation: A Journal of Rhetoric, Writing, and Culture*. http://www.enculturation.net/naming-affrilachia.

Webb-Sunderhaus, Sara. 2016. " 'Keep the Appalachian, Drop the Redneck': Tellable Student Narratives of Appalachian Identity." *College English* 79, no. 1, 11–33.

Wilson, Greg, and Rachel Wolford. 2017. "The Technical Communicator as (Post-Postmodern) Discourse Worker." *Journal of Business and Technical Communication* 31, no. 1, 3–29.

Zelenko, Laura. 1990. "High Hopes on Hillbilly Highway." *American Demographics* 12, no. 3, 55–6.

CHAPTER 7

"Are Y'all Homos?": Mêtis as Method for Queer Appalachia

Caleb Pendygraft and Travis A. Rountree

With a few exceptions prior to this *Queer Appalachia* collection, queer methodologies have rarely engaged the overlap between Appalachian studies, ruralism, queerness, person- and place-based research, and rhetorical theory (Gradin 2016). This essay offers such an example of how queer storytelling can begin to extend rhetoric, composition, and literacy methods in queerer, more nuanced ways. We tell two narratives of the same startling experience that happened to us during person-based research in Appalachia. Similar to other coauthored essays using storytelling, our two narratives are "not contradictory but rather in tension" (Alexander and Rhoades 2012, 189). This essay is a dialogic exploration of methodology and the many complexities that comes along with person-based research. By drawing from our different embodied experiences, we recuperate the rhetorical construction of mêtis—strategic cunning intellect—into person-based methodology.

Our views of the singular situation, we think, are important to begin with to explain how mêtis can be different for individual queer scholars. Our initial responses to the situation, bolstered by previously lived experiences, are in stark contrast and should both be told. Mêtis is largely an embodied rhetorical construct, as we explain later. As such, we argue that mêtis should be grounded in embodied experiences if we are to develop it as a method. In this case, our stories provide two points of view on a single event from which we retrospectively apply mêtis as a potential methodological tool. In other words, mêtis could have been used differently for Caleb compared with Travis.

Despite our differing points of view, we argue that mêtis as a method for queer scholars in Appalachia relies on what we call performative precarity: conducting research with the understanding and awareness that it's always precarious; and performative disidentification: embodied practices that resist certain systems while not overtly rejecting them. In our conclusion, we gesture to the future of mêtis as method more broadly. In the spirit of Appalachian storytellers and cultural rhetorics scholars, and to queer the genre conventions of scholarly writing, we begin with our stories.

Caleb's Story

In the heat of the summer, Travis is about to embark on a road trip to Virginia to conduct person-based research. I've recently wrapped up my first year of PhD work and have ambitiously filled my summer: two independent studies, a pile of neglected readings, and editorial board duties for my university's student writing publication. Plus I am responsible for compiling teaching materials for next year's graduate cohort. I'm sharing these details because they set the stage for what will become one of the most singular lessons of grad school for myself and my boyfriend; it's a lesson we were not equipped to handle, not personally and not as academics.

The work I was doing that summer I can do anywhere with an adequate internet connection, because my computer, files, and readings can easily be carried along with me in my travels. It followed, naturally, that I could tag along with no hindrances to Travis's work or my own. At least, that's what we figured before the six-hour car ride to the research site.

I packed light: tank tops, flip flops, and plenty of shorts. Despite being deeply invested in my rural roots, during the sunny months you would think my proclivity to minimal clothing would deem me a West Coast queer. I also packed light because I did not anticipate that Travis would need me to be with him during the interviews, the tours of critical research sites, or any reason that would take me away from the hotel room. Company for company's sake: boyfriends on a trip across a few state lines, not spending time alone in the hotel room, maybe not eating alone four-hundred miles away from our homes. That certainly wasn't the case. Travis, to anyone who knows him personally, has an enthusiasm that sometimes risks optimism. I am one to view the world as a glass half empty, or even question why there's a glass in the first place. I had my doubts that everything would be fine considering two gay men, two out-of-towners, two academic-outsiders were walking around a community they didn't belong to and wanted the town to supply them with something. We were there for a purpose, and we soon found out that others could tell we were outsiders.

Travis wanted my support in coming along for the interviews and to be next to him in the archives. It was unnerving that I couldn't conceal my queerness— the tattoos, the piercings, the tank tops and shorts—in a town of just under 3,000 people. I realize that I should be careful when I speak of my queerness in such a way that could evoke shame or guilt, perhaps insinuating that we should all want to hide behind facades in potentially dangerous settings. It may even be dangerous to suggest to an academic audience that hiding one's queerness in rural settings is stereotyping those settings—in this way, I could be considered both a part of and creating a wrought contradiction in my academic privilege. That is, I could potentially be speaking for a rural setting that isn't homophobic and isn't dangerous, and by writing this I wanted to hide my othered status to perpetuate long-standing prejudices of Appalachians and rural Americans. What I am left with is an earnest answer: I'm not trying to color or perpetuate any negative views of Appalachia. I grew up in Kentucky, in twelve different places. Between the Appalachian mountaintops, the bluegrass-that-isn't-so-blue, and the Appalachian knobs, I know what trauma can come to a homeless Kentucky queer when you're outed and register queer on the homophobic meter. I am left saying: I was scared of being othered again during the research trip, in a possibly dangerous area, because I grew up experiencing those dangers in rural Kentucky. I have witnessed the homophobia, the hatred, the physical assault from being openly queer in areas where queerness seems to mix like oil and water.

So I went along with Travis in spite of my malaise—we support each other's research, so I tried to be as open-minded as I hoped the town would be. I stood next to him when he walked the site of his work, he and I spoke and met with the archive coordinator, and we drove through the hills and mountains to visit various people and places essential to his work. We stayed for three days. The first two nights were not exceptionally eventful as far as rendering ourselves as a gay couple. A sideways glance at dinner. The selling of Trump paraphernalia on the street corner. Subtlety suspect, but not overtly damning. On the last evening, Travis was feeling high on being able to do the work he loves and we were reflecting on a meaningful trip. He wanted to attend a town-wide event that happened to be taking place during our last day.

The cheap beer must have been the best part for me as we walked around the town, listened to a local band, and eventually found a bar and grill to eat dinner. We had been to the restaurant earlier that day to grab a quick drink before the event took place. It was a modest, two-story, mom-and-pop kind of joint. The bar was upstairs. On our first visit we had a few glasses of wine and shared the bar with an older gentleman with a long gray beard, wearing a frayed, cut-off denim vest, complete with a large patched emblem on the back. Before we finished our wine, two more men arrived to accompany our vested bar-mate. We paid, left, and ventured out to engage with the town.

With a failed attempt to find another restaurant for dinner, we returned to the bar an hour later. This time more comrades of our gray-bearded bar-mate, all wearing the same denim vests with the oversized insignia on the back, crowded the upstairs. All the booths were filled at this point, and considering the amount of people in lawn chairs along the streets and walking about, this wasn't surprising. We sat at the same seats as earlier.

We ordered salads and glasses of wine. During our wait, one of the denim-clad men, at least four beers in as we observed since our arrival, meandered over to our end of the bar. Immediately I regretted the wine. It shouldn't have been the first thing I worried about, looking back. Perhaps I should have been more concerned with how all these men and the few women were all strikingly similar to the motorcycle clubs I grew up around down in the knobs of Kentucky. That should have been the moment we asked for the check. After the guy briefs us with the expected country niceties, he asks, "Do y'all mind moving to the end of the bar? We got a couple more people coming up to meet us. Y'all don't mind do ya?"

We moved. A few more of the clan arrived, and our interlocutor pays us another visit.

"I got a question for y'all. Don't get me wrong, I'm looking out for ya. Are y'all homos?"

This seemingly innocuous statement was delivered with an insidious smirk. The level of sticky sweat, the perspiration produced when you're confronted with a fight-or-flight moment was immediate. It stuck to my tank top and the creases behind my knees. Without any reservation, Travis answered, "Yes."

Could the man have genuinely been inquiring into our queerness? Sure. But his body language said otherwise: he fidgeted, looked over his shoulder, and wore a snide smile. There was some rapport between our newly acquainted inquirer before he strolled off to the opposite end of the bar. I could tell that Travis was uncomfortable and, in the moment, did the only thing he figured was the best move: telling the truth. I didn't engage in conversation when we were asked. Too many conversations have begun in a similar way when I was younger, and the best thing to do is assess the likelihood of getting your ass beat before coming out, again, to a complete stranger. Now that Travis and I were sitting there othered, looking like we were dressed for the beach, sipping our glasses of wine, all I could muster to Travis was a muffled *fuck*.

Our new acquaintance makes a third and final approach as our food arrived. The first thing that comes to mind as our salads are being sat down in front of us and as the now clearly drunk man approaches us is *Why the hell did we order salads? Why couldn't we have ordered a burger or a steak?*

"Listen. Listen," he begins. "I'm on y'all's side. My brother he's a homo. So I'm on y'all's side, but listen. See, I'm looking out for ya. We have about eight more people coming. They're gonna get here in about twenty minutes, ya know what I'm saying?"

Travis says, "Sure. That's fine. No problem. We'll be done by then." At this point I don't want to look at this man, let alone speak to him.

"All right, all right. Ya know, I'm just looking out for ya because my brother he's a homo and we've got people coming here in about twenty minutes."

This was their spot, and two queers were in it. The twenty minutes were a warning to leave. He was threatening us. It was obviously a laughing matter for his group, as they cajoled and tilted their heads back in laughter every time he went back after talking to us. Maybe not explicitly, but it was obvious that we were being told, in a matter of speaking, that we weren't welcome there. Moreover, that bar space belonged to them, and we were alien. Once he walked away, laughter erupted from the group and almost half went downstairs and presumably out the door. Did they leave in anticipating two queers coming through the front door? Were they waiting for us?

Immediately Travis asked me, "You want to go?"

"Fuck, yeah."

There was a door out the back of the second floor we were on. However, it was closed, shutting down the connected patio over the concert playing below. Explaining to Travis that I didn't want to risk running into the members of the club downstairs outside the front door, we would sneak out the back and down the patio. We hurried for our check, piled our food in to-go boxes, and rushed out the back door, hopping over the chain that closed down the patio.

We walked back to the car, taking a long route around the main street, thinking it best to avoid as many people as possible. After returning to the hotel, we recognized that we had just been threatened and run out of town. We had come to a town to conduct research and our safety was put in jeopardy because our queerness was visible and legible.

Travis's Story

My upbringing in Virginia was vastly different from Caleb's in Kentucky; my experiences led me to react differently to the situation. Hailing from Richmond, Virginia, I never considered myself Appalachian or queer growing up. In Richmond, I witnessed the Confederacy everywhere. I attended a private high school in the fan district near downtown Richmond. On the track team, I ran down Monument Avenue, which was adorned with Confederate statues. I visited the museum of the Confederacy with my family several times. I left to attend college at James Madison University in the Shenandoah

Valley. It was only a short distance from Richmond (and only three hours from Hillsville), but there was still a Confederate stronghold in the small Virginian mountain town. I took a history course there where we visited Civil War battlefields and talked mostly about the Confederate side of the war. Because of these experiences and Virginia's complicated history of Virginia, there were several times (and still are) when the voice of Faulkner's Quentin Compson echoes in my head saying, "I don't hate it! I don't hate it!" (Faulkner 1986, 303). When I moved to attend graduate school in Boone, North Carolina, at Appalachian State University, there was a different South that included Appalachia. Unsurprisingly, although there were Confederate flags in the outskirts of town, there was a more liberal stronghold within the circumference of the university. Because of this stronghold, I was comfortable to finally come out of the closet at age twenty-six. Unlike Caleb, I never felt threatened because of my sexuality in the town.

Leaving the mountains, I began my doctoral studies at the University of Louisville, where I researched the courthouse shootout in Hillsville, Virginia, for my dissertation. I started this project as a graduate student at App State and was fascinated by the rhetorical constructions of the event ever since. Hillsville was clearly Appalachian—it fell within the confines of the Appalachian Regional Commission's geographic borders, and it retained the Confederate roots I was familiar with in Richmond. This overlap of the identities of my research fascinated me because they coincided with my complicated relationship to the South and Appalachia.

On top of meshing southern and Appalachian identities, I had another problematic personal layer toward this project. In researching the shootout, I discovered the possibility that I could be connected to it through my maternal grandfather. He first introduced me to the shootout when he told me that he, my grandmother, and some friends visited Hillsville in the 1960s. Someone approached him and asked if he was an Allen. The Allens were the family that contributed to the courthouse shootout. When my grandfather said "yes," the man told him to "get the hell out of town." My grandfather, grandmother, and their friends quickly left soon after. My grandfather said that his father had been an orphan and was, more than likely, from Hillsville. Hearing this story not only contributed to the complexity of retelling memory in my dissertation, it also provided me with a personal link to the town. During my research, I was hesitant to disclose the possibility of this connection. There was still tension between those who were for the local government side of the shootout and those who were for the Allen side. Though not directly from the small mountain town I was researching, I still felt it was home because it was in Virginia and because of this possible familial link. My personal ties to the town and the research made the confrontation Caleb and I experienced even more hurtful.

On the morning of the interaction, I had an interview with one of my informants. I got dressed that morning and put on a salmon-colored T-shirt. After putting gel and hairspray in my hair in what my paternal grandfather called a "pompadoo," I began to question if I was performing straight, rural academic researcher. I went to the interview and put on my best mountain performance, complete with local vernacular of "y'all" and "yeah, yeah, yeah" like I'd heard local Jack Tales teller Orville Hicks say.

After the interview, Caleb and I decided to drive to another museum. On the way we stopped at a local flea market and vegetable stand—one of those you see on the side of the road in most Appalachian towns as you're going up the mountain. The shop included rebel flags as well as a hillbilly on the store sign complete with jug, beard, big shoes, and a floppy hat. Caleb was reluctant to enter the store. Feeling at home in Virginia, I didn't feel the same hesitation. I went in while Caleb waited in the car. I encountered the typical flea market trinkets: a Jesus behind glass who looked like he was praying to get out, North Carolina moonshine jugs, T-shirts with Confederate flags and hillbillies on them. The middle-aged woman stood in front of the counter with rebel flags of all shapes and sizes behind her. I didn't stay in there long since we wanted to get back to town. I felt I understood the lives of these folks: they were Virginians. I had heard the stories of Robert E. Lee, of Stonewall Jackson, of the burning of Richmond, of the piles of shoes that remained at the Battle of Manassas. I was able to pass here. While uncomfortable, I knew the discourse to use to engage, but most important I was visibly read as straight. Boots. Tucked-in collared shirt. George Jones belt buckle. Although I disagreed with the racial overtones the flag suggested, I related to these people. They could be members of my family, friends, folks I went to school with; I felt a sense of home in both the South and the mountains.

After we got back to the hotel, I changed clothes because it was too warm for khakis and boots. We decided to go into town to watch the local car show. There was going to be music and other festivities. We arrived a little early, so we decided to get a drink at the local bar. We sat there for about an hour when a man walked in who looked almost exactly like the stereotypical man we saw on the store sign. He had a big hat, overalls, and a beard pulled down and tied with some sort of hair tie. He declared his presence by hollering, "The mountain man is here!" when he walked in. We sat there and finished our drinks and then went outside where the band was going to play.

The band wasn't supposed to go on until seven, so we decided to get a beer from the beer tent and sat and talked. We started to get hungry and went back to the restaurant to eat dinner. Sitting at the same place with the same waiter serving us, we ordered one more glass of wine. As we sat there, we noticed that others came to join the mountain man who was sitting there earlier. He was clearly chugging Bud Light, bubbling it halfway down every time he took a sip. My boyfriend and I suddenly became aware of our surroundings and how we were performing. I noticed earlier that we were calling each other "babe" instead of our names. I now had on a small Northside Cincinnati T-shirt. I wore khaki shorts and recognized that I had on flip-flops. Caleb had on a black T-shirt printed with cats playing pool and denim shorts. Although the denim shorts most certainly fit in with the local dress code, the cat shirt was edgy. It wasn't for the local sports team or for NASCAR. It was different. Othered. Queer. He also wore flip-flops. As we walked around earlier at the car show I noticed that only two other men were wearing flip-flops. The rest had on clunky dress shoes, muddy tennis shoes, or cowboy boots.

As more men began to arrive at the bar, we noticed they wore denim jackets with the sleeves cut off with their gang's emblem on the back of the jacket and their name on the front. Caleb and I ordered two salads: mine a house, his a Caesar. A medium-height man wearing the gang haircut came over:

"Where y'all from?"

I said, "Kentucky."

Caleb remained silent and avoided eye contact.

"My brother lives in Kentucky and raised horses. He runs a camp for special needs kids. I have one myself and it's real nice he goes there."

"That's great and really nice of your brother."

"Oh, yeah, my brother looks out for my son."

We waited, and the guy wandered back over to his group. The group started conversing among themselves. While I didn't hear exactly what they were saying, I did hear them include racial slurs and the phrase "they got what they deserved." The man came over a second time after a significant number of men—numbering closer to eight or ten now—had started to gather.

"Well, I just have to ask because I'm looking out for you guys, but are y'all homos?"

This was a moment I had never encountered in my life. I have *never* blatantly been asked this question. Caleb and I sat there like the tackily painted stone deer that were posed outside of our hotel room. I was determined to correct him, so I said in an attempt to correct him:

"Yes, we're gay."

"Well, that's okay. My brother is homo and he's got a little lisp. And I think that's just fine. I'm okay with it."

He wandered back. Our salads came out, making us seem even more othered because we didn't order ribs or burgers. As we got them, he came over a third time, staggering a little from the beers that he had drank.

"Hey, the rest of us are going to be here in about half hour so y'all need to move or there's going to be trouble. I'm just looking out for you. I don't want nothing to happen. I'm just looking out for you."

Although verbally this doesn't sound threatening, we knew he implied a threat of violence. We were strangers in a strange place where the atmosphere was shifting.

We said, "Sure, sure, sure."

I gave the waiter my credit card without getting the check and asked for a couple of boxes.

Knowing that the rest of the gang had headed down the front steps, we got our food and then headed down the back steps. We went right in front of the band that had started to play and walked quickly to our car.

Before this trip I never separated my identity with where I'm from and who I am. I am southern. I am Appalachian. I am queer. Looking back, I know that we were truly afraid. To me, this interaction was much more than getting run off because I was gay—it was a betrayal of place. Passing at the flea market falsely reassured me that I could pass anywhere in a state and region I considered home. After growing up in a hometown with such deep roots in the Confederate South and spending a significant amount of my life in Appalachia, I could hear remnants of my parents and grandparents in my interviewees' voices. I could hear home in their voices. I felt included in my construction of the local event I was researching; the participants and I constructed a story together and shared a desire to remember it. Hillsville was not only my research site, it was what I considered my home. These were *my* mountains, too. But I realize that my queerness wasn't home here. The rejection was more than just a covert gay threat, it was a rejection of me from the region. I was betrayed, and it stung terribly. I am hesitant to return to my on-site research in fear of rejection and possible violence against my person and my conception of home.

Some Queerly Suggested Methods

We left the next day, thinking we had learned some things from our trip that may be valuable for others in our fields. We weren't equipped with how to handle research in areas that can prove contrary to our identity. By providing our different Appalachian histories and queer points of view, our aim was to demonstrate how we respond individually and why we acted the way we did. In retrospect we realize that our individual ideas of Appalachia, doing research, and being visibly queer were in tension with one another. We hope that by sharing two unique perspectives of one story, we can offer methods for other queers in our field to do their research. In this case, no amount of coursework or theory could have prepared us for being forced out of a town because of our queerness. The experience led us to the rhetorical concept of mêtis as a construct of embodied, cunning intellect, which the following section of deals with in detail. First we feel it's important to explain how our positionality as queer researchers and as a queer couple doing research positions us in that research.

We acknowledge that we are writing from a position of privilege. We had funding to make the trip: Travis had approval and support from his university, and Caleb was able to work remotely for his institution. We are both cisgender, white men, which come with a set of cultural and economic positions that we refuse to overlook. We cannot write for queers who can't "pass" in areas where we found ourselves, whether that is through racial legibility or for those who are queer and do not choose to pass as straight in certain contexts. We write our experience aware of our positionality in hopes of cultivating open conversations with other queer Appalachian scholars to develop new methods for the future. There is also the fact that heinous acts of violence have been committed against queers; being run out of a bar with insidious threats may not compare to the physical violence that has occurred to other queer family. We approach this essay as we begin to think of methods that reach out and potentially address these acts of unkindness, perhaps before they happen.

To begin thinking through how we can use our unfortunate experience productively for other queer scholars in Appalachia, we start with the premise that writing is a social act. As Roozen (2015) has put it, "Writing puts the writer in contact with other people, but the social nature of writing goes beyond the people writers draw upon and think about. It also encompasses people who have shaped the genres, tools, artifacts, technologies, and places writers act with as they address the needs of their audiences" (18). We would like to extend these claims to methodology. If writing is always already social, it follows that the research we do in the field of composition and rhetoric studies is social as well. In other words, methods are as much about the research we conduct as with whom we conduct it.

This obviously includes the participants in community-based research, but we suggest that this goes further than our participants. Our methodologies and methods must also accommodate the places that are constructed socially wherein we do our research and those interpersonal relationships that we foster as queers in academia, personal, or otherwise. Jeff Grabill (2012) may help here, with what he has called the research stance: "the single most important issue to consider when researching in or with communities and needs to be better understood in any conversation about research methodology" (211). Grabill's notion of research stances allows us as queer academics to reevaluate why we do our research and how our participants and our perspectives affect our methods and methodologies.

We note our use of terminology. We are in agreement with feminist scholar Sandra Harding (1987) that method and methodologies are theories and analyses "of how research does or should proceed" (3). *Methods* refers to the techniques "for (or way of proceeding in) gathering evidence" (Harding 1987, 2). In short, methods are what you do during research, whereas methodologies explain why you perform your particular methods. We also recognize that these concepts are not stable, nor always fixed. Grabill (2012) defines research stance as an answer to these three questions to identify three specific aspects of being a researcher:

1. Researcher identity: Who am I personally? as a researcher? in relationship to my discipline?

2. Purposes as a researcher. Why research?

3. Questions of power and ethics. What is my commitment with respect to research? (Grabill 2012, 215)

Extending these three areas, in accordance with our claim that methodology is socially constructed, Grabill makes the claim that relationships are important to research (2012, 214). We hope that through our stories we have exposed our research stance. What's more, it is through our storytelling that we pose a counternarrative to introducing new methodologies. We hope that by beginning with the story, we can expose our varied research stances without adhering to the traditional modes of scholarly writing.

Travis's identity as a researcher was threefold: he attempted to function as a southerner, then function as Appalachian, and then hide his queerness. Recognizing that his queerness could possibly deter his informants from participating, he aimed to pass as straight. Though ethically and personally questionable, passing enabled him to gather research for his project; however, this passing did not work in a social setting outside of his research, as the instance in the restaurant illustrates. It should be noted that Travis's choice not to divulge his queerness and to attempt to pass as straight was not intended to purposefully deceive his participants. His research did not involve queer research, and he thought it best not to be labeled as such. Despite his attempt to pass, his queerness became apparent. Even though it didn't have an effect on his research, it did have an effect on him as a researcher. The residual effects of the experience taint his future possibilities of continuing research about the event.

In this particular case, Caleb was not the researcher but was there as emotional support and a queer companion. Although Caleb wasn't conducting research, we argue that if writing and rhetoric research are tethered to social relationships, his relationship to Travis and to the field of rhetoric and composition acts as a site we can use as research in this essay. Following Grabill's second question, "Why research?," we would like to point out that we are placing our relationship as a queer couple central to this essay. To answer why: by looking at the queer couple as a social construct in Appalachia, we offer our personal experience to develop alternative methods for other queers who find themselves in comparable situations.

In many ways, what we are doing by positioning ourselves as queer researchers with sometimes differing views along with using our relationship and experiences as a queer couple, agrees with William Banks's claims that "regardless of how distant we can get ourselves from the embodied experiences of our lives, if we do not find ways back to those bodies, those experiences, we run the risk of impoverishing our theories and pedagogies. More specifically, when we ignore the 'embodied' in discourse, we miss the ways in which liberation is always both social and individual, a truly symbiotic relation" (Banks 2003, 22).

Methodologies and methods don't spring forth from theory alone, but as we have been suggesting and as we would like to add to Banks's claims above, methods reveal themselves from doing. The research stance is important in sharing our methods and how they shape our methodologies. Much as we expected Travis's research not to involve outing us as a couple, the failure to recognize a methodology that could accommodate such a possibility inspires new ways of doing and thus new methods. From our experience, then, we propose the rhetorical construct of mêtis as a methodological frame that can emerge from queer researchers telling their stories from Appalachia, the basis of our argument so far—and even for queer research in Appalachia. Next we explore mêtis as a historic figure and its more recent use in rhetorical theory. From its rhetorical uptake we propose that mêtis can be not only be theoretical but an enacted practice: mêtis can be a method. Through the lens of performativity, we then suggest mêtis as method relies on precariousness and disidentification.

Mêtis: Performative Precarity and Disidentification

We pose a few questions to help frame a queer methodology for queers in and for Appalachia. What does it mean to do research in the field of composition and rhetoric as queers in rural areas, often rural places where queerness is deemed other? How does identity, safety, and person-based research overlap with and in many ways contradict methodological frames in the field? What happens when your research poses a threat to the social spheres you do not belong to? How can queer theory help further intersectionality with rural studies in the field and offer new ways of doing research?

We may not have all or complete answers, but in reflecting on our research stances, we agreed that we may have acted differently when confronted by the man at the bar. Thinking about it rhetorically, we came across mêtis in our research. Mêtis was a mythological figurehead, a goddess of the Greco-Roman pantheon and first wife of Zeus. Zeus became threatened of her cunning wisdom, transforming her into a fly and swallowing her in fear that she would usurp him. Her namesake evokes themes of wisdom and cunning and is always a referent to embodied threat that her female power posed to Zeus.

Detienne and Vernant's (1978) *Cunning Intelligence in Greek Culture and Society* has played a critical role in recovering the term as a "complex but very coherent body of mental attitudes and intellectual behavior" (3). They relocate mêtis as "a type of intelligence and of thought, a way of knowing," recognizing that their research of the word is in part "a linguistic study, an analysis of the semantic field of mêtis" (Detienne and Vernant 1978, 3). Notice that their focus is epistemic—not embodied and certainly not methodological. Mêtis is a quality of intellect, not necessarily a mode of being. Mêtis "implies a complex but very coherent body of mental attitudes and intellectual behavior which combine flair, wisdom, forethought, subtlety of mind, deception, resourcefulness, vigilance, opportunism, various skills, and experience acquired over the years" (Detienne and Vernant 1978, 3).

Mêtis as a rhetorical construct is concerned with knowing how to outwit, particularly in rough situations. It is a slippery if not flat-out a tricky term because it only reveals itself when necessary situations come into being. Or, as Detienne and Vernant (1978) phrase it, mêtis is bound up with "the world of becoming, in circumstances of conflict—takes the form of an ability to deal with whatever comes up, drawing on certain intellectual qualities: forethought perspicacity, quickness and acuteness of understanding, trickery, and even deceit" (44). This definition relies on kairotic situations, always in anticipation of the moment where cunning can lead to an escape from a problematic situation. For example, when we wrote in our narrative that when we were confronted by the man with the question "Are y'all homos?," we experienced the fight-or-flight reaction. Mêtis, arguably, could have been enacted at this moment; the situation wasn't anticipated, in other words, it emerged.

Our application of mêtis adds to recent scholarship in rhetoric and writing studies where mêtis is theorized as an epistemic device but also through ontological understanding. Karen Kopelson (2003), for instance, uses mêtis as a pedagogical strategy of neutrality in the writing classroom. She argues that by performing neutrality via mêtis, instructors can enhance "students' engagement with difference" and "minimizes their resistance to difference in the process" (Kopelson 2003, 188). In the context of the writing classroom, Kopelson emphasizes how neutrality is a space of potential for instructors; neutrality as never fully or quickly taking sides of issues allows mêtis to play out according to what unfolds.

Jay Dolmage perhaps has done the most work with the term, and looks to mêtis as a concept to broaden rhetoric studies to include bodily difference among gendered and ableist lines. He explains, "The mêtis stories refute a canonical view of rhetorical history that not only overlooks the body but also explicitly vilifies the female body and that uses disability as a master trope of disqualification" (2009, 1). More particularly to our project here, Dolmage uses mêtis as part of a "reclamation project"—"cunning, adaptive, *embodied* intelligence. The word mêtis means wise and wily intelligence" (Dolmage 2009, 5). Mêtis has been associated with "the trickster, the trap-builder," Dolmage points out (2006, 119). Mêtis seeks to use a difficult situation to one's advantage.

Adding to these perspectives, and in agreement with Detienne and Vernant's understanding and framing of the mêtis, we want to complicate the concept. Mêtis is limited to the intellectual as "an informed prudence" (Detienne and Vernant 1978, 12). Never in action, only in thought, mêtis is the wit to assess a potentially dangerous situation. As Detienne and Vernant frame it, it doesn't offer much in the way of an actual escape. Whereas rhetoric scholars like Kopelson and Dolmage have incorporated mêtis as a pedagogical and embodied rhetorical concept, we argue that mêtis can be brought into the realm of doing, not just becoming. Mêtis is as much about a state of mind as it is about ways of reacting. We'd like to offer an alternative, queer understanding of mêtis as a method.

We use mêtis not just as a rhetorical construct of embodied intelligence, being both cunning and adaptive, perhaps even sly, and we propose mêtis as a performative and in turn a method. Mêtis isn't merely a quality you can embody, but it can be a tool you enact. Particularly, mêtis offers a strategy for queers who work in areas where their queerness sometimes conflicts with the communities they find themselves in—we would even go as far as saying that one's bodily safety can rest on mêtis as a method. How does mêtis as method work outside understanding that intelligence always has an embodied position? We would position two more theoretical terms beneath mêtis to demonstrate this performative: precarity and disidentification.

The notions of precarity and disidentification are in many ways already examples of mêtis, or cunning, adaptive intelligence. The way we see them working together is not exclusive nor independent from one another. We also add that they are not sequential as methods; one does not enact or perform precarity or disidentification in any particular order. Instead, we see precarity and disidentification working simultaneously, as though they are two nodes on the axis of mêtis. Either end of the axis may be activated at any time, together or alone, while relying on all that underscores mêtis as a methodological framework. We will return to specific moments in our stories to offer concrete ways these methods could have been used before we explain how to enact and perform these concepts. It is also essential that the two terms have philosophic and theoretical genealogies and our attempt here isn't to track down these genealogies but to move these terms vis-à-vis mêtis into the realm of methodologies and methods.

How do you move from abstract theorizing into enacting methods? We suggest that you do so through performance. Much as Butler (2009) has done with gender theory, we draw from Austin's concept of a performative "in which to *say* something is to *do* something; or in which *by* saying or *in* saying something we are doing something" (12). For instance, when Travis responded to the question "Are y'all homos?" with a "Yes," he not only spoke but did something in that certain context. He performed his queerness. Through the utterance, we were othered. We place "performative" to extend and gather the concepts of precarity and disidentification into the scope of methods. As a result, and as we explain shortly, precarity becomes performative precarity, and disidentification moves to become performative disidentification.

Judith Butler (2009) has been expanding her theories of gender to include a conversation on precariousness. She writes that "precarity also characterizes that politically induced condition of maximized vulnerability and exposure for populations exposed to arbitrary state violence and to other forms of aggression that are not enacted by states and against which states do not offer adequate protection" (Butler 2009, ii). Here she is speaking of preciousness on the level of populations and law, but it highlights an important element that applies to our use of the term when she writes of "vulnerability" and "protection." We argue that the same can be applied on the local, isolated level where and when individuals find themselves in precarious situations with their research. This applies to our stories with Caleb's lack of "proper" wardrobe and Travis's willingness to include Caleb in his research without considering the dangers of making us vulnerable. In short, we were precarious subjects in our own research, and in retrospect we should have performed that precarity in more cunning ways.

Elsewhere, Butler (2011) elaborates her notions of precariousness and explains that the term "characterizes every embodied and finite human being, and non-human beings as well. This is not simply an existential truth—each of us could be subject to deprivation, injury, debilitation or death by virtue of events or processes outside our control" (12–13). The driving principle of precariousness that informs Butler's understanding, then, rests on the instability of events to unfold, a certain unknowingness, so to speak. We aren't attempting to solve and account for all free radicals that can make a subject precious insofar as their research is concerned; instead, performative precarity would acknowledge the precariousness of one's research. Performative precarity would seek a cunning intelligence to ensure that when conducting research as an outsider, you pay close rhetorical attention to how you embody your research.

Caleb would have considered bringing his boots and a pair of jeans to minimize the chances of being othered for the sake of Travis's research. Travis could have understood the precarious nature of entering a space where being a visibly gay couple may interfere with the research overall. Entering new spaces may contradict your stance as a researcher—in our case, being a queer couple and queer researchers, acknowledging precarious circumstances, and taking measures to prevent foreseeable (as possible) events that may threaten your own safety.

We make another brief note on why we've been placing precarity before disidentification. To disidentify, as we are about to explain, presupposes a state of precarity. That is, precarity is already assumed once one has to disidentify. We use *disidentify* here in the lineage of José Muñoz. To disidentify rejects the binary thinking that you can identify with or against.

Disidentification purports that you can reject structures of identification while always working within those systems without completely or overtly

rejecting them. Muñoz (1999) elucidates on creating this third mode of identification: "The first mode is understood as 'identification,' where a 'Good
Subject' chooses the path of identification with discursive and ideological
forms. 'Bad Subjects' resist and attempt to reject the images and identificatory
sites offered by dominant ideology and proceed to rebel, to 'counteridentify'
and turn against this symbolic system. . . . Disidentification is the third mode
of dealing with dominant ideology, one that neither opts to assimilate within
such a structure nor strictly opposes it; rather, disidentification is a strategy
that works on and against dominant ideology" (453–59). It's crucial to point
out here that disidentifying does not require a counteridentification, and, in
fact, rests on the notion of working within certain structures. We carry on
these ideas into the realm of methods.

We suggest that disidentification is a particular form of mêtis wherein the
scholar can adapt wisely to their surroundings when doing person- or place-
based research. Performative disidentification distills mêtis as a method by
acknowledging that some parts of identification can be contradictory and even
momentarily deniable. We mentioned in our stories how we negotiated our
queerness; looking back, we realize that if we were to perform disidentification, we could have avoided the conflict and threats we experienced. Travis
could have disidentified and answered "no" to "Are y'all homos?" He could have
disidentified with our queerness momentarily for the sake of avoiding conflict;
however, that would raise ethical and personal issues, such as the rejection of
his queer self in public, rendering feelings of guilt and shame for not being
honest. In addition, saying "no" may not have an effect on what the group of
bikers already understood as operating as queer in the restaurant. By way of
mêtis as performative disidentification in the hypothetical situation, we would
have certainly been working within the structure we found ourselves in. Muñoz
(1999) is clear that disidentification also works on and against dominant ideology, and this is where mêtis presents as a unique strategy for queers doing
rural research.

Mêtis as Method: Possibilities of Precarity and Disidentification

By making use of that threatening experience—our failure to rhetorically
adjust to the context we found ourselves in at the restaurant—we are working
against the notion that we shouldn't find academic value in it. In other words,
we could have just brushed it off as a bad experience; instead, we turned it
into something productive. By writing through the experience, we imagine
that mêtis methods include others doing the same in academic writing. Put

another way, mêtis as method may include writing about how we perform precarity in our academic writing and how we may disidentify in academic writing space.

We have aimed to create room for discussion and room for the experience to operate as a study in methods and methodology. Although the production of this experience is valuable to the study of research, our personal experiences demonstrate possible conclusions that resonated from this experience.

Caleb wrote in his story that he was worried about being labeled as a stereotype or denying his own queerness. This is one way through which performative disidentification can help us understand the layered, nuanced issues when two or more parts of a researcher's identity are at odds. The constant negotiations involved with performative disidentification seem to contradict the scholarly progress in our field. That is to say, we anticipate that a rebuttal to our proposed methods may be that we are simply lying about our queerness to conduct research.

We wouldn't ask this of anyone, but we want to highlight the sticky and sometime dangerous risk that emerges when queerness and rural Appalachian identity brush up against one another. If Travis had answered "no" instead of "yes," would that have been lying? On a base level, one can assume that it was a lie. However, when one's own safety is threatened, would it be best to tell the truth or disidentify to remove oneself from such a precarious situation? This question is as tricky as the situation at hand. Mêtis acts an anchor to intellectualize these contradictions. As we have been arguing, it also helps us act through those contradictions during person-based research, in sharing academic writing, and in our queer lives.

In addition, Travis's experience demonstrates the place-based emotional and ethical predicament of disidentification. He felt he could not choose to identify as southern, Appalachian, *and* queer; instead, he had to choose two of the three. Expressing his queerness to his informants in the mountain town had the potential to detrimentally affect his research. Although his informants would probably not have the same threatening reaction as the men at the restaurant, they could have withheld valuable information. Travis did come out as queer to one informant over email. She and her mother provided information about the event because he was "family." These two women, unsurprised by the confrontation in the small mountain town they once called home, were still saddened by it. Reading these participants' responses through the lens of mêtis, we speculate that it is likely they figured it best to disidentify with certain parts of identity that pose a potential threat in our particular circumstances.

These situations demonstrate that we also realize these methods may be used on much more benign levels. Not all queers conducting research in Appalachia will face the threats that we have, but we offer our experience in hopes that it prevents similar ones for other Appalachian and rural queers. While there is an emerging history of fiction and nonfiction queer Appalachian writers (e.g., Jeff Mann, Silas House, Jason Howard, Tennessee Jones, Doris Davenport), rhetoric and composition scholars such as Sherrie Gradin and Eric Darnell Pritchard are opening up Appalachia and rural sites as a site of critical queer scholarship. We hope this chapter adds to these fruitful discussions. Our methodology of mêtis is not meant to detract from the progress of visibility but highlights the precarious nature of the sometimes risky work we have to conduct as queer scholars in rural Appalachian spaces. Working through queer relationships with each other, our sites of research, and our research participants may sometimes require us to disidentify parts of ourselves, but that does not mean we reject the queerness that brings us together.

BIBLIOGRAPHY

Alexander, Jonathan, and Jacqueline Rhodes. 2012. "Queerness, Multimodality, and the Possibilities of Re/Orientation." In *Composing(Media) = Composing(Embodiment): Bodies, Technologies, Writing, the Teaching of Writing*, edited by Anne Frances Wysocki and Kristin L. Arola, 188–212. Logan: Utah State University Press.

Austin, J. L. 1962. *How to Do Things with Words*. Oxford, UK: Oxford University Press.

Banks, William. 2003, September. "Written through the Body: Disruptions and 'Personal' Writing." *College English* 66, 21–40.

Butler, Judith. 2009. "Performativity, Precarity and Sexual Politics." AIBR *Revista De Antropologia Iberoamericana* 4, no. 3, i–xiii.

———. 2011. "For and Against Precarity." *Tidal: Occupy Theory, Occupy Strategy* 1, 12–13.

Detienne, Marcel, and Jean-Pierre Vernant. 1978. *Cunning Intelligence in Greek Culture and Society*. Trans. Janet Lloyd. Chicago: University of Chicago Press.

Dolmage, Jay. 2006. " 'Breathe upon Us an Even Flame': Hephaestus, History, and the Body of Rhetoric." *Rhetoric Review* 25, no. 2, 119–40.

———. 2009. "Mêtis, *Mêtis, Mestiza*, Medusa: Rhetorical Bodies across Rhetorical Traditions." *Rhetoric Review* 28, no. 1, 1–28.

Faulkner, William. 1986. *Absalom! Absalom!* New York: Vintage Press.

Grabill, Jeff. 2012. "Community-Based Research and the Importance of a Research Stance." In *Writing Studies Research in Practice: Methods and Methodologies*, edited by Lee Nickson, Mary P. Sheridan, and Gesa E. Kirsch, 210–19. Carbondale: Southern Illinois University Press.

Gradin, Sherrie. 2016. "Can You See Me Now?: Rural Queer Archives and a Call to Action." *Pearson*. https://www.pearsoned.com/pedagogy-practice/can-you-see-me-now-rural-queer-archives-and-a-call-to-action/. Accessed September 14, 2017.

Harding, Sandra. 1987. "Introduction: Is There a Feminist Method?" In *Feminism and Methodology*, edited by Sandra Harding, 1–14. Bloomington: Indiana University Press.

Kopelson, Karen. 2003. "Rhetoric on the Edge of Cunning; or, The Performance of Neutrality (Re)Considered as a Composition Pedagogy for Student Resistance." *College Composition and Communication* 55, no. 1, 115–46.

Muñoz, José Esteban. 1999. *Disidentifications: Queers of Color and the Performance of Politics*. Minneapolis: University of Minnesota Press.

Roozen, Kevin. 2015. "Writing Is a Social and Rhetorical Activity." In *Naming What We Know: Threshold Concepts of Writing Studies*, edited by Linda Adler-Kassner and Elizabeth A. Wardle, 17–19. Logan: Utah State University Press.

CHAPTER 8

Queering Trauma and Resilience, Appalachian Style!

delfin bautista

It has been five years since I moved to Athens, OH, and even today I am still asked, "Why Athens from Miami, FL?" My answer remains the same—as a queer person and professional, to me the narratives of the Midwest, Appalachia, and rural areas are sources of transgressive inspiration and resilience. What excited me about southeast Ohio and what continues to inspire me are the rich narratives of queerness and LGBTQ-ness in a region of the United States that has been largely ignored by the mainstream equality movement. These past five years of living in Athens and traveling around the region have offered many opportunities to become immersed in the challenges and celebrations of a rainbow community that has claimed and continues to claim and reclaim lesbian, gay, bisexual, transgender, queer, plus (LGBTQ+) identities with pride. This dynamic keeps me here and keeps challenging me to expand my own understanding of creating safer, braver spaces of belonging. Despite being overlooked and neglected by the national LGBT rights movement, queer and LGBTQ+ individuals and communities in rural, Appalachian, and rural Appalachian areas are not only surviving but thriving.

Poet Richard Blanco (2014) shares this story:

> I'm six or seven years old, riding back home with my grandfather and my Cuban grandmother from my tia Onelia's house. Her son Juan Alberto is effeminate, "*un afeminado*," my grandmother says with disgust . . . "Better to having a granddaughter who's a whore than a grandson who is *un pato* faggot like you. Understand?" . . . All I know is she's talking about me, me; and whatever I am, is bad, very bad. Twenty-something years later, I sit in my therapist's office, telling him that same story. With his guidance through the months that follow, I discover the extent of my grandmother's verbal and psychological abuse, which I had swept under my subconscious rug. Through the years and to this day I continue unraveling

how that abuse affected my personality, my relationships, and my writing. I write . . . in the shadow of my grandmother—a homophobic woman with only a sixth grade education—who has exerted (and still exerts) the most influence on my development as a writer. (48)

These words reflect the intersectional realities of what it means to be LGBTQ+ in rural parts of the United States. Blanco poetically represents the question this essay explores—what are the experiences of hardship and resilience (or in my radical queer wording, bad-assery) of LGBTQ+ people in rural settings based on my experiences working and living in an Appalachian college town? His words also embody the reality of intersectionality that I explore later in this essay; Blanco is an LGBT Latino who lives in a rural area. As an LGBTQ+ movement, we have made much progress in the past twenty years. We have experienced changes in policy from *Lawrence v. Texas* in 2003, which struck down sodomy laws; to the repeal of "Don't Ask, Don't Tell" in 2010 allowing gay and lesbian service people to openly serve in the military; to the Supreme Court's 2015 decision in support of marriage equality in all fifty states. We have seen an increased presence in the media of LGBTQ+ people, characters, stories, and advertisements.

We have made great strides; however, much of the focus of these past two decades has revolved around the experiences of LGBTQ+ people on the coasts of the United States, specifically Los Angeles, San Francisco, New York City, Miami, Washington, DC. Media representations, such as the TV shows *Will & Grace*, *The L Word*, *Orange Is the New Black*, and *Transparent*, all depict queerness in metropolitan areas, creating what some scholars are now calling "metronormativity" (Detamore 2010). When the media depicts rural communities, those representations often follow the trope of the rural, small-town LGBTQ+ person fleeing the horrors of home to bask in the Oz that is the big city. We have neglected the experiences of the Midwest, especially when it comes to rural spaces.

In the past five years, and I would argue perhaps even longer, we have seen a shift in conversations around sexual and gender diversities to include experiences of people and communities in rural areas. Many of our national LGBTQ+ equality organizations are located in large coastal cities; however, regional organizations such as Southerners on New Ground are emerging. Plus we are rediscovering organizations such as the Southern Poverty Law Center that have been actively engaging rural communities for a number of years. Not only are we beginning to recognize work that has been happening in rural areas of the country and exploring ways to support new efforts, as a movement we have also recognized the biases and misrepresentations of these regions, especially in Appalachia. There are specific hardships in spaces within and beyond Appalachia, and there are multiple narratives and dynamics of resilience that reflect "locally owned and grown" queerness.

We are becoming mindful as a movement that although we have made a lot of progress, there is still much work to be done across the United States. Various studies reflect the unique contexts and hardships experienced by LGBTQ+ individuals and groups in rural America; few, however, acknowledge how LGBTQ+ people are not only getting by but also challenging the stereotypes of what it means to live in a rural setting simply by being who they are. To borrow and adapt the words of activist and actress Laverne Cox, our existence and everyday living are acts of resistance in settings that say we should not exist. The goal of this essay is to raise awareness regarding the experiences of LGBTQ+ individuals, specifically college students, in rural America by exploring both resiliencies and challenges of "rural queerness."

Rural Queers and Queering the Rural

Often when people are asked to describe the LGBTQ+ community, the first things they respond with include night clubs, drag queens, sexual exploits, lavish parties, interior design, gay best friend or pocket gay who is stylist to the stars, and other colorful descriptors revolving around large metropolitan and urban areas. When asked to describe rural areas, people often respond with words such as *conservative*, *closed*, and *anti-LGBT*. Although some of these descriptions hint at certain realities, generally they misrepresent the diverse realities in LGBTQ+ communities and geographic locations. In *Queering the Countryside*, Johnson, Gilley, and Gray (2016) reflect:

> Rural is first and foremost a name we give to an astoundingly complex assemblage of people, places, and positionalities . . . in this respect, rural is not entirely unlike queer itself, a term that surely carries with it both a troubled and troubling past, but one that was actively reclaimed by LGBT activists and scholars beginning in the 1990s precisely because it is indeterminate and unstable, as well as because frankly, it had often been used as a term of derision, one that was meant to shame gender and sexual non-conformers in much the same way that terms like hay-seed, redneck, and hick have been used to shame uncouth non-metropolitans. (8)

On a basic and perhaps abstract level, many understand that LGBTQ+ lives in rural America have existed for a long time—sexual and gender diversities are not limited to any one geographic location or more accurately geocultural location. LGBTQ+ people have lived and continue to live in rural parts of the United States, some under the radar, some out in the open, and some a mixture of both. On an intellectually abstract level, the existence of the "rural queer" has been known, but the unique realities of challenge and celebration of rural queer narratives has received little attention.

More and more the meaning of the word *rural* is not limited to geographic areas that are less populated or more agricultural; as Johnson, Gilley, and Gray (2016) explain, ruralism is becoming a worldview, much like queer, and is expansive in its definition but generally it revolves around conservative values. Many people stereotype rural America as highly orthodox and rigid in its understanding of sexual and gender diversities. With this assumption of conservatism comes the assumption of hostility toward LGBTQ+ people.

Though anecdotal and scholarly research reflects some or limited truths within these claims, many of us in minoritized communities know the dangers of stereotypes and generalized assumptions that limit and dehumanize people; as an activist scholar, I attempt to balance generalizations as starting points with experiences that contradict these generalizations. Many rural areas in Appalachia tend to be skeptical of outsiders due to the close-knit, interdependent dynamics of smaller communities. These dynamics present challenges for coming out but also unique resources to support coming out, especially for those raised in and who continue to live in certain communities. In an essay based on a series of interviews, Kelly Baker shares the experience of one of her interviewees: "people just kept treating me like me . . . they just said, 'you know, it's somebody who we've known forever, and she is who she is' " (2016, 38). Even those who move to rural locations express that although there may be some initial hesitancy in embracing their presence, with time their involvement and work in the community has led to their being respected and valued— they are claimed as one of the community's own. Because of the dynamic of interdependence in many rural areas, difference is not always seen as a threat but as a celebrated factor that strengthens the community.

A question to introduce that requires further study elsewhere: are LGBTQ+ folks who are accepted into rural communities playing into respectability politics, knowingly or unknowingly? Often rural communities are not diverse and there is an unofficial or official expectation to conform to certain standards, so many LGBTQ+ folks struggle with "fitting in" and not drawing attention to themselves. I wonder if "out and overt" LGBTQ+ people would be accepted as much as those who pass as heterosexual who just happen to be in a same-sex relationship? Family and familiarity grant access to the formal and informal resources within the community; being different is perceived as a threat. At the same time, LGBTQ+ people are using this dynamic of familiarity to be embraced and silenced by their rural communities. Family and kinship are grounded in the ability to be recognized in the network of "who you know/are related to." Queer folks in rural areas are (not "could be") related to someone in the community who has standing that opens the door to hope-filled acceptance and access to the necessities of everyday survival (Gray 2009). I am mindful of the judgmental undertone of my own query. Who am I to judge why a person acts in a certain way? LGBTQ+ individuals in Appalachia may be reflecting heteronormative and homonormative dynamics to survive, which is a feat to be affirmed. Some just are the way they are, and it is not fair of me to undermine a person's beingness through dissection. Folks who are out have a certain level of privilege that needs to be acknowledged; those who are not out overtly are finding ways to embrace who they are with and in pride.

When an LGBTQ+ person seeks support services in rural areas, they are often confronted with social and mental health services that lack multicultural awareness and training in supporting people with multicultural identities. Historically, many LGBTQ+ adults migrated to more urban areas seeking safer havens and opportunities for community; however, not everyone is able to leave, wants to leave, or should have to leave. Given the lack of culturally competent resources in rural areas, where is a person to go for help of any kind? According to Snively (2004), "literature on the subject of social services for gay persons in rural areas has emphasized the need for service providers to act as advocates and community organizers instead of providing more traditional mental health services" (103). Because of the lack of services, many queer youth are faced with the difficult and overwhelming decision of deciding between living in silence at home or risking a move to a larger, more urban area, a decision that assumes economic and social mobility, which in itself is a problematic dynamic concerning privilege. Many in Appalachia have deep ties to the region because it is not just a physical location but an integral part of one's identity. How does one reconcile rural identity with queer identity when rural areas alienate sexual and gender diversities and queer spaces demonize rural areas?

LGBTQ+ Experiences in School

The Gay, Lesbian, and Straight Education Network (GLSEN) issued a report in 2012 called "Strengths and Silences: The Experiences of Lesbian, Gay, Bisexual, and Transgender Students in Rural and Small Town Schools"

(Palmer, Kosciw, and Bartkiewicz 2012), and although research in this area is growing, many articles and reports focus on just a few of the identities under sexual and gender diversities. The GLSEN report is one of the few that is comprehensive in focus and national. The study was based on raw data collected in the 2010–11 National School Climate survey, which included the experiences of 8,584 LGBT secondary school students, 2,387 of whom attended schools in rural areas. The report yielded alarming statistics and provided student testimony regarding the increased frequency and risk of anti-LGBT experiences in rural schools compared with urban schools. Another reality reflected in the data was the regional differences of rurality with the South and Midwest being more hostile toward LGBTQ+ young people than were communities in the Northeast and West. The GLSEN report stated that "more than 98% [of students in rural areas] heard sexist remarks, 'gay' used in a negative way, or other homophobic remarks at school, and more than 90% had heard racist remarks or negative remarks related to gender expression" (Palmer, Kosciw, and Bartkiewicz 2012, 5).

Young people experiencing anti-LGBT incidents in rural areas, and several studies have highlighted the lack of resources to address these biased incidents. School climate is not just a result of how students interact with other students; it is also influenced by the interactions among faculty and staff members, faculty/staff with students, and school/university with local communities. As noted in the GLSEN's study, "if the use of biased language goes unchallenged in the school setting, then it can be signal that such language is acceptable for use in the school and perhaps in other public spaces . . . on the other hand, if staff members intervene when they hear such language, then they may be sending a message that such language is unacceptable" (Palmer, Kosciw, and Bartkiewicz 2012, 7). However, LGBTQ+ students reported that school staff members would intervene when racist comments were said but were less likely to do so when an anti-LGBT comment was said. Because of the lack of response from employees, many LGBTQ+ students do not report incidents involving anti-LGBT comments or behaviors.

The lack of response was also reflected in the lack of intervention from other students. Research and anecdotal experience reflects that a peer-to-peer interaction may have more of an impact than if a superior were to intervene; however, frequency of intervention is quite low and minimal. I interact with students as director of the LGBT Center at Ohio University, and I notice that some of the resistance to intervening is grounded in people fearing that others would think they were LGBTQ+ or that any hostility would be directed toward them. At the same time, I have witnessed transformative dynamics of privilege when students own their voices and call out problematic comments and behaviors—dynamics that create a sense of solidarity for students who feel isolated and disconnected from others. Students and other activists are starting to use the language of "calling in" rather than "calling out," as the latter does not reflect inclusivity or an invitation to dialogue.

Compared with suburban and urban students, rural students report feeling unsafe at higher rates due to perceived or actual sexual orientation or gender identity. These experiences have caused many to avoid spaces such as restrooms, locker rooms, and even a cafeteria or dining hall. The majority of rural students report being verbally harassed, ranging from slurs to graffiti to lies or rumors being spread about them. Nearly half of students stated that they experienced physical harassment such as pushing, shoving, or shouldering in the hallway—this was reflected in GLSEN's study and through my informal interactions with students from Athens High School and Ohio University. These findings were reinforced and supported by GLSEN's follow-up study, *From Teasing to Torment: School Climate Revisited* (Greytak et al. 2016), that again showed that students in rural areas, the South, and the Midwest experience higher rates of biased experiences.

Although the majority of the existing research on LGBTQ+ young people focuses on high school, anecdotal experience and the few studies that look at college/university students suggest that experiences in higher education do not vary much from those in primary and secondary education. Because of the hardships that LGBTQ+ students have experienced prior to enrolling at a college or university, students are coming to campuses with emotional traumas that affect their ability to fully embrace the college experience. Often prior experiences are retriggered or intensified because of similar dynamics occurring on college campuses.

Because of the geographic isolation of rural and Appalachian communities and schools in rural communities, stressors for LGBTQ+ individuals are intensified because of the lack of ability to connect with a larger rainbow community. There is also a lack of access to resources for supporting individuals who are coming out or transitioning. There are conversations within the food justice realm that identify certain spaces as "food deserts" due to the lack of grocery stores and other places for the community to obtain fresh, healthier food options. Similarly, there are many "queer deserts" in the United States where LGBTQ+ individuals are in isolation, live in fear, and do not experience support because of the lack of local resources. Many who reach out to Ohio's LGBT Center share that they have to travel an hour or more to reach Athens and even longer to access resources in Columbus. One of the challenges of queer deserts is sustainability for individuals and groups traveling to neighboring communities for resources; being able to make the trip is perhaps a possibility in the short term but can become costly (time wise, financially, and emotionally) in the long term.

As high school students transition to college life, levels of stress and anxiety increase, especially for LGBTQ+ students. A study of the student body at a public Midwestern institution reflected that lesbian, gay, and bisexual students reported depression at three times the rate of heterosexual students, a situation made more intense by the lack of support services for those coping with anti-LGBT bias (Williams 2012). On top of the common university stressors, such as rigorous academic courses and living away from family for the first time, LGBTQ+ students also deal with issues related to coming out, affirming their identity development journey, discovering new identities or changes in identity, internalized and external dynamics of homophobia/biphobia/transphobia/sexism, and the constant wrestling match of conforming versus rocking the boat or challenging hegemonic dynamics across identity categories. In addition, many trans and gender creative/expansive students experience being misgendered at all levels of the university, are frequently confronted with their deadname (legal name or name given at birth) in class rosters and emails, have to navigate physical spaces that are based on rigid and limited definitions of gender, and are targets of verbal harassment and physical assault. Williams (2012) notes: "The classroom is a social setting in which the LGBT college student must assess the risk level of self-identifying . . . it comes as little surprise that LGBT college students experience high levels of stress when they are faced with faculty, staff, and students that believe LGBT individuals are sick, sinful, or unnatural in addition to students who tear down posters displayed by LGBT student organizations yell hostile remakes and slurs such as 'hey, faggot' or "bash them back into the closet!" (8).

Often in discussions regarding sexual and gender diversities, all nonheterosexual and noncisgender identities are lumped together without any recognition of the unique needs, challenges, and experiences of specific identity groups. Historically the lives of transgender and bisexual people have been overlooked because of the focus on gay and lesbian individuals (and then often only white gay and lesbian lives). Indeed, the lack of attention toward trans and bisexual communities is not limited to just the heterosexual, cisgender community but also exists within gay and lesbian communities. Over the past ten years, especially the past five, there has been a shift in LGBTQ+ discourse that is raising awareness of the realities of transgender people. There has been increase in media representation of people such as Chaz Bono, Laverne Cox,

Caitlyn Jenner, Jazz Jennings, and Aidyn Dowling; the violence toward trans women of color has ignited outrage within many communities; and debates over policies such as bathrooms and name/pronoun usage have sparked conversations around gender diversity in different sectors of society, including health care settings, educational institutions, the legal/criminal system, faith communities, and public policy.

We have begun to witness an increase in the visibility of bisexuality as individuals and communities become aware of the dynamics of bi erasure. One study suggests that "once at college, individuals who identify as bisexual reported difficulty of making new friends as well as loss of old friends making their college experience much more difficult" (Whiting, Boone, and Cohn 2012, 514). Many who identify as bisexual and pansexual express that they are often told to "pick a side" or have their bisexual identity undermined based on who they are in a relationship with, often being told that they are now gay/lesbian or straight. Bisexual people who already experience a challenging college environment are made to feel even more uncomfortable by being treated differently because of misunderstandings of their sexual orientation and being marginalized within student groups, including LGBT-focused groups. Bisexual and pansexual students are often placed in the position of educator regarding all things in "middle sexuality" for students, faculty, and staff, furthering their inability to enjoy being a student. These experiences intensify feelings of isolation, leading to increased feelings of vulnerability and a higher risk of destructive behaviors.

Trauma Queries

Name-calling, being assaulted, being rejected by one's community, daily reminders of one's second-class citizenship—all of these experiences overwhelm a person's well-being by fracturing their ability to cope. This overwhelming and all-consuming dynamic is what I refer to as trauma. Trauma is unique to the individual and their reality—what is traumatic for one person may not be traumatic to another. Traumatic events in the life of LGBTQ+ people may have profound disruptive effects in self-care, relationships, mental health, spirituality, career, or physical health as their ability to cope or resist is shattered. Unaddressed traumas or prolonged exposure to trauma can lead to the development of posttraumatic stress disorder due to the body's inability of responding to stress in a way that minimizes traumatic impact or integrates the event in a healthy, constructive way into a person's lived experience (Balog 2016).

Herman (2015) states that "traumatic events are extraordinary not because they occur rarely but rather they overwhelm the ordinary human adaptations to life" (33). When we are traumatized, our inherent and innate abilities to confront a perceived or actual threat become altered and disorganized, leading to their ongoing exaggerated activation long after the danger has ended. This prolonged "on" state causes profound changes in emotional and physical well-being and memories; our bodies no longer respond to triggers and other stimuli in an integrated or coordinated way. Because of the pervasive nature of trauma that causes an experience to begin but not end, a person's vitality is drained because of the energy needed to constantly try to repress the incident.

Traumatic experiences can lead a person to wrestle with conflicting ideas of what to share, wanting to share their identity and any negative experiences while also trying to keep some experiences secret. LGBTQ+ people want to come out while also desiring to stay hidden, struggling with living in a place of shame, ultimately creating a reality of a double closet, one for their LGBTQ+ identity and the second for their experience of victimization and trauma (Rosenberg 2000). Although Rosenberg's research on the impact of trauma is around twenty years old as of this writing, his notion of the double closet or what other scholars refer to as double thinking remains true today (so much so that his work was republished in 2014).

Many LGBTQ+ people wrestle with balancing being "out and proud" and remaining in the closet to avoid public scrutiny. This is further complicated by the pervasive dynamics of discrimination of our beingness as our personhood and lives are debated within legislative bodies, courts, education systems, civil government, health care systems, religious communities, and mainstream media. As Balog (2016) notes, "LGBT individuals are constantly subject to subtle, inadvertent, or insensitive attacks on the core of their very nature, even by people who profess no disdain or disrespect for them" (58). Institutionalized stigma coupled with internalized prejudice contribute to higher rates of self-destructive behaviors, suicide, and depression, which are all amplified by the lack of safer spaces and queer-inclusive resources in rural areas.

Study after study and report after report demonstrate the higher rates of suicide attempts and deaths by suicide by LGBTQ+ people. Some studies indicate that as high as 40 percent of LGB youth and almost 50 percent of trans youth have made a suicide attempt or have died by suicide. Though suicide is complex and often associated with other chronic mental health issues, at its core suicide is frequently about an individual's (in)ability to cope with a perceived never-ending problem and being so overwhelmed and shattered that death is seen as the only way of ending the pain. Much like responses to trauma need to be intersectional and wholistic, so must our engagement of suicide in the LGBTQ+ community.

On a very basic level, if a person does not feel safe, they cannot learn or grow or be challenged to consider different ideas. Experiencing verbal or physical harassment or assault affects LGBTQ+ students' ability to concentrate on their academic performance. The impact goes beyond their ability to be mentally present in class but often physically as they begin to avoid places where they were victimized, such as restrooms and the classroom. Higher rates of absenteeism mean that a student's grade suffers, and their overall academic experience goes from transformative to destructive. Studies show that the severity of the harassment directly affects educational outcomes; the more violent or traumatic an experience, the more likely a student will begin to miss class, leading to drops in their GPA and overall desire to be in school. Anecdotally, several LGBTQ+ students at Ohio and other universities have shared that they do the bare minimum to pass so as not to attract too much attention from their schools and families.

In many Appalachian communities, the topics of sexual and gender identities and diversities is often treated as a "don't ask, don't tell" issue. The dynamics of sexuality and gender are not to be discussed directly or in public, creating a culture of silence and by extension a reality of isolation—"we just don't discuss those things in polite company." Fischer, Irwin, and Coleman's (2014) study of LGBT health outcomes in rural communities, specifically in Nebraska, discovered that rural LGBT people had lower rates of social engagement, especially in terms of being out to others, as a result of stigma and silence around sexual and gender diversities. Southeast Ohio is not so different. This lack of engagement is a result of a culture that silences conversations on sexuality and believes gender to be connected to an individual's decreased ability to accept themselves, leading to higher rates of depressive symptomology and damaged physical well-being.

Another dynamic to acknowledge is the intimate nature of violence in rural communities toward LGBTQ+ individuals. Studies show that assaults are often perpetrated by a person known to the victim. In rural areas, the chances of a complete stranger attacking a person or group is lower because of the close-knit and familiar dynamic in many rural communities. The impact of the violence is deeper because it was perpetrated by "one of our own." Because trauma can sever relationships or isolate a person, the small-town dynamic can also be a source of reconnection and healing because mistreatment is less likely to go unnoticed. Because "one of our own" was mistreated, solidarity and support may be easier to achieve, helping an individual overcome traumatic pain and rebuild their sense of self through connections with others. On a practical level, unlike the labyrinth of larger cities, smaller and rural communities offer the ability for a person to better understand what places to avoid.

Though LGBTQ+ individuals represent only a fraction of the population across geographic locations, they use mental health services at higher rates compared with heterosexual individuals (Williams 2012). Many rural areas uphold self-reliance, patriarchy, stigmatization of mental illness, and acceptance of poor health under the guise of "it could be worse." These dynamics often intensify the stress experienced by LGBTQ+ people. The double stigma based on their sexual and/or gender identity and their desire to seek professional help increases the experience of low-esteem and depression. This is further complicated by lack of access to resources based on finances and no organization that specializes in (or is at least knowledgeable of) sexual and gender diversities.

At Ohio University, we are fortunate that our counseling center employs therapists and counselors who are not only trained in sexual and gender diverse cultural competency but are also committed to gender and sexual justice. Given the number of students seeking mental health services, people power in the counseling center is limited and not able to respond to the growing need and demand. Students could turn to community providers; however, the few providers in the area are already understaffed and are often not equipped to engage LGBTQ+ identities.

Despite some of the hardships experienced in Appalachian areas, there are also many transgressive dynamics of resilience that reflect a long history of queerness. At a time when there are many conversations and butting of heads around gender-inclusive language, many in Appalachia have been using gender-inclusive language knowingly and/or unknowingly. For example, in parts of Appalachia, many use *y'all*, and as the slogan goes, "y'all means all." In other parts, *yins* or *you-ins* is used, which like *y'all* also means all. It is important that we affirm the narratives in Appalachia and not just import coastal narratives that do not acknowledge the lived realities of trial and triumph in Appalachia.

Intersectionalizing Rural Queerness

As individuals, we do not exist in isolation from each other or within our own selves. A person's experiences of injustice and resilience is colored and filtered through the multiple identity groups to which the person belongs. Critical legal race scholar Kimberlé Williams Crenshaw coined the term *intersectionality* in 1989; however, "the themes of intersectionality have long historic roots within and beyond the United States . . . black activists and feminists, as well as latina, post-colonial, queer, and Indigenous scholars have all produced work that reveal the complex factors and processes that shape human lives" (Hankivsky 2014, 2). The concept of intersectionality is grounded in the understanding that humans are shaped and influenced by the interactions of our various social locations and these interactions happen within systems of power that, like our social locations, are interconnected and interacting.

LGBTQ+ people are not just their sexuality or their gender—they are people of color, people of different national origins, socioeconomic status, abilities, geographic locations, religious affiliations, sizes, and more. These identities are happening within and around the individual—a borderland of crossings that conflict and coexist. The lives of not only LGBTQ+ people but *all* people are multifaceted and beautifully complicated. LGBTQ+ individuals in rural settings and/or attending schools in rural areas are challenged by the unique hardships of their location and enriched by the strengths present in those same locations.

One of the central themes of intersectionality is that individuals experience both privilege and oppression. Applying this dynamic to rural LGBTQ+ communities, one is able to explore how rurality may reflect isolation as a challenge as well as the interdependence of the community because solidarity that does not always happen in larger cities. Rurality is both a rich factor and strength. Like Appalachia and rural parts of the country, social locations are challenges and spaces of resilience, as challenges are being overcome in obvious ways and ways that have yet to be uncovered.

As narratives are claimed and reclaimed, we create spaces identifying with multiple aspects of self in an integrated and conscious journey. Living and working in Appalachia has taught me to affirm my life being a trans person of color living in rural America who also lives with depression and is married. It has taught me how to extend this dynamic into creating safer and braver spaces for folks to embrace with pride their multiple isnesses. For many LGBTQ+ people, identities are dynamic, reflecting an organic fluidity that can and may change over time and be influenced by social location/context. The understanding of ourselves as sexually and gender-diverse individuals is not an end product but an ongoing process and journey—a continual process of becoming. LGBTQ+ people affect their rural context and the rural context affects LGBTQ+ people with the mutual, ongoing resistance, challenges, and transformation of systems of inequity and oppression.

Scholars such as LaToya Eaves (2016) are addressing the need for expanding the conversation of rural queerness to include the dynamics of race, and

I would add other identities such as religion, ability, and class—all of which enrich and complicate the conversation. In her essay "Outside Forces: Black Southern Sexuality," Eaves (2016) writes: "The sociocultural mythology of the South often homogenizes its regional discourse as a site of abjection, or a culturally backwards space that reeks of plantation culture, Jim Crow, and Bibles . . . this mythology is problematic because it insinuates a strict regionalism that does not acknowledge the opportunities, realities, and experiences of the entire US South" (147). There is a need for intersectional conversations regarding how sexuality and gender affect other aspects of identity and how other aspects of identity affect sexuality and gender to engage individuals and communities more holistically. Several sources and studies used in this essay reflect that LGBTQ+ people in rural areas experience feelings of isolation; when applying an intersectional lens to this dynamic, LGBTQ+ people of color experience not only sexual or gender isolation but also racial isolation.

Eaves (2016) shares the experience of an interviewee: "Asheville [North Carolina] seems so progressive . . . beautiful and open, but when you get down to the nitty gritty, it's not diverse at all . . . there is limited racial and ethnic diversity of predominantly white Asheville, which is accompanied by a lack of exposure to perspectives brought about by those lived experiences" (152). The dynamics of feeling disconnected from community are reflected in not feeling welcome within the LGBTQ+ community as a person of color, within the larger community for being a person of color, and as an LGBTQ+ person in the South. The realities of -isms and discrimination exist in all communities; there are LGBTQ+ individuals who are racist, Islamophobic, classist, ableist, and so on.

Trauma-Informed and Intersectional Resilience

Trauma-informed practices are intended to provide a safe and empowering space where traumatized individuals can heal and begin to feel free and whole again. Much like the principles and practice of intersectionality, trauma-informed care engages the whole individual, recognizing how various systems are affecting the person and how those systems are affected by the person. As stated by Carello and Butler (2015): "To be trauma informed is to understand the ways in which violence, victimization, and other traumatic experiences may have impacted the lives of the individuals involved and to apply that understanding to the design of systems and provision of services so they accommodate trauma survivors' needs and are consonant with healing and recovery" (264). As a former clinician who worked with victims and survivors of violent crime, and in my role as director of the LGBT Center, I present the following guidelines, which are grounded in my professional training, personal experience, and academic research. I share them as suggested best practices for university counseling centers to better and more holistically support not only LGBTQ+ individuals but also all the people a center serves.

1. Understand the multifaceted nature of sexual and gender diversities, especially as they intersect with rural identities and other aspects of human identity. The reality is that our understanding and engagement of sexual and gender diversities is constantly changing and evolving. Although it is not possible to know everything, we must be mindful that individuals we encounter may have a different nuanced and lived understanding of sexuality and gender. This difference does cause confusion but also a more wholistic opportunity to support individuals on their journey.

2. It is important to recognize the impact of oppression and injustice on the people we serve. Individuals who have experienced trauma have also experienced powerlessness as a result of their experience. Many LGBTQ+ individuals from rural areas have been stigmatized by their communities, and therefore it is important that counselors be educated on how to avoid problematic language around sexual and gender diversities and how to address mistakes that are likely to occur throughout the therapeutic partnership.

3. Language mindfulness is important not only when speaking but also in how we create physical spaces. It is important that we indicate or advocate for gender-inclusive spaces such as restrooms and ensure that language on intake forms affirms how people identify and how they want to be identified.

4. Integrate ongoing trauma-informed competency training, LGBTQ+ cultural competency, and rural inclusivity for all staff.

5. Recognize the rippling effects of recovery across all levels of the center. Practitioners gain inspiration through the stories of recovery and healing shared by clients; clients feel courageous by realizing they are not alone, and they come to a compassionate perspective of who they are in the present (Herman 2015).

One of the central tenets of intersectionality and trauma-informed care is the expertise of the people we serve. In this light, university counseling centers are the experts in their realities and strengths. The foregoing guidelines are suggestions, and counseling centers must incorporate perspectives, policies, and practices that make sense for their context—the research on trauma-informed care is growing and easily adaptable to multiple settings and situations.

In Conclusion, We Need More Queries!

Additional research is needed that explores how trauma-informed practices can be infused not only in mental health settings but throughout all levels of a university, from programming to policy initiatives to curricular pedagogies. Carello and Butler (2014) state that "as educators we undoubtedly need to teach about trauma; at the same time, we must also be mindful of how we teach it as well as how we teach trauma survivors . . . trauma may be endemic to our present political, social, and private world, but marching it into the classroom to be prodded, provoked, and endured . . . is not to transform trauma but to potentially recapitulate it" (163).

I am mindful that asking more of faculty is tricky because of the current demands of teaching, scholarship, and service. Trauma-informed care offers the opportunity to approach current work with a different perspective, not as an additional burden. Recent studies in the field of higher education have shifted the focus from student affairs professionals to student interactions with faculty, from academic advising to social connections. These limited studies reflect that positive interactions with faculty have led to higher GPAs and increased class participation even when students experienced anti-LGBTQ+ sentiment on other parts of campus. A study completed by Linley et al. (2016) found that "faculty perceived as supportive facilitated positive in-class experiences, mentored and advised students, and served as allies in out-of-class activities created an environment for LGBTQ students that moved them from the margins to the center of the higher education experience" (61).

At a time when trigger warnings and safer spaces are questioned and dissected in an attempt to discredit them, trauma-informed pedagogies can help those who oppose these practices better understand how micro-aggressions and blatant aggressions can affect all aspects of a student's well-being and learning. It is not about sheltering a student or avoiding difficult conversations; it is about creating an environment and giving everyone the tools to live through the conversation and do so in one piece. As stated earlier, if a student does not feel safe in every sense of the word, they cannot learn and embrace their inner possibilitarian.

This essay attempted to explore multiple aspects of LGBTQ+ identities, rural identities, rural LGBTQ+ identities, and LGBTQ+ identities in rural settings through a framework grounded in intersectional and trauma-informed perspectives. However, I am mindful that this essay is limited and there is more to explore, write, and practice. Much like our understanding of sexuality, gender, and identity is evolving, so is our understanding of how to support this evolution within individuals and communities, especially around trauma and resilience in rural and queer communities. We began with the words of poet Richard Blanco, and I close with his words because they summarize and contextualize the goal of this essay and my response to why I moved to and continue to live on the foothills of Appalachia—to raise the experiences of LGBTQ+ folks by exploring both resiliencies and challenges of rural queerness.

> Would I have become a poet regardless of my grandmother's abuse? Probably, but not the same kind of poet, nor would I have produced the same kind of work, I think. Nevertheless, in the end her ultimate legacy was to unintentionally instill in me an understanding of the complexities of human behavior and emotions. I could have easily concluded that my grandmother was a mean, evil bitch, and left it at that. But through her I instead realized there are few absolutes when it comes to human relationships. People, myself included, are not always good or always bad. They can't always say what they mean, and don't always mean what they say. My grandmother loved as best she could, the way she herself, was loved, perhaps. Her trying to make me a man was an odd, crude expression of that love, but it inadvertently made me the writer I am today. And for that I feel oddly thankful. (Blanco 2014, 52)

BIBLIOGRAPHY

Baker, Kelly. 2016. "Out Back Home: An Exploration of LGBT Identities and Community in Rural Nova Scotia, Canada." In *Queering the Countryside: New Frontiers in Rural Queer Studies*, edited by M. L. Gray, C. R. Johnson, and B. J. Gilley, 25–48. New York: New York University Press.

Balog, David. 2016. *Healing the Brain: Stress, Trauma, and LGBT/Q Youth*. Schenectady, NY: A Thousand Moms.

Blanco, Richard. 2014. "Making a Man Out of Me." In *The Queer South: LGBTQ Writers on the American South*, edited by D. Ray, 48–52. Little Rock, AR: Sibling Rivalry Press.

Carello, Janice, and Lisa D. Butler. 2014. "Potentially Perilous Pedagogies: Teaching Trauma Is Not the Same as Trauma Informed Teaching." *Journal of Trauma and Disassociation* 15, 153–68.

———. 2015. "Practicing What We Teach: Trauma-Informed Educational Practice." *Journal of Teaching in Social Work* 35, no. 3, 262–78.

Detamore, Mathias J. 2010. "Queer Appalachia: Toward Geographies of Possibility." University of Kentucky Doctoral Dissertations Paper 57.

Eaves, LaToya E. 2016. "Outside Forces: Black Southern Sexuality." In *Queering the Countryside: New Frontiers in Rural Queer Studies*, edited by M. L. Gray, C. R. Johnson, and B. J. Gilley, 146–60. New York: New York University Press.

Fisher, Christopher M., Jay A. Irwin, and Jason D. Coleman. 2014. "LGBT Health in the Midlands: A Rural/Urban Comparison of Basic Health Indicators." *Journal of Homosexuality* 61, 1062–90.

Gray, Mary L. 2009. *Out in the Country: Youth, Media, and Queer Visibility in Rural America*. New York: New York University Press.

Greytak, Emily A., Joseph G. Kosciw, Christian Villenas, and Noreen M Giga. 2016. "From Teasing to Torment: School Climate Revisited—A Survey of U.S. Secondary School Students and Teachers." *Gay, Lesbian & Straight Education Network*. https://www.glsen.org/sites/default/files/TeasingtoTorment%202015%20FINAL%20PDF%5B1%5D_0.pdf. Accessed April 2016.

Hankivsky, Olena. 2014. "Intersectionality 101." *Institute for Intersectionality Research and Policy, SFU*. http://vawforum-cwr.ca/sites/default/files/attachments/intersectionallity_101.pdf. Accessed April 2016.

Herman, Judith. 2015. *Trauma and Recovery: The Aftermath of Violence—From Domestic Abuse to Political Terror*. New York: Perseus Books.

Johnson, Colin R., Brian J. Gilley, and Mary L. Gray. 2016. "Introduction." In *Queering the Countryside: New Frontiers in Rural Queer Studies*, edited by M. L. Gray, C. R. Johnson, and B. J. Gilley, 1–23. New York: New York University Press.

Linley, Jodi L., David Nguyen, G. Blue Brazelton, Brianna Becker, Kristen Renn, and Michael Woodford. 2016. "Faculty as Sources of Support for LGBTQ College Students." *College Teaching* 64, no. 2, 55–63.

Palmer, Neal A., Joseph G. Kosciw, and Mark J. Bartkiewicz. 2012. "Strengths and Silences: The Experiences of Lesbian, Gay, Bisexual and Transgender Students in Rural and Small Town Schools." *Gay, Lesbian and Straight Education Network*. https://www.glsen.org/sites/default/files/Strengths%20%26%20Silences.pdf. Accessed April 2016.

Rosenberg, L. G. 2000. "Phase Oriented Psychotherapy for Gay Men Recovering from Trauma." In *Gay Men and Childhood Sexual Trauma: Integrating the Shattered Self*, edited by J. Cassese, 37–73. Binghamton, NY: Haworth Pres.

Snively, Carol A. 2004. "Building Community-Based Alliances between GLBTQQA Youth and Adults in Rural Settings." *Journal of Gay & Lesbian Social Services* 16, nos. 3–4, 99–112.

Whiting, Erica L., Dominique N. Boone, and Tracy J. Cohn. 2012. "Exploring Protective Factors among College-Aged Bisexual Students in Rural Areas: An Exploratory Study." *Journal of Bisexuality* 12, 507–18.

Williams, Erin E. 2012. "Help-Seeking and Stressors among LGBT College Students in Rural College Settings." Honors thesis, Eastern Illinois University.

PART IV

Queer Media: Radical Acts of Embodiment and Resistance

CHAPTER 9

Working against the Past: Queering the Appalachian Narrative

Tijah Bumgarner

This image that I had stitched together like an Appalachian quiltmaker began to fray, the pieces and seams of my denial unraveling like broken thread.

—Jason Howard (2015, 88)

The notion of home often brings up thoughts of open arms and welcome signs, a comfort one cannot find elsewhere. Now imagine being born in a place, absorbing its cultures, and identifying with what it means to belong, only to find out that you are absent from the written history, stories, and representations that define this place. Appalachia is one such place. The dominant narratives of Appalachia celebrate the promises of capitalism, traditional family, and the trope of the hillbilly. These images thrive at the cost of erasing the multiplicity of lives and entangled materialities. The questions of who is Appalachian and what it means to be Appalachian are often framed through these dominant narratives. However, as this essay explores, behind these narrative scenes are stories and individuals who challenge and complicate what being Appalachian means.

Katie Algeo (2003) embarks on the question of belonging in Appalachia through her essay, "Locals on Local Color: Imagining Identity in Appalachia." She examines the constructed and enduring stereotypes often associated with the Appalachian region. Algeo looks to the insider/outsider dichotomy to where "outsiders" largely write these stereotypes into actuality through short stories, novels, and scholarly work. Historically, the master narrative perpetuates "the social construction of Appalachian identity as silent and passive, objects of description and scrutiny who themselves contributed little to the popular conception of Appalachia" (Algeo 2003, 28). This silence has paved the way for the popularity of the insider/outsider dichotomy in Appalachian studies, which claims that outsiders, through capitalism and power, have named the region. However, even the often-cited insider/outsider dichotomy is grounded in the monolithic, master narrative. If outsiders are accused of having constructed the popular image of Appalachia, what is the contribution of an insider perspective? More important, what is at stake when an insider perspective is responsible for creating an exclusive narrative as well? There is not necessarily a dominant culture of Appalachia, but there are the multiplicities that lack representation. This is where structures of power intersect. An examination of what and who are included and excluded in the stories of Appalachia, past and present, needs to be explored. These pieces, connections, are like the quilt Jason Howard speaks to in the epigraph—an image of Appalachia created as a monolithic story in need of being unraveled to create a space for different and diverse narratives. To do this, an intersectional approach is necessary to unpack the multiplicity of Appalachia.

Throughout this essay, I investigate how minor voices and the less common stories of Appalachia challenge the authority of a single master narrative within the region. Whereas the definition of Appalachia was once "white mountain men," the contemporary experiences of Appalachians are anything but homogeneous. Using theories of intersectionality to investigate this notion, I take up the reworking of dominant narratives by Affrilachian poets and explore this disruption at the Appalachian Queer Film Festival and through student queer films. Ordinarily, such communities are nowhere to be found in the popular image of "Appalachia." I disrupt this image by bringing marginalized Appalachian stories to the forefront. By highlighting these underrepresented positions and stories the question arises: how is contemporary Appalachia being reworked from those on the ground? Moreover, do these minor stories and voices have the ability to shift the master narrative of Appalachia? The discussion around diversifying economies (as a transition from coal) mirrors the shift discussed in this essay. Using this postcoal Appalachia landscape as the social backbone of the conversation, I take up the ways queer artists, citizens, and others respond to these changes and the master narrative of Appalachia. After beginning with an overview of Appalachian history, as a constructed master narrative, the essay moves into the need and examples of listening to the multiple narratives.

The coal industry has played a major role in shaping the master narrative of Appalachia. By structuring the stereotypes, we know today, the industry held the power of naming to control people in the region. For example, in 1885, Mary Murfree writes about a young Appalachian girl in her novel *In the Tennessee Mountains*, saying, "when a sudden noise in the terrible loneliness of the sheeted woods suggested the close proximity of a wild beast, or perhaps, to her ignorant, superstitious mind, a supernatural presence, — thus she journeyed on her errand of deliverance" (149). Emphasizing the stereotype of people as uneducated and fatalist, this story and many like it were the beginning of constructing the cultural landscape and an identity for the people of Appalachia. As Algeo (2003) points out, "local-color writing is a style of fiction or travel writing that takes as its starting point a place or region and attempts to convey the essence of that locale through detailed depictions of the geographic setting and through characters that supposedly represent essential qualities of the place" (30). The use of these essentialist qualities in literature— both geographically and culturally tied to coal—began in the late nineteenth century and continues to plague the region.

Today this naming takes place in popular slogans such as "Friends of Coal" and "War on Coal" as major players in the current narrative. This is an example of a dominant rhetoric of Appalachia used by the government and powerful coal industry. To create multiplicities in the dominant narrative, "images of place [must] be approached not only from the standpoint of reading the place through the lens of the representations, but that texts and images [must] also be read through the lens of the problems and priorities of particular places" (Powell 2007, 153). The problems and priorities for Appalachia are wrapped up in the contention of pride and shame. On one hand, Appalachian identity takes up the tropes created in local color writing, while others work to oppose such qualities. Either way, Appalachian identities outside of the mainstream image created by these tropes, whether characterized by pride or by shame, have been silenced so that the imagination of this space remains homogeneous. What is at stake when some voices within the region, especially in rural spaces, are silenced and groups of people are made invisible?

These rural spaces—most recently cast as "Trump country"—have become center stage in the media once again. The notion of the urban/rural divide has been added to this conversation to explain the popularity of Donald Trump in "coal country" as a barrier between urban (*there*) and rural (*here*). This barrier of the urban/rural divide has a long history in the creation of what makes this region "Appalachia." While the rural coal miner in contemporary Appalachia may find their worth as the backbone of America, having sparked the Industrial Revolution here, the media perpetuates the worthlessness of Appalachia through tropes of ignorance, backwardness, and being uncivilized. Appalachians take on these identifiers and become, in a way, defensive of the "urban" view. As Nick Mullins (2007) writes in his blog, *The Thoughtful Coal*

Miner, "The dehumanization of its people has allowed for the exploitation of its vast energy and timber reserves and putting Appalachians down has often been a means of lifting others up: 'I may not be rich, but at least I'm not a hillbilly.' " These forces have made maintaining our dignity a constant struggle. Mullins is a ninth-generation coal miner living and working in West Virginia. This complicated past and present he speaks of becomes muddled in the imagined and structured knowledge of Appalachia. This building of the narrative, often through structures of power, has been based on coal extraction. Therefore, coal, extractive as both a fossil fuel and cultural sign, has held the power of naming the region. Michel Foucault's work on space and power is important to note here. Specifically, his notion of heterotopia, as a space of otherness, can be applied to Appalachia as a constructed notion of a place—in other words, an invented space. This means that the writers, politicians, filmmakers, and others created the images of Appalachia known in the world today by hierarchies of power. Those who shaped the narrative had the power and opportunities to do so. This notion of a complicated past in Appalachia's creation mimics the contemporary conflict with minor narratives. The integrity of difference and those who appreciate it are demarcated as either part of the problem or not Appalachian. However, by expanding a meaning of Appalachia, the past and present narratives may coexist in the public imagination.

Currently, Appalachia is transitioning away from a coal economy and, to some extent, away from a coal culture, allowing for a re-representation of the homogeneous tropes. This transition creates a gap to be filled by minor narratives of Appalachia offering multiple perspectives that deviate from the universal, stereotypical tropes. Kathleen Stewart (1996) emphasizes this notion in her book, *A Space on the Side of the Road*. She postulates "how to imagine and represent cultural differences that make a difference in a way that might itself begin to make a difference" (5). Meaning, how can work being made in/about the region be used to highlight the minor narratives? The works discussed in this essay represent cultural differences that are often hidden away within the master narrative of Appalachia. Therefore, they are working to make a difference. By taking up intersections of identity, the Appalachian Queer Film Festival and student queer films engage the master narrative of Appalachia to poke holes in it and let stories of difference seep through. Across these works, counterrepresentations become a catalyst in addressing difference and contention in the cultural understandings of Appalachia. These representations, often muted voices, are part of the narrative of West Virginia, in a media haze of Trump country. However, their work and stories still operate within the framework of a constructed Appalachian identity.

In Appalachia, like many other places, stories play a critical role in shaping space. Whether told by outsiders or insiders, stories make claims on the space and those who occupy it. Therefore collectives, artworks, films, zines, and other objects must be made to tell stories that matter and make a difference, stories that entangle the multiple voices in this historically constructed space of Appalachia. There is an opportunity in our contemporary moment to make these voices heard to recognize the multiple narratives as part of region. This multiplicity creates an identity and representation of this "world got down" (Stewart 1996, 58) in a postcoal landscape. However, deeply embedded power structures work against those seeking to change the course of the narrative. Although the conversation of a postcoal Appalachia landscape is not a new concept, the actuality of it seems to be our present condition. This moment has created a space where the past narratives collide with contemporary experiences. Approaching these narratives in a way that resists the authority of the master narrative is necessary. Moreover, the multiple should be examined through a diversity of approaches, such as intersectionality. By taking this method of examination into account, the layers that structure the master narrative can be dismantled. This calls for an examination that is more complicated than understanding only the history of Appalachia or the history as separate from the experience. More important, an examination of the complicated contemporary narrative is in order. What about the pieces of Appalachia left outside the official history? What about the occluded voices that are not prominent in Appalachian studies? To think about the power of stories and the multiple ways to tell them, a different approach is necessary. I am not claiming to be the first to make such an assertion, but I am working to point out the possibilities that require further investigation and a platform to be heard. To contest these master narratives of the region, to understand the complicated work in brandishing the multiple narratives, it will take as much effort, determination, and resolve as naming the region since late nineteenth century.

To approach these possibilities of inclusion and multiplicities within the narrative, I take up Kimberlé Crenshaw's (1989) notion of intersectionality as a way to investigate the overlooked intersections of identities within Appalachia. This approach offers a framework in exploring how race, class, sexuality, and Appalachian identities are entangled. Because of this entanglement, it becomes difficult for a singular identity to encompass the multiple ways identities take shape. As Crenshaw explains, "this focus on the most privileged group members marginalizes those who are multiply-burdened and obscures claims that cannot be understood as resulting from discrete sources of discrimination" (140). In particular, Crenshaw (1991) points to singular strategies toward social justice as problematic "for those whose lives are shaped by a different set of obstacles" (1243). At the 2016 Appalachian Studies Association (ASA) conference, Affrilachian poet Frank X Walker (2016) said, "homogeneity is more striking than diversity" for the Appalachian region. This constructed notion of Appalachia as a space of "white mountain men" has characterized through tropes of hillbillies and whiteness in the US cultural imagination, thus perpetuating an essentialist master (male) narrative. Walker addressed this narrative in 1991. Negotiating the intersection of being African American and Appalachian, Walker coined the term *Affrilachian*. This was in response to the overlooked intersection that made up his identity. With Appalachia's definition often converging on whiteness, Barbara Smith (2004) points to assumptions of generic identities of white as normative in Appalachia in her article, "De-Gradations of Whiteness: Appalachia and the Complexities of Race." Emphasizing this point, Smith eludes to an alternative way to see Appalachia through a historical lens, a perspective that is not just white. This perspective is rooted "within much of Appalachian labor history, which has focused above all on the coal industry, [and] there has been a tendency to view race and class as competing and mutually exclusive forms of allegiance" (Smith 2004, 44). Therefore, overlooking these intersections mark some people and their voices as invisible if not part of the homogeneous narrative.

This homogeneous framework is bound to a distinct culture wrapped up in coal. A shift into a postcoal Appalachia may rupture this narrative. With Appalachia marked as a sacrificial zone, there is a lack of import in representing identities outside of mainstream assumptions, disregarding any injustices in these spaces. Appalachia has been a sacrifice zone for fossil fuel, particularly coal, since its inception. Some spaces were constructed around seams rich in coal and around stories of what sets this region as a place apart. The essays in *Mountains of Injustice: Social and Environmental Justice in Appalachia* take up the urban/rural divide through the lens of capitalism (Morrone and Buckley 2013). To this, Jedediah Purdy (2013) writes in the afterword, "There is no equality among American landscapes: some are sacred, some protected against harm, and some sacrificed" (183). Purdy notes how this concept reflects inequality for Americans. Some spaces reap the benefits of the electricity, such as urban New York City, whereas blown-off mountains in Appalachia made that electricity possible by coal extraction. The mountains are gone, that piece of the landscape and cultural landscape, but the shining billboards remain. This ruining of the place is acceptable as a way to continue the "way of life" so well preserved in a place that never seems to change. What is visible? What is made invisible? During his talk at the ASA conference, Walker contended that media and entertainment shape the perception of those who live in Appalachia. The capitalism of fossil fuel extraction and the extraction of stories in mainstream entertainment—for example, the *Buckwild* (2013) TV series and the *Wrong Turn* film franchise—take from the region without giving in return. The notion of what is *not* represented is more important. To examine what is not represented, notions of Appalachian studies may use a broader framework in examination. Although Crenshaw's focus concerns the intersection of race and class for women of color, her ideas are applicable in furthering the conversation of LGBTQ+ communities in the rural spaces of Appalachia toward social justice.

The Appalachian Queer Film Festival

Our mission is to bring queer films and filmmakers to the beautiful state of West Virginia, break down stereotypes and broaden minds in the Appalachian region.

—AQFF mission statement

What is not represented is often what constitutes the need for change. The thought of heritage and folk is often in conversation with basket weaving and fishing, however, as Gina Mamone (2018) states, those tasks are performed by queer people, too. So how can this narrative of "being around," in history and contemporarily, make its way into the master narrative of what constitutes Appalachia? One attempt in this task is the work of the Appalachia Queer Film Festival (AQFF). The fact that *Appalachia* and *queer* appear in the same title is a feat in and of itself for this region. This site, like other sites of queerness, is not meant to be misleading and suggest equity for the LGBTQ+ community, but operates as one visual representation of queer/ness in the space of Appalachia. The representation of queerness in Appalachia often takes place in designated spaces, such as a specific film festival. With lack of representation, the narrative of unhappiness as a queer person in the region remains mainstream. In her book *The Promise of Happiness*, Sara Ahmed (2010) aligns the representation of the unhappy queer to the unhappy endings of queer films and literature. For Ahmed, "there is no doubt that heterosexual happiness is overrepresented in public culture, often through an anxious repetition of threats and obstacles to its proper achievement" (90). This notion in relation to Appalachia points to the representation of happiness in the master narrative of the hard-working coal miner providing for his family. Here, happiness is obtained through the obstacle of hard work in the heteronormative trope of Appalachia. Heterosexual love in obtaining this "good life" drives the Appalachian narrative, therefore, "it is difficult to separate out narrative as such from the reproduction of happy heterosexuality" (Ahmed 2010, 90). Addressing and responding to the homogeneous narrative of Appalachia is the AQFF. Started in 2014, the Appalachian Queer Film Festival works to represent and showcase these often-occluded voices of Appalachians.

I made the three-hour drive to Lewisburg from Charleston, WV, to attend my first AQFF. Along the curves that hug the large mountains of Appalachia, I am reminded of the scarring of the land that sits just above the ridges. West Virginia has recently rebranded itself as a tourist destination. This space created for tourists has come into focus as a way to bring revenue into the state. However, the space created for the narrative alongside this tourist space is constructed around the "wild and wonderful" landscapes. Along my drive, there are particular bare spots that peek through the late fall landscape. At these junctures, I glimpse the broken, brown ground where mountaintops once stood. This is where mountaintop removal is taking place. The shades of red, yellow, and orange leaves attract tourists for the beauty while attempting to keep the destruction of these mountains away from the tourist's gaze. Peter Adey (2009) speaks to the politics of mobility by questioning how and why certain spaces are constructed. For example, he questions the role of a car driver as believing they are autonomous, one who thinks that they control their journey or destination, when they are limited by seatbelt laws, speed limits, and other drivers. For Adey, there is a strategy used by those who shape and direct space. In this instance, the destruction of the mountaintop is secluded just out of sight to create a facade of beauty for tourists. Along I-64, up on the former mountaintop, sits a deep crevice that was carved, exploded, and dredged to extract coal. It is not visible from the interstate. The destruction of what makes West Virginia "the Mountain State" is hidden away to continue the narrative of "wild and wonderful West Virginia" or "almost heaven," as state slogans have claimed. This concealment mirrors the tendency to conceal voices that do not fit the structured "mold" of the Appalachian narrative. This "mountain state" has hidden destructions, capitalist endeavors, and hidden narratives. The ridges are the dirty black of coal—permeating a sense of hurt for the land and people. This notion of the tourist narrative and the mobility of the travel is structured through a protected story of Appalachia. This thought and these connections are made clear as I travel to the AQFF.

Once in Lewisburg, voted America's coolest small town in 2011, I noticed some older white people holding neon yellow and pink signs. They waved at vehicles, and some blow their horns in accordance with their signs. Aware that the AQFF was happening and also aware of my conceptions of Appalachia,

I naively assumed they must be protesting the film festival. As I got closer to them, I was pleasantly surprised to find words of encouragement for the festival (see fig. 9.1). As much as I resist the master narrative of the region, I had let my own assumptions of Appalachia shape the situation I experienced.

The AQFF aims to shift these notions and create a space giving voice to the silenced queerness in Appalachia. In *New Queer Cinema*, B. Ruby Rich (2013, 37)

Figure 9.1. Advocates of the Appalachian Queer Film Festival hold signs on the busy streets of Lewisburg, WV, in 2016 (Photos by author)

points to gay and lesbian film festivals as creating a community within a larger society. This is a goal for the AQFF in that Jon Matthews (2016), a filmmaker from West Virginia and cofounder of AQFF, hopes the festival will become the "queer Park City of Appalachia." Isolation for the Sundance Film Festival creates an experience of not just the films being screened but also the place. Matthews works to program films he hopes will represent a marginalized group in the region while showcasing the space of small-town West Virginia to "outsiders." To accomplish this, he strives to bring as many of the filmmakers as possible. He hopes to "bring in outsiders to show off our progressive small town" (Matthews 2016). Although Matthews considers Lewisburg a progressive town, there were concerns for the word *queer* in the festival title. However, Matthews says that people are invested and root for the small festival underdog. From the AQFF website, the Lewisburg mayor, John Manchester (Appalachian Queer Film Festival 2015) says: "The festival broke down some barriers and showed that a large influx of the LGBTQ community coming to town was really not that different from any other group of people who come to town to enjoy what we have to offer. What's not to like about more people coming to town to celebrate the arts, shop, eat, spend money and have fun?"

What does it mean for the city of Lewisburg to take in money from a queer film festival when being queer is "often seen as threatening key social institutions: their lack of family orientation compromises such things as community and civil society, while their 'sterile' and non-reproductive 'lifestyle' endangers capitalism, which so depends on labor and wealth accumulation" (Kapoor 2015, 1613). Manchester sells the festival as an economic influx of cash for the town, whereas the LGBTQ community may focus more on breaking down barriers. Ilan Kapoor (2015) takes up this conversation of queerness and capitalism in their article, "The Queer Third World." The positioning of a space as "Third World," in relation to coal mining, mirrors the lack of agency in the historic notion of outside buyers profiting off those living in the mined spaces of Appalachia. Even as some notions of queerness are accepted, such as through fairness acts and marriage equality, there is still a need for structural change in these politics of domination.

Although the AQFF takes up power in occupying the space and shouting "Queer" from the marquee, the entanglements of history can still prevail. The mayor's sentiment draws on "what we do know about film festivals in general is that they are frequently symbols of sociopolitical ambition" (Rich 2013, 36). This ambition, as presented by the mayor, plays into the imbalance of wealth created by outside sources who would buy land from poor Appalachians to keep them poor. These constraints of profit-making also constrain opportunities, which is presented on the artistic side of the festival. This barrier is between the films screened at the festival and locally produced queer films available. Of course, the lack of funding and appreciation for art-making points back to the constrained opportunities in a state owned by coal. In their first year AQFF screened the local films, *Ladybeard* (Smith 2013) and *Welcome to Dragalachia* (Fugate 2013). Matthews says he would like to have more locally produced films, but, because of the small market for these films and lack of funding for filmmakers, the festival currently makes up this lack by creating a space to screen films not housed in other theaters in the state. This space is one way a narrative is being written to fill the gaps of representation in Appalachia. The festival addresses the intersectionality of queer and Appalachian identities within the same space in order to address the silenced representation of queered identity.

In April 2017, *Vice* published an article titled "Rural Film Festivals Are the Next Frontier of LGBTQ Tolerance" (Valentini 2017). The article explores how the AQFF is using public space in Appalachia as support for the LGBTQ community. By emphasizing rural communities as places to organize, the article recognizes AQFF as a tool of visibility for the LGBTQ community: "When we think of LGBTQ gatherings and celebrations, we conjure images of Provincetown's Carnival Parade or the massive OutFest film festival in LA. But outside Christopher Street or the Castro, film festivals like AQFF and other events are playing a vital role in galvanizing rural LGBTQ communities, where opportunities to celebrate one's identity are limited—and not solely because of intolerance, as one might assume."

Growing up queer in a space such as Appalachia does not always afford the comforts of home. Bradley Milam (2016) grew up in this type of space. In a small West Virginia town in Raleigh County, he felt that his identity as a gay man and as a West Virginian could not coexist. After graduating high school, he "left the state for college that he had a romanticized idea of coming back to West Virginia and helping the state to make it more open for queer folks" (Milam 2016). For Milam, the festival opens up a space where his identities "of being from West Virginia and an openly gay man" could intersect. He emphasized how he feels that the festival gives members of the LGBTQ+ community "a lens into the availability of openness that would otherwise not seem like a place that would welcome a queer film festival." With West Virginia as a vulnerable place for negative representations, the AQFF "incorporates art and openness and tolerance." His partner, Tim, is the cofounder of the film festival. They have decided to stay in the region to help make it a more open space for people like them and make it attractive for other people who do not consider visiting this part of the country.

I was able to watch three films at the 2016 festival. The one that most represented the rural in this rural setting was a short documentary titled *These C*cksucking Tears* (Taberski 2016). The film follows Patrick Haggerty, creator of the first and only gay-themed country music album. The album, *Lavender Country*, was released in 1973. As Haggerty says in the film, "I am as country as they come and if you challenge my credentials of my 'countryness' you will do so at your peril." Just as West Virginia takes on the narrative of rural in the urban/rural divide, so does country music. The film explores this notion as Haggerty claims he was denied access to Nashville because "a conservative political conscience captured Nashville and dominates it." That is, because Haggerty is an openly gay man, he is denied access into the master narrative of country music. The camera then follows Haggerty to his childhood home, where he speaks about his father seeing him in a dress with glitter and lipstick on for the first time. He says he hid from his father, but his father said, "Whoever you run around with in drama school . . . don't sneak like you did today. If you sneak, it means you think you are doing the wrong thing . . . so, don't sneak." This is a moving moment in the film that describes the acceptance of his identity by his father in the 1950s. The film ends with Haggerty saying, "Sing your truth." Feeling and showing your truth, as Haggerty references, is part of the larger conversation of tolerance in rural spaces. The intersectionality of identities as queer and rural are part of the master narrative, however, some find difficulty singing their truth because of social and safety concerns.

After watching the film, I spoke with festivalgoer goer Chris Gang. Originally from suburban Connecticut, Chris has lived in Boone County, WV, for three years as an environmentalist for the Radical Action for Mountains' and People's Survival Campaign in Whitesville, WV. Identifying as queer, Chris says he struggles being a queer person in Appalachia and misses the opportunity in big cities to see queer cinema. He feels the AQFF "is exciting and a way to push forward the conversation of what it means to navigate and hold to both parts of that identity." Chris was curious whether the marquee would display the word "Queer" and feels the film festival is, unfortunately, being gently promoted, referencing the lack of newspaper, television, radio, and other local ads and promotions for the festival. However, he appreciates that it is geared toward the queer community. Chris feels that attendance was low and thinks it may be because of the travel and location. In June, massive floods ripped through Greenbrier County, where the festival takes place, causing a shift in focus and funding on rebuilding towns rather than already planned events. Therefore, less visibility of the festival exists and in turn less visibility for LGBTQ+-identifying people in the area to attend. Queerness is not part of Chris's identity when he does environmental work in small West Virginia spaces. His heart goes out to Appalachian queer youth living in isolated spaces of West Virginia because the models for LGBTQ+ visibility are urban-based. For Chris's parting words, he says, "The festival is a fucking big deal."

Amplifying Student Voices

As queer people, you learn so many life skills that young kids should not have to know or shouldn't have to rely on to successfully navigate through life.

—Joelle Gates

In fall 2017, I began teaching full-time at Marshall University in the School of Journalism and Mass Communications. Being from small town West Virginia, I had dreamed of this day since I became interested in filmmaking and teaching. By teaching documentary and narrative video production, I am in a position to nurture multiple student stories, most of which are local to the region. During my first year, I had a student who made it her mission to structure each project around trans issues in Huntington, West Virginia. When Joelle Gates (2018b) showed her first film, *Effeminates*, I knew she had a unique voice on our campus and was using her knowledge and experience to make a difference that makes a difference, to again borrow the words of Kathleen Stewart. In *Effeminates*, Gates explores her transition by sharing deeply personal moments of doubt and euphoria. The above epigraph is a quote from her film juxtaposed over footage of Gates lying topless on a medical table, flinching at each use of the laser hair removal tool on her face. Not only does Gates explore her own LGBTQ+ story, she takes up what it means to be queer through stories of multiple Marshall students during the sensitive moment of coming out. Gates took this project and created a collective called the Effeminates (2018). Their mission statement points to the work needed to work against the past of Appalachia: "Being queer and growing up in Appalachia has never been an easy task. Our Christian heritage combined with abundant poverty has created countless obstacles that often prevent LGBTQ+ individuals from living authentically. In an attempt to bring about acceptance, our mission is to share stories of queer Appalachians to educate, advocate, and inspire change."

Gates was able to first share this film with the public during a symposium I cocreated, "Appalachian Narratives: Notes on Identity." During a participatory event in this symposium, with queer Appalachia and short Appalachian queer films, Gates shared her film. This opportunity points to the collective's mission statement as a moment of educating while highlighting the obstacles of being home to/in the region with a queer identity. In her book *Feminism without Borders: Decolonizing Theory, Practicing Solidarity*, Chandra Mohanty (2003) explores the power and appeal of "home" as a concept in connection to identity (85). She writes, "the historical grounding of shifts and changes allows for an emphasis on the pleasures and terrors of interminable boundary confusions, but insists, at the same time, on our responsibility for remapping boundaries and renegotiating connections" (87). Appalachian artists, such as Gates, are doing just this. Gates points to Christian heritage as a barrier to acceptance of her queer identity in the region; by taking up this type of historic grounding of place, Gates's work renegotiates the past within a present context.

In another of Gates's films, *02/20/18: Being Normal* (2018a), she takes a simplistic avenue with driving visuals juxtaposed over dialogue with a friend on an ordinary day, hence 02/20/18. The entirety of the film shows only what is outside of the car: the familiar streets of Huntington, where Gates resides for school and, for now, calls "home." This familiarity is met with discussion of not fitting into this place. Tracing the city where she has come to live is met with her inability to fit into a college experience that is often expected, often "normal." By tracing the geography of Huntington streets, Gates retraces the streets, emphasizing a queered perspective as if mapping a new perspective. As a remapping of the extracted landscape becomes visible in the region through broken factories, store fronts, and mountains, so does a remapping of an Appalachian culture. Mohanty's (2003) chapter "What's Home Got to Do with It?" takes up a discussion of Minnie Bruce Pratt's (1991) autobiographical narrative "Identity: Skin Blood Heart". Mohanty claims that Pratt's narrative is essential in addressing political questions surrounding identity politics (88). I find this reading useful in exploring how contemporary Appalachian artists are confronting a shift in identity politics, such as through student films. Gates and other aspiring filmmakers in my classes are using their talent and their voices to shift the monolithic Appalachian narrative. By grounding work in this geography, their relationships between home and identity are connected to the local histories of exploitation and struggles while deeply commenting on contemporary struggles of belonging.

Conclusion

In her book, *Out in the Country*, Mary L. Gray (2009) emphasizes the agencies available for LGBTQ+-identifying people living in cities compared with those living in rural America. This availability is a problematic notion of mapping by the urban/rural divide, which pushes people further into the margins. The intersectionality of Appalachian and LGBTQ+ identities is useful in approaching Gray's point of LGBTQ+ people living in rural America and problematizing the presumptions of queerness's proper place. As Gray (2009) notes, visibility and political dissent do not operate across a universal space and time (7). Cultural understandings of Appalachia are painted as homogeneously white and heteronormative, making only one narrative of this space visible. Therefore, spaces, politics, and subjects of rural Appalachia must be recognized as embedded in a history of this place and constructed through these tropes. Within the singular narrative of Appalachia, "gay visibility is simultaneously given a spatial location and a social value in this formation"

(Gray 2009, 9). Addressing the social value of this visibility, Fairness West Virginia, a statewide civil rights organization, works to represent the diversity of Appalachia. The organization works to create visibility for LGBTQ+ identifying people in the region to address the issues that Gray points to as political and social implications of invisibility. Small Appalachian communities operate within ties of kinship and everyone knowing everyone, and there is fear in pushing too hard for visibility. As Gray (2009) explains, LGBTQ+ people in Appalachia risk "seeming out of place in communities that materially depend on familiarity [and therefore] outweigh the tangible benefits of making oneself queerly visible" (165). Therefore, this apprehension toward visibility poses problems not just for individual people but also for the possibility of furthering the larger conversation of rural diversity.

In addressing these rural diversities, the AQFF and films discussed herein are creating what Stewart (1996) describes as a difference that makes a difference by creating ruptures in the master narrative: these ruptures are the multiplicities that make Appalachia what it is. As Ahmed (2010) says about happy narratives, "happiness scripts could be thought of as straightening devices, ways of aligning bodies with what is already lined up" (91). This line is constructed in Appalachia through the metaphor of roots. Often the phrase "my roots are in Appalachia" is used to stake a claim in being home. What becomes problematic is the hierarchy associated with such a deep and embodied notion of place. Rather than roots, Deleuze and Guattari's (1987) notion of rhizome works as "principles of connection and heterogeneity: any point of a rhizome can be connected to anything other and must be. This is very different from the tree or root, which plots a point, fixes an order" (7). As Ahmed (2003) points out, "to deviate from the line [root] is to be threatened with unhappiness" (91). This deviation creates what Ahmed refers to as a perverse promise of unhappiness. For example, Gates (2018a) references getting used to the feeling of being outside of society: "I wonder if it actually gets better . . . or you just don't give a shit." She reminds us of the possibility of eternal unhappiness. This association of unhappiness and place is a point of contention for Gates and other Appalachian queer artists working to make a difference as "they blur the boundaries of who belongs where and who has claims to be members of one's community" (Valentini 2017). As we look into the moments of upheaval in the Appalachian region, these artists propose an alternative view for future discussion through their work.

"Homogeneity is more interesting than diversity" (Walker 2016) is both quote and critique. As artists contend to create minor narratives of Appalachia, there will always be a historic context of coal and stereotypes that mark a past within the present. I looked at examples that take up these notions and deconstruct an essentialist trope of Appalachia as a singular existence. Queer communities are not spaces marked with the largest number of gay bars, they are in the everyday spaces that are often made silent (Long 2016). Representations of these spaces are at work in contemporary Appalachian film, which explores notions of "being home" and "not being home" (Mohanty 2003). What I do not have is a name for these new representations, this Appalachian Renaissance. Naming and narratives have mapped the region of Appalachia as a place apart, but as the physical landscape shifts away from coal, so does the cultural landscape. The queer basket weavers, the queer folk singers, they've been around. What might hopefully happen within the economic–cultural shift will be these narratives taking center stage, as opposed to the minimal side story from the past. In the shift, this gap remains a space not to necessarily rewrite history but to discuss how this history is taken up and reevaluated in the present.

BIBLIOGRAPHY

Appalachian Queer Film Festival. 2015, July 31. "Q&A with Mayor John Manchester." *AQFF*. http://aqff.org/uncategorized/588/.
"AQFF." 2019. Appalachian Queer Film Festival, 84 Agency. http://aqff.org/.
Adey, Peter. 2009. *Mobility*. New York: Routledge.
Ahmed, Sara. 2010. *The Promise of Happiness*. Durham, NC: Duke University Press.
Algeo, Katie. 2003. "Locals on Local Color: Imagining Identity in Appalachia." *Southern Cultures* 9, no. 4, 27–54.
Crenshaw, Kimberlé. 1989. "Demarginalizing the Intersection of Race and Sex: A Black Feminist Critique of Antidiscrimination Doctrine, Feminist Theory and Antiracist Politics." *University of Chicago Legal Forum* 1, no. 8, 139–67.
———. 1991. "Mapping the Margins: Intersectionality, Identity Politics, and Violence against Women of Color." *Stanford Law Review* 43, no. 6, 1241–99.
Deleuze, Gilles, and Félix Guattari. 1987. *A Thousand Plateaus: Capitalism and Schizophrenia*. Minneapolis: University of Minnesota Press.
Effeminates. 2018. "This Is Effeminates: A Celebration of Queer Appalachia." *Effeminates*. https://effeminates.wixsite.com/home.
Fugate, Oakley. 2013. *Welcome to Dragalachia*. Film. https://www.youtube.com /watch?v=urZCwKxbuok.
Gates, Joelle. 2018a. *2/20/2018: Being Normal*. Film. https://www.youtube.com /watch?v=DxKId5iU4qI.
———. 2018b. *Effeminates*. Film. https://www.youtube.com/watch?v=mQcUMfor1d4.
Gray, Mary L. 2009. *Out in the Country: Youth, Media, and Queer Visibility in Rural America*. New York: New York University Press.
Howard, Jason. 2015. "Bastards and Ghosts." In *Walk till the Dogs Get Mean: Meditations on the Forbidden from Contemporary Appalachia*, edited by Adrian Blevins and Karen Salyer McElmurray, 85–93. Athens: Ohio University Press.
Kapoor, Ilan. 2015. "The Queer Third World." *Third World Quarterly* 36, no. 9, 1611–28.

Long, Elliot. 2016, April. Discussion with Tijah Bumgarner.

Mamone, Gina. 2018, February 6. Discussion with Tijah Bumgarner.

Matthews, Jon. 2016, April. Interview by Tijah Bumgarner.

Milam, Bradley. 2016, October. Interview by Tijah Bumgarner.

Mohanty, Chandra Talpade. 2003. *Feminism without Borders: Decolonizing Theory, Practicing Solidarity*. Durham, NC: Duke University Press.

Morrone, Michele, and Geoffrey L. Buckley, eds. 2013. *Mountains of Injustice: Social and Environmental Justice in Appalachia*. Athens: Ohio University Press.

Mullins, Nick. 2017, April. "Stereotyping Appalachians Feeds Only the Coal Industry," *Yes!* https://www.yesmagazine.org/new-economy/stereotyping-appalachians -feeds-only-the-coal-industry-20170410. Accessed November 4, 2018.

Murfree, Mary. 1885. *In these Tennessee Mountains*. Boston: Houghton, Mifflin, 1885.

Powell, Douglas Reichert. 2007. *Critical Regionalism: Connecting Politics and Culture in the American Landscape*. Chapel Hill: University of North Carolina Press.

Pratt, Minnie Bruce. 1991. "Identity: Skin Blood Heart." In *Rebellion: Essays 1980–1991*. Ithaca, NY: Firebrand Books.

Purdy, Jedediah. 2013. "Afterword: An American Sacrifice Zone." In *Mountains of Injustice: Social and Environmental Justice in Appalachia*, edited by Michele Morrone and Geoffrey L. Buckley. Athens: Ohio University Press.

Rich, B. Ruby. 2013. *New Queer Cinema: The Director's Cut*. Durham, NC: Duke University Press.

Smith, Barbara. 2004. "De-Gradations of Whiteness: Appalachia and the Complexities of Race." *Journal of Appalachian Studies* 10, nos. 1/2, 38–57.

Smith, David. 2013. *Ladybeard*. Film.

Stewart, Kathleen. 1996. *A Space on the Side of the Road: Cultural Poetics in an "Other" America*. Princeton, NJ: Princeton University Press.

Taberski, Dan. 2016. *These C*cksucking Tears*. DVD.

Valentini, Valentina. 2017, April 28. "Rural Film Festivals Are the Next Frontier of LGBTQ Tolerance." *Vice*. https://www.vice.com/en_us/article/pgjjvn/rural-film -festivals-are-the-next-frontier-of-lgbtq-tolerance.

Walker, Frank X. 2016, March. "Escape from Negro Mountain: Writing History, Righting Wrongs." Keynote plenary at the Appalachian Studies Association Conference, Shepherdstown, WV.

CHAPTER 10

Writing the Self: Trans Zine Making in Appalachia

Savi Ettinger, Katie Manthey, Sonny Romano, and Cynthia Suryawan

Identity is ubiquitous to the everyday life of writing centers.

—Harry Denny (2010, 137)

Embodiment

This piece contributes to a queer/ing of Appalachia by theorizing the risks and rewards of writing about and embodying trans by creating and circulating of zines (self-published, often activist publications) by offering vignettes of an interview between a cis professor and three trans students. We end the piece with the first issue of a student-produced zine, titled "Trans Embodiment," that works through what it means to be trans at a women's college in Appalachia. Before we go any further, we want to introduce ourselves:

Savi (they/them or he/him) is a queer and trans student currently working toward a double major in English and creative writing with a concentration in poetry and an interest in multimodal writing and visual literature. They recently finished their first year as a writing consultant, with previous volunteer experience at the Salem College Writing Center.

Cynthia (she/her or they/them) is a nonbinary, biracial, queer student currently studying mathematics and statistics at Salem College. She completed an internship and is now a volunteer at the Salem College Writing Center.

Sonny (he/him or they/them) is a blue-haired, queer, mixed kid from Cincinnati currently majoring in rhetoric and composition with a concentration in zine history, preservation, and archiving, with a double minor in professional writing and art history at Salem College. They recently finished their first year as a writing consultant at the Salem College Writing Center.

Katie (she/her) is a white, cisgender, young(ish), able-bodied, fat, queer woman. She is an assistant professor of English and the director of the Salem College Writing Center.

Our story takes place in 2016 at Salem College in Winston-Salem, NC. Salem College was founded in 1772 as a school for girls and women. It prides itself on its mission of offering higher education to historically marginalized populations. Salem is small, with about eight hundred traditional-age undergraduate students. The school is 51 percent white, and a large percentage of students are first-generation college students. Although there are no official data about sexual orientation, the LGBTQ student organization, Open Up, has about one hundred members. Salem is a women's college (currently, traditional-age undergraduate students must select the "female" box on the application form for admission to be considered), but there are many students on campus that do not identify as women.

Conversations

For many years, there has been a push for Salem to have an official policy about transgender students.

Katie: Do you all feel that there are currently spaces on campus for trans or nonbinary students?

Sonny: No.

Savi: Very little.

Cynthia: We're open to try and we have the "Alphabet Support Group" [Alphabet Soup-port is a LGBTQIA+ support group that has been running for about a semester. It was started by and co-facilitated by trans people, though it is open to all queer people.]

Savi: But that's not a trans-specific space. I think a lot of that comes from the fear of it being a no-trans policy.

Cynthia: True.

The current lack of a trans policy at Salem makes being out as trans (and writing about it) a potentially dangerous act.

Katie: How have you all felt about the risks associated with a project like this where you are, in essence, outing yourself to the world?

Cynthia: I'm not out to my parents or anything, but I feel like if they were to find out, it wouldn't necessarily be that bad. I don't know. Then when it comes to Salem, I don't know. I feel like for at least a number of trans people on campus, pretty much all of campus already knows, including faculty and staff and all that stuff. The biggest worry would be actually being kicked out or something for being trans, but again, they can't do that without visiting a trans policy, which they're not going to do. I think there isn't as much risk as it could be, I guess.

One place that has become safe for trans students is the Salem College Writing Center. Historically, writing centers offer tutoring services to students who want help with their writing in colleges and high schools and are part of academic support services. Although writing centers are often seen as remedial, writing center scholarship advocates for seeing the centers as collaborative spaces for writers of all levels and identities (Gellar et al. 2007; Denney 2010). Some centers are staffed with professional tutors, but many use a peer-consulting model. The Salem College Writing Center is one of the latter. When Katie became the director in 2015, there were three peer tutors. In the span of a year, the staff grew to sixteen. During that year, we collaboratively crafted a new vision statement to help the campus understand that we were more than a "fix it" shop: "At the Salem College Writing Center (SCWC), we welcome any student who needs a sounding board or help with expressing thoughts. We work with any form of writing from resumes to love letters. Because we view you as whole people, not just sessions, we work to make better writers, not just better papers. This is a safe space, so bring your work, grab some candy, and take a seat!"

Savi: Honestly, this is a very different job than the job I thought I was applying for.

Katie: What did you think you were applying for? I'm interested to know.

Sonny: I thought low-key and thought I was just going to come and edit people's papers. That's all I was going to do. I thought I was just going to show up and edit people's papers and trade snarky jokes like when I worked at the library. It's very different than that. I like it.

Cynthia: Yeah. I didn't expect as many projects to be going on, I guess. In the writing center, you're working on how to express yourself through different avenues like your papers. It's more than just papers. It's creative things, too.

Savi: I think, especially in the context of the writing center, so many people think of us as the place to go for essays, so it's not really associated with fun often times. I think that's a big misconception about writing in general. It's supposed to be enjoyable and fun. It's supposed to be expressive.

Sonny: The writing center is our treehouse. It's where we go to do the thing, but it's also home. I definitely feel more comfortable in the writing center than I would just meeting at a coffee shop or something to work on this.

One of the powerful things about writing centers is that they make space for collaborative work to happen organically. At the SCWC, consultants are expected to have a "side project" they work on when they don't have appointments. These range from filing papers to updating handouts to research projects. In 2015, a senior consultant proposed an interview-based research project to collect stories about being a trans writing consultant. The project (slowly) continued this year, and staff members were able to sign up to continue to work on it.

Katie: So, how did this project get started?

Savi: We really didn't know how the project was going to happen. We [were in the writing center and] got to talking about just off-subject stuff. I was thinking about putting out a poetry zine at the time. The ideas converged upon themselves. It led to us thinking about the Trans Embodiment research project through the scope of zines.

Sonny: I was like, "This one [the Trans Embodiment research project] seems really cool and also only has one person signed up for it so far," so I will put my name on it. Then Savi and I met at the first meeting and were talking about how we maybe wanted to do it. Then Savi was like, "Why not a zine?"

Cynthia: I was signed up for a lot of different projects, so especially the first couple of times I was meeting with the other projects because they're more time-sensitive, I guess. Then when I finally met with them, they were talking about the zine. They had pretty much already basically come to the conclusion that the zine was going to be a thing. I was like, "That's cool. I don't know what a zine is, but that's cool." Then I think they asked if I wanted to be a part of it. I was like, "Yeah, that's cool."

Zines and Trans Embodiment

Before we go further, we want to address what Cynthia brought up: not every-one knows what zines are. Zines as a medium lack definition, but not for lack of trying. In her essay, "Zines in the Classroom: Reading Culture," Rebekah Buchanan (2012) defines zines as "independent, self-published works created for pleasure that earn little or no profit" (71). Although broad, the defini-tion does not account for zine presses and small publishing companies that perform the same function as larger publishing houses, except on a scale and in a manner that lends themselves to zine work. Other definitions of zines include a wide variety of other qualifying identifiers, one describing zines as "handmade, noncommercial, irregularly issued, small-run, paper publications circulated by individuals participating in alternative, special-interest com-munities" (Radway 2011, 140), and another description focuses on content, calling zines "quirky, individualized booklets filled with diatribes, reworkings of pop culture iconography, and all variety of personal and political narra-tives" (Piepmeier 2008, 214). However detailed and helpful, no definition fully captures the entire potential of zines; instead, they only capture the usual qualities of zines, which zinesters may choose to subvert, as long as it can still be called a zine.

Ultimately zines are personal creations in which often unconventional topics may be explored, works that are purposefully noncommercial and small run. They often take the shape of booklets, but they are far from the typical traditional literary experience. Many times, they explore topics that traditional literature shies away from and subvert expectations to create a unique aes-thetic, which allows for a personalized creation. While zines are not commonly assigned in college writing courses, we argue that they have a place in college writing and therefore in college writing centers. In 2005, the National Council of Teachers of English (2005) issued a statement on the importance of "multi-modal literacies," which include creations of texts that engage all five senses; since then scholars (Piepmeier 2008; Helmbrecht and Love 2009; Liming 2010; Radway 2011) have written about the importance of this genre of writing in academic settings.

There is a growing body of scholarship focused on taking writing centers beyond the classroom and viewing them as sites for social justice work. As Harry Denny explains, "The writing center is a place to make a more immedi-ate, different impact than conventional activism . . . writing centers them-selves intersect with notions of identity and the complications that come along with them. Identity is central to writing centers, and not just because they are institutional units occupied by the individuals within them—people with multiple identities that impact on everything they do. Writing centers take on the politics of identity and questions of face because how they present themselves has symbolic and material implications that represent a whole range of relations" (2010, 312). This perspective offers writing centers as spaces where students are encouraged to see their writing as something that is an intrinsic part of themselves—a sort of "embodied" production. Our "Trans Embodiment Zine" (https://trans-embodiment-zine.tumblr.com) is an example of this:

Cynthia: I liked the idea of having an outlet for trans and gender-nonconforming people to have a space to talk about their identities.

Savi: I like it being on trans people's terms. This is by and for trans people, and gender-nonconforming people and anyone who doesn't fall under the label of "cis," basically. It's just really interesting to have this space where this is solely for these people of this marginalized identity. It's really cool to get to set that parameter and say, "this is our space."

Sonny: It's been really nice being able to feel like I'm being self-indulgent, even though what I'm doing is important work.

The fact that personal manners and experiences are expressed in a way that destabilizes the traditional sphere, such as zines do, demonstrates how zines use the idea that the personal is political—and even this idea is not safe from the zinesters' tendency to explore and break open that which is stable. As Sonny commented, it sometimes feels "indulgent" to critically examine the self; however, as Duncombe (1997) explains, zines "broach political issues from the state to the bedroom, but they refract all these issues through the eyes and experience of the individual creating the zine" (33). Issues are approached with consideration of the inner thoughts to the world government, examining and identifying what is valuable to justice and what must be dismantled. Some zines do this in an explicit fashion, outright advocating for social, economic, and political justice for various marginalized groups or educating on nuances in thought or on how one can better treat people of specific identities. Zines may also speak directly to certain groups of people, as a rallying cry to action or as a way to raise awareness on new or hidden information; this creates a publication that does not serve or follow the dominant culture whatsoever. Rather, it is created by and for people left out of traditional media.

Katie: What do we gain from creating spaces for composing opportunities?

Cynthia: I guess in the context of the zine itself, trans people around the world get the benefits in a way because they can see, especially through social media, just all the submissions that they could identify with from different people around the world.

Cynthia: In the context of having it in the writing center, it benefits the students who don't have a space elsewhere on campus. It excludes cis people, but at the same time, like you said, having this start in the writing center allows opportunities to open for other similar projects to occur for other groups of people on campus . . . This is a creative thing. With the whole creative space, the idea of creativity is really important on a college campus in general. Having the writing center offer creative opportunities for people, that's quite the contribution as well.

Savi: I think it's important to remember, specifically with North Carolina, being trans in North Carolina in itself is pretty revolutionary.

Sonny: It's a radical act.

Savi: It is a radical act. It's just really important to realize whenever we make spaces like this for trans people, we ourselves are committing a radical act. We're doing something we know people are going to oppose eventually. It's also the right thing to do. I know that's silly. It sounds silly to say, making this zine is a radical act, but it is.

Sonny: That's what zines have always been.

Savi: Exactly.

Sonny: That's literally the history of the art form, is radical acts.

Zines are a decidedly activist genre of literature and rhetoric. They are only one of the ways craft can be activist work. This use of craft for activism, or "craftivism," is defined by Betsy Greer—who coined the term—as "a way of looking at life where voicing opinions through creativity makes your voice stronger, your compassion deeper, and your quest for justice more infinite" (Williams 2011, 306). Through craft, people may come into their own, articulating the experiences of various identities, which is considerably helpful to marginalized people. Making and crafting allows for distributing ideas from voices that have been previously silenced using the means of traditional press. Though it is true that zinesters use mannerisms and practices that are "steadfastly middle class" (Liming 2010, 134), the same can be said of those who create pamphlets and broadsides. The dissemination of suppressed information among both the masses and smaller circles tends to be a middle-class endeavor. Even though the impoverished and the wealthy sometimes turn to craftivism, the middle class has the most widespread use of craftivism, due to economic stability allowing them extra free time, and intersectionality and dissatisfaction with those wealthier than them may spur the desire to take part in resistance movements. Zines are an activist form of literature not only because of their form as self-published and subversive works, but also because of the stories they tell—even when they are not just telling stories—and whom they speak to. They refuse to fulfill capitalist standards of creation, thus engaging in a more genuine form of creation, and undermine traditional means—an inherently activist act.

Because of how zines can be used to resist, and perhaps even because of their predecessors in broadsides and pamphlets, a number of marginalized identities and activist movements are represented throughout zines. Zines are works that promote and vocalize those who inhabit third-space lives. With a third space being defined as "a space that materializes what borders serve to divide" (Licona 2012, 11), zines are the manifestation of experiences in such spaces. The rhetoric they use ultimately works to break down the labels that have been forced on them, then repurposing and reclaiming the very language once used to oppress. This makes zines especially useful as tools to educate and promote sociopolitical topics, such as equal rights and justice for those of all races, ethnicities, nationalities, sexualities, genders, religions, classes, and abilities. As stated in the leaflet *Queers Read This* (1990), produced anonymously, for those who identify as queer, "everyday you wake up alive, relatively happy, and functioning as a human being, you are committing a rebellious act." The same stance can be taken for a wide range of marginalized identities. By embracing and promoting diversity and providing a platform on which it can flourish and be heard, zines commit multiple rebellious acts simply by existing.

This project began in the SCWC and has grown to touch the lives of people across the world. After publishing the first introductory volume of the "Trans Embodiment Zine" on Tumblr (a social media blogging platform which, according to Business Insider, heavily engages people ages sixteen to twenty-four; see Cooper 2013) people began to respond through messaging and emails. Hundreds of people found something to relate to or though the information was worthy of passing on, and we received more than three hundred reblogs in the span of a few weeks. This social media activity led to an international audience far greater than anticipated. There was an initial shock over the sheer amount of interest the zine had amassed; however, it only helped us understand the potential scope of the zine.

Cynthia: I feel like seeing the response we've had, especially before making the second edition [of the zine], helped validate the project because I know when we were first starting, at first we were just thinking, "Salem people can submit and it will be a Salem thing." That was cool, but I was just a little concerned about how many submissions we would get because there aren't a whole lot of trans people on campus. Then when you started going online with social media, that definitely broadens the scope and makes it a bit more real, I guess.

With our newfound confidence and availability of submissions, we produced the second and then third issues with relative ease. We took a risk applying to a local zine fest, an hour or so away in Durham, NC, and our table was accepted. Zine culture exists as a counterculture, and thus led to intrinsic knowledge and understanding of how we functioned personally and professionally in these spheres. For those of marginalized identities, these spaces can be crucial.

Although hiding any identity is not ideal, we admit that there are times when it is necessary for survival. Even in our small corner of Appalachia, at a women's college known for its liberal ideas, where plenty of people are out and proud, there are still a handful of people who are in the closet or have their foot in the door but can't come out completely. This hesitancy to be fully out has to do with the lack of a trans policy on campus, allowing there to be an air of ambiguity and the overhanging threat of a sudden exclusive policy.

Sonny: If they [the administration] were to explicitly say no [to having trans students on campus], then several students on campus would have to leave.

Katie: Better to live in ambiguity than to explicitly say no.

Savi: Yeah, exactly.

Katie: I was going to say, but what does that ambiguity do for your everyday life as people who exist here?

Savi: It's stressful.

Sonny: Even the four of us in this room, as visibly queer as we all are, we could all say we're allies if we so chose.

Savi: Yeah. No one can tell.

Katie: Exactly. In that moment, how do you prove it? There's not a blood test. It's not a DNA test. It's not any of the institutional markers for definitions of queerness.

Savi: I feel like in my lifetime, they'll try and figure one out, though.

Katie: Yes, probably, especially if you stay in North Carolina.

We posit that being queer in Appalachia is itself a radical act because there are so many forces opposing our existence. Being trans, especially outwardly and "not passing" trans, can make us incredibly vulnerable because our existence is visible; trying to hide runs the risk of extreme dysphoria and negatively affected mental health. We see our zine as a step in the process of making space for all people to survive and thrive in Appalachia.

Savi: I think that's ultimately what this zine is working toward, is having these experiences written down.

Katie: Of bumping up against things and then helping to redefine them?

Savi: Yeah, exactly, of dismantling old definitions in place of new ones.

You can find all of the zine's volumes at http://trans-embodiment-zine .tumblr.com/. We hope that you will read, share, and consider contributing to this method of making space for queer people in Appalachia.

BIBLIOGRAPHY

Buchanan, Rebekah. 2012. "Zines in the Classroom: Reading Culture." *English Journal* 102, no. 2, 71–77.

Denny, Harry. 2010. *Facing the Center: Towards an Identity Politics of One-to-One Mentoring*. Logan: Utah State University Press.

Duncombe, Stephen. 1997. *Notes from Underground: Zines and the Politics of Alternative Culture*. New York: Verso Books.

Geller, Anne Elizabeth, Michele Eodice, Frankie Condon, Meg Carroll, and Elizabeth H. Boquet. 2007. *The Everyday Writing Center: A Community of Practice*. Logan: Utah State University Press.

Helmbrecht, Brenda M., and Meredith A. Love. 2009. "The BUSTin' and Bitchin' Ethe of Third-Wave Zines." *College Composition and Communication* 61, no. 1, 150–69.

Licona, Adela C. 2012. *Zines in Third Space: Radical Cooperation and Borderlands Rhetoric*. Albany: State University of New York Press.

Liming, Sheila. 2010. "Of Anarchy and Amateurism: Zine Publication and Print Dissent." *Journal of the Midwest Modern Language Association* 43, no. 2, 121–45.

National Council of Teachers of English. 2005. *Position Statement on Multimodal Literacies*. Last modified November 2005. http://www.ncte.org/positions /statements/multimodalliteracies.

Piepmeier, Alison. 2008. "Why Zines Matter: Materiality and the Creation of Embodied Community." *American Periodicals* 18, no. 2, 213–38.

Queers: Read This. 2009. New York. Leaflet. Republished 2009. http://www.qrd.org/qrd /misc/text/queers.read.this.

Radway, Janice. 2011. "Zines, Half-Lives, and Afterlives: On the Temporalities of Social and Political Change." *PMLA* 126, no. 1, 140–50.

Smith, Cooper. 2013, December 13. "Tumblr Offers Advertisers a Major Advantage: Young Users, Who Spend Tons of Time on the Site." *Business Insider*, http://www .businessinsider.com/tumblr-and-social-media-demographics-2013-12.

Williams, Kristin A. 2011. " 'Old Time Mem'Ry': Contemporary Urban Craftivism and the Politics of Doing-it-Yourself in Postindustrial America." *Utopian Studies* 22, no. 2, 303–20.

CHAPTER 11

Queer Appalachia: A Homespun Praxis of Rural Resistance in Appalachian Media

Gina Mamone and Sarah E. Meng

Bryn Kelly was the first transgender woman I, Gina Mamone, met decades ago in West Virginia. Her Pentecostal parents kicked her out when she was sixteen and only let her take one grocery bag full of items with her. Having no place to go, she looked up "gay" in the local phone book. It was the early 1990s and the only thing that sounded like an actual resource in the Huntington, West Virginia, phone book was the Marshall University LGB office. It was so long ago, our acronym only had three letters. Bryn didn't call; she took her paper bag full of everything she owned and came straight to the office. I was working there under a work-study grant. Looking back, it seems irresponsible and inappropriate to staff a resource office with students without any train-ing. At the time, I desperately needed the work-study hours because of my own situation.

The other students who staffed the office and I sat down to sort out our options. Bryn was a minor and perhaps we should have called the state. How could we? An effeminate sixteen-year-old in the foster system in rural Appalachia at that time didn't have a chance. Maybe she'd make it in the foster system of a large city, but not where we were in West Virginia. We knew Bryn would face mental and emotional abuse in foster care, and we couldn't imagine the physical ramifications of putting a child like her there. This was a long time before curriculums of inclusion and tolerance. I don't remember if we voted or if we argued. All these years later, I just remember we decided Bryn would become one of us. She crashed with all of us here or there, but in time settled with Ryan and Steve. They had a spare bedroom that doubled as an office. Bryn had her own room, and Ryan and Steve had been together almost two years. The LBG office staff and I were barely old enough to drink; two years sounded like a rock solid eternity. Bryn finished high school, and we all chipped in to make it work. When I graduated, I left for the Pacific Northwest and lost touch with Bryn. Later, I moved to Brooklyn where we were reunited as friends and became professional collaborators.

Bryn thrived in Brooklyn. She was a Lambda Literary award winner, her work was featured at the Whitney and MoMA, and she was the host of the Gay Ole Opry. But art doesn't always pay the bills. Being an HIV-positive trans woman without consistent professional access to physical and mental health resources takes a toll when mixed with depression and alcohol. Bryn Kelly killed herself on January 13, 2016. In the wake of her death, the same people who took her in all those years ago started taking steps to preserve her memory and celebrate her vision of a publication documenting the rural queer culture that gave birth to her, to all of us.

Bryn Kelly was a HIV-positive trans woman who grew up on the West Virginia/Ohio border in the late 1980s and 1990s. She fell in love with zines and feminist writing at the age of sixteen. She wrote her first zine at the age of seventeen. *Granny Witch Squares* explored the nuanced correlations of the AIDS Quilt and her Appalachian folk art roots. For the entirety of my friendship with Bryn, she was in a constant state of hypothetical curation of a zine that she was going to make one day. Our emails and texts often included articles that have yet to be written with titles like "I Love Wendell Berry but I Still Like to Get My Dick Wet on Instagram" or "Oral Sex Tips from Shape-Note Singers." Bryn would be overcome with a wave of inspiration, and I would get a G-chat or text message explaining to me how academia was no longer a ladder out of Appalachian oppression unless you're white or she was going to get a ramp stamp tattoo on the small of her back so she could be in the centerfold of her own zine.

After her death, we set about trying to bring Bryn's vision to life in a way that would benefit our community the most. We are people who love Bryn. We are queers living together in these hills and sometimes also living so far apart from one another. Isolation is a primary violence we face, a weapon that has taken the lives of too many queer folks in Appalachia. It's easy to wonder how we survive; it's easy to wonder how we create a place for ourselves. At first we were just an Instagram and Facebook account, which was enough to get started. As we put feelers out, more people got involved; some of them knew Bryn, others only knew of her, and either way it was her vision to bring people together. We are not sociologists or archivists, folklorists or scholars. We are the collision of intersectional feminism, folklore, pop culture, queer takes on homespun traditions, art, and community. We survive and even thrive by sharing tales of wildcrafting our queerness, foraging for pieces of ourselves within the intersections of coal mines and class, race and religion, food justice and colonialism. We are Queer Appalachia. We have been collecting ourselves.

Around the beginning of spring 2016, the first transphobic bathroom bills began to hit state legislatures in Appalachia and the South. West Virginia was first, and within weeks almost every state in the region had similar legislation introduced in some way. Organizing efforts began in West Virginia by the queer community and our allies. Queer Appalachia's Facebook page became a centralized focal point of the organizing. It was a way for anyone doing any type of organizing to get their messages out. As a result, organizers from different states began to connect with each other and collaborate to build a rural resistance. Organizers and community members began relying on our Facebook feed to weed out fake and sensational news, instead providing accurate, relevant, regional information. Around the same time, Kim Davis refused to issue marriage certificates for same-sex couples in Rowan County, KY, and religious freedom laws were introduced into the legislature. That's when the world started to see Appalachia and how they treated their very own queer community and kin. Whether it was about the liberal left not shaming Davis for her appearance or mass boycotting the state of North Carolina over its bathroom bill, a multitude of national headlines were talking about Appalachia. This was just the beginning. The rest of the country was just starting to talk about our rural regions, and we were about to enter into an election cycle that would put Appalachia in the headlines regularly. Major international media conglomerates from the BBC to Al Jazeera sent production teams to Appalachia in 2017 to document the region that appeared to have enough political power to decide the highest office in the country but cannot make a better life for itself. Unfortunately, four to six minutes of a news segment cannot accurately depict the nuanced truths of intergenerational poverty, systemic racism, toxic masculinity, absentee landlords, geographic isolation, the opioid epidemic, and what century after century of politicians instead of leaders can do to an isolated region.

While the world felt like it was falling apart, a small piece of the Internet felt like it was coming together on our Instagram page. The facilitators of our online media, largely led by Gina Mamone, a first-generation riot grrrl; we've seen zines change the world, and we've seen revolutionary zines ignored. We had no idea how traditional print media would go over in our digital age. So many great zines beg for content until people give up on them. This was a big fear, but within the first few weeks of the Queer Appalachia Instagram launch, this fear quickly subsided. People started to send content. Every day more and more came in. The submissions were unique, personal, and sometimes just broke my heart. In addition, our number of followers skyrocketed.

By November 2018 our combined social media presence was 130,000, many of whom were rural queers below the Mason–Dixon line.

The submissions meant the zine did not lack for interesting, thoughtful, and articulate content; neither did our social media. By the end of our first month online, we had enough content to fill thirty zines. This is how the Queer Appalachia Instagram became submission based. Everyone needs to see positive images of themselves represented in every form of media, and rural queers are no different.

Every day we received dozens of submissions from people who identified with the project, people who were ready to share images of themselves sporting gold lame booty shorts and a backward camo cap while squatting to send fresh milk from a goat's udder into a mug of coffee. The images were a feast for the eyes, depicting the nuanced juxtapositions of queerness and rural Appalachian life. "Southern Sunday Best" was reinterpreted and redefined not just with every same-sex marriage and blended family in the region but also every formal event. It seemed like whatever people were reinterpreting had one foot planted in the past and in tradition, and the other foot planted just as firmly in contemporary queer identity. It didn't matter if these queer peoples' communities and neighbors were voting away their safety and identity, these queer people knew who they were. Who we are has never been in danger the way our safety has been. Queer Appalachians understand the small victory of leaving the house looking queer. Queer Appalachians understand what medicine it can be to see people like you in the world no matter what age you are. Our ancestors were hellbent on carving out a life in these beautiful and unforgiving mountains. So are we.

People were willing to give unfiltered access to their lives. Submissions often included the hashtags people wanted us to use. Living in extreme poverty, in the buckle of the Bible Belt in Trump's America, these amazing people found a way to make art and community. Not being able to afford "art," one follower collected mirrors from every junk store and antiques mall in the area and created a "wraparound peekaboo instillation" to experience with his Grindr dates. He agreed to not show their faces in his photography, and the majority of his dates agreed to be photographed spending time with him in his room. He's very upfront on why he hosts. Commenting on what it's like shopping for mirrors he said, "I like to imagine all the MawMaws that owned these before me, how boring their life was and how exciting it is now." This man follows the Instagram account of every major trending museum on the planet, including the Whitney Biennial.

As submissions poured in for our print edition and social media, we started

Figure 11.1 (*left*). #goldlame #bootyshorts & #livestock! @amarahollowbones is living their best life with fresh milk in the coffee! DM/tag us in your pictures of #queersinnature in warmer times to help get us through the winter. #queerappalachia #electricdirt (Photo courtesy of Amara Hollowbones Maceachern)

Figure 11.2 (*right*). "Cuntry girls make do" @lilperc666 / @the.farm.show #queerappalachia #electricdirt (Photo courtesy of Helena St. Tearer)

to learn about the people who were following us through daily interactions. They started asking how to get involved, where to buy the zine, and when the zine would be out, but some questions were of a more personal nature. Folks wanted to know where we were located and why we were doing this. We wanted to know who they were, too. As time went on, we realized the people following Queer Appalachia daily could, for the most part, be sorted into five different categories.

Rooted: You stayed within the immediate geographic vicinity of your birth.

Uprooted: Your birth region is socioeconomically devastated, such as some areas of extraction states like West Virginia and Kentucky. The only work available is in shrinking, dying industries like coal and fracking. Your family, education, and community have raised you to leave for your survival. In central Appalachia, young children learn sayings like "Reading wRiting and the Road to Roanoke."

Migrated: The location of home is not something that changes even though your address might. You may put down roots outside of Appalachia, but you always feel connected to the earth and dirt that bore you.

Came Back Y'all: You were uprooted or migrated, but you came home.

Traveler: Maybe your grandparents lived in the region and you visited during summers, maybe it's a 4-H camp you went to every year, or maybe you attended college in the region. Because you called it home for a while, you will never not be able to recognize Appalachia as a home.

We've learned that there are so many reasons people have spent time in Appalachia and formed a connection to its mountains and dirt. At first we truly underestimated the number of people who fit into the migrated category and still very much identified with the Appalachian region. Even though these folks form an identity attachment to their new homes, the new attachment does not diminish the emotional connection to the region.

Bryn's vision was an intersection of queers in nature, art, homespun cultural traditions, bad-ass intersectional politics, pop culture, and accessibility. People began sending in biographies and family histories along with the photo submissions.

Slowly, we got a peek into rural queer culture throughout Appalachia by firsthand accounts. Every submission felt like a field note in real time.

With such unfettered access, we started to be able to make connections about the larger community as a whole. Each submission and email added to an expanding picture of the unique relationships between identity, politics, and roots happening in queer Appalachia. It was nothing we set out to do intentionally; we had accidentally created the first virtual queer rural community. Even though cutting-edge technology and rural broadband brought us together, what connected us was a place where we shared a collective knowing of one another, a place where Dolly Parton was recognized not just as a country music star but also a patron saint. When family doesn't treat you like family, the cultural touchstones you agree on are even more dear and sacred. Queer Appalachians submitted photos with their own DapperQ moments in the dressing rooms at the Tractor Supply Co. Queer Appalachians were fucking the binary at every bingo hall, state fair, and Elks Lodge around. With three hundred or three dozen followers, these queer as fuck experiences were documented in some way for social media. On the average day, queer Appalachians come in contact with countless messages telling us we are not wanted and this is not our home. We know better, and we hold strong to a deep reverence and passion for our mountains.

Sometimes the submissions celebrated the absurdity of rural life in the modern world. Others captured the absurdity of what it's like to live with one

Figure 11.3 (*left*). "It's hard these days but I just try to love everyone" Ms. Pauline. Ms. Pauline is an 85 year old farmer who still works from sunup til sundown. When @badnursecontest wrote me about Pauline Frazier, I found myself smiling the rest of the day. "She is truly a role model as one of the most big hearted, kind, loving and supportive people I know, loves the earth and all her creatures." #queerappalachia #elders #femalefarmer #femalefarmers #elderreverence #homespunriotgrrrl #mawmawcore (Photo courtesy of Flinn Fulbright)

Figure 11.4 (*right*). From local_._honey "I got drunk last night and started talking about my mom, something I rarely do anymore. I grew up taking care of her, and at certain points in my life when I feel exhausted or like my needs are a burden to friends, I think about what it would be like to be mothered. To have someone make you scrambled eggs at noon when you finally get out of bed after crying all night, someone to drive you across town to that movie theater with the big chairs you like so you can stay in the dark but come out laughing, someone to tell you it's going to be okay even when it won't be. My mom is mentally ill, and last night I repeated my childhood vow to never have a daughter, because all the women in my family are sick like that, crazy to everyone not related to us. But today when I pulled out this packet of photos, one of the handful I have from my childhood, I saw how life has made us that way, made our fears and hesitations and craziness blossom into trailers in the woods, on porches covered in feral cats, in borrowed rooms we never got to call our own. And now I see that for all her lack of mothering, my mom gifted me with the power to survive. The fact that she's still surviving somewhere gives me strength, gives me comfort, feeds me at noon when I finally get out of bed. Next time I'm drunk, don't let me discount that. It may be the most valuable thing I'll ever own." (Photo courtesy of Amanda LaFollette)

foot in Appalachia and one foot in the contemporary modern world with everyone else.

After the electoral college election of Donald Trump, queers who had never been politically engaged began writing to the Queer Appalachia social media accounts, scared and looking for resources. They realized their families were not treating them like family and they, along with their neighbors, coworkers, friends, and community, had voted their rights and safety away. Some were angry, some were livid, and some were just so hurt. They couldn't understand how the people who invited them into their homes for dinner are the same folks they see every weekend at the lake and could have such blatant disregard for their safety and basic right to exist. Of the Appalachian queers who wrote to our social media accounts during that time, almost all mentioned rights and a few mentioned the constitution, but the messages always came down to the same thing: not just feeling but literally being unsafe and unwelcome in the places they called home.

Queer Appalachia start to organize in real time, just as they had when the bathroom bills were first introduced but now through the connections of our social media. Queer Appalachia followers had sign-making nights in their homes, inviting people they had never met before. Queer Appalachians started carpooling and road tripping to the marches, rallies, demonstrations, and actions. Queer Appalachians started making weekly trips to their state leaders' offices on congressional and senate levels. Queer Appalachians gathered up Confederate flags and started burning them in 2016. We saw all of these things because queer Appalachians took pictures and video of it in real time and sent it to us to share. They were using the infrastructure our social media was built on to organize and connect with each other. Everything has always been handle-based: we tag the submitter in the image along with the text from what was submitted. Every now and then someone wants a submission to be anonymous because it's illegal or they aren't out like that. It's very easy for people to talk to each other and connect after meeting in the comments section or seeing a post someone sent in.

As the days after the election wore on, we signed every petition we could. We didn't think it would do a lot of good as much as we needed something to do. We noticed that the ages of the people reaching out to Queer Appalachia got younger and younger in those days. Sometimes the youngest people would send the shortest messages. "How do you know you're gay?" Sometimes looking at the profile of the person who sent the message, we would be terrified to write back because they were so young. Reading these messages from younger queer Appalachians affected by the election—people who were not even old enough to vote—we realized how selfish we could be as queers who were very connected to other queers. It's easy to focus on our own feelings when forced to drive past a neighbor's home, with the lawn littered with Trump-Pence signs or to be angry when stopped behind a Trump bumper sticker in traffic. The messages from youth revealed a whole generation of queer kids who are growing up riding in the cars with those bumper stickers on them, living in the

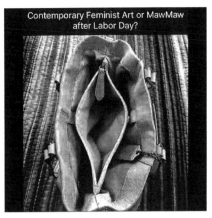

Figure 11.5 (*left*). "Ruth Bader Hensburg does not dissent to her new jabot (fancy judicial collar). Thanks to Ashley Carpenter for humoring me and custom making this for her!" #ruthbaderginsburg #ruthbaderhensburg #feministchicken from @lizzie9208 & @anytree #queerappalachia #queersouth #electricdirt (Photo courtesy of Elizabeth Hartman)

Figure 11.6 (*right*). "Contemporary Feminist Art or MawMaw after Labor Day?" That #mawmaw life y'all #judychicagochurchpotluckseries #nohotsaucehere #feminist #feministpotluck #queerappalachia #electricdirt (Photo by Mamone)

homes with those signs in the yard. Some of them are still in the process of coming out to themselves. They already know there's no place for them in their family of origin to be themselves. They already know they are not welcome. There's no reason to even entertain the thought of coming out to their families. Some queer Appalachian youth understand that if they want to have a family, if they want to still have a place to sleep at night, they need to keep such things to themselves. Some feel they must do anything and everything they can to change themselves, to try to fit in with their family's expectations. It runs the gamut from parents who want to be supportive to those who are looking for a "cure." The saddest conversations have been with queer people who know they are queer and want to change it. Queer Appalachia has some amazing social workers and therapists who are part of the collective and can help connect young queers to resources.

Minorities in Appalachia are in the trenches of the culture war. The entire region is addicted to fossil fuel and, as of November 2016, the coal industry has affected every person in this country in a new and profound way because of the election. However, the coal industry employs fewer people than the Arby's fast food chain (Ingraham 2017). We are transitioning to a postcoal region and have been for some time. After social class, the issue queer Appalachians who contacted us are concerned with most is isolation and addiction. Isolation and addiction are especially relevant to those in the coalfields because of the brain drain phenomenon in the region; those who can get out because of access to resources have already left. The queer Appalachians who stay, the majority of whom have no choice, tend to be the very definition of working poor/blue collar, living paycheck to paycheck.

There are some opportunities for younger queers with access to a car who are within driving distance of LGBTQ nonprofits and college towns, but many groups in these areas have cut-off ages for their clientele. The older you are, the less likely you are to qualify for resources or to be able to participate in groups. Due to lack of access, older queer Appalachians are also less likely to be familiar with technology. Combined with often being poor and not having access to the latest technology (including broadband—even if you can afford the technology, the infrastructure is not always there for it to work), gaining exposure to technology may not be as much of a priority for older people as it is for younger folks. Intimidation also plays a role. We were told "forty-four-year-olds that flunked out of their GED and technical school don't feel comfortable playing around and figuring it out" as we were trying to talk someone through submitting some of their art for our print edition.

Although isolation affects everyone in Appalachia, the impact on queer folks is specific and unique, even more so now with restrictive bathroom bills and religious freedom laws. Religious freedom laws are nothing new. Businesses have been finding creative ways to let us know we're not welcome long before now, but state-sponsored isolation and denial makes it scarier. We're familiar with navigating these things from time to time, but giving these practices legal protection is terrifying. People have been making huge shareable Google docs with safe bathrooms on maps or through the region down to North Carolina. These lists included items like "constant garden being tilled," "new manager here," and "not safe anymore." This was the beginning of being able to see a whisper network start to appear, a network that has become stronger over time and with each passing and well-executed antifascist action and demonstration.

So often with underdocumented cultures and communities there is a gate-keeper—an archivist, sociologist, anthropologist, or historian who decides what is documented and who is omitted from history. This person has access to higher education and resources that many folks, especially in our impoverished region, do not have. That does not happen with Queer Appalachia. The underrepresented and misrepresented represent themselves. We get to define

Queer Appalachia with our own images and truths. By embracing a combination of contemporary technology and social media, we are in a constant state of documenting our culture, community, lives, and herstory/history. Queer Appalachia is a place for us to share our truths and find each other. We offer a unique and special way for people to interact and build community. Folks often swap art, exchange recipes, and pass along beloved mementos in our comments section. Recently, someone's family autoharp from Georgia found a new home in Virginia. In summer 2018 we hosted our first meetup in Asheville, North Carolina. We had more than two hundred people and got national press in a photo essay of the event in Autostraddle.

In the summer of 2019 we hosted Farm Show, our first weekend event gathering more than two hundred people on a private farm in West Virginia. Workshops ranged from harm reduction to how to make sustainable walnut ink. Games and creek swimming filled the day. At night regional bands gave way to a DJ around 2 a.m. A field was plowed to create a dance area. As the DJ played, art installations and porn were projected onto the tree line above the crowd.

In fall 2019 we conducted a winter coat drive, raising over $4,000 in less

Figure 11.7. Two queers embrace in a field in front of an old barn in West Virginia at Farm Show, a weekend of workshops and music in 2019 (Photo by Jenny Revilla)

Figure 11.8. We're back! @the.farm.show was SO magical y'all! What a special thing to be a part of & help make happen. The barn stage wooed me, the #deeplez #bonfiresingalong was dreamy, I got healed in the waters & new moon eclipse open field dance party complete with a billion stars. We want to thank the group of folks that made this happen & let us be a part of it. We can have things like this in our region if we work together to make them a reality. #ruralresistance is not just #bannerdrops & #actions, we need things like this to survive here too & lift our quality of life. Thank you to the organizers, workshop leaders, campers, artists, AND a special shout out to the kitchen crew, y'all made three meals a day for over a 100 people w/ a vegan option & brought it on the dance field! I loved how everyone shared everything they brought & how multigenerational it was! Real pictures coming from our photographer @jennyreville (we missed you @shooglet feel better) @spinstersounds spotted by the pool w #unioncrocs 🐊 #electricdirt #queerwestvirginia #queerappalachia #thefarmshow (Photo courtesy of Jenny Revilla)

than forty-eight hours to buy coats for our community. Every time we give our virtual community and opportunity to show up offline, from camping weekends to praxis of mutual aid, they exceed our expectations. As our followers increased in numbers, our on-the-ground resource building increased, and so did our opportunities to connect and collaborate with organizations. We were very nervous to find ourselves in a meeting with the executive director of the Foxfire Fund. Like many people from the region, we were raised with Foxfire books, taught to have reverence and respect for those pages because that was the history of our people and how they survived in such unforgiving geography for so long. When we announced our community partnership with the Foxfire Fund, we again realized Queer Appalachia was more than a zine project. Our followers simply being themselves and documenting their lives was enough to get the attention of Foxfire. In every printed issue of *Electric*

Figure 11.9. A #bigassthankyou to everyone that came out to our panel @ #afsam18! / @ americanfolkloresociety It was SO amazing to have a conversation in real time about our #communitypartnership with @foxfireorg. We also talked about the work being done to diversify @westvirginiafolklife & @tnfolklife! I encourage y'all to follow & $upport these two organizations that are working hard to include our #ruralqueer voices in their work. w/ @thehousepie, @ southsidesupervillain and @atl_urbanfarmer #ruralresistance #queerappalachia #electricdirt (Photo by Mamone)

Dirt, there will be a dedicated Foxfire section with the introduction handwritten by the executive director. We have the unique opportunity to write our ancestors back into the annals of Appalachian maker culture. In 2019 we traveled to the national folklore conference in Buffalo, New York, and presented a panel discussion based on the collaboration of our organizations and what this partnership means for traditional heritage-based arts and folklore.

Our growing numbers have garnered the attention of SAGE, the country's largest and oldest organization dedicated to improving the lives of LGBT older adults. SAGE flourishes in urban areas, yet their outreach plummets in rural areas for reasons such as limited accessibility to technology and limited broadband infrastructure. By partnering with SAGE, we have the opportunities to provide new resources to older rural queer adults. So much effort and resources are put into our youth for obvious reasons, and as a result older adults and the elderly can easily get lost in the grant shuffle of bottlenecked regional resources. There's just too much to do and not enough resources. Partnering with SAGE is a way we can help. We are gearing up for our first SAGE Table in fall 2019, a local meal that is shared intergenerationally. This event can be held at a restaurant or in a home, with at least four and up to as many people as you want. Building these real-life connections can make all the difference for isolated rural adults. So far we have thirty different communities hosting these intergenerational meals in Appalachia!

Some people have been kind enough to share their professional expertise with us as we navigate people's questions and requests. Jessica Halem, the head of LGBTQ outreach and engagement at Harvard Medical School, has been amazing with every type of referral for any medical thing you can think of, especially rural-based transitioning. It is unprecedented for someone without any insurance in rural Kentucky to have access to the person in charge of the queer medical curriculum at Harvard Medical School. In addition, with Jessica's help, SAGE has started working with us to develop a list of resources for LGBTQ seniors in Appalachia and across the South.

Perhaps the most unique community partnership we have is through our community micro-grant program. All of those followers we've been telling you about, who are so kind to share private moments of their lives with Queer Appalachia, are also happy to $upport the project as well. When we launched the GoFundMe in 2017, we were worried a goal of $3,000 was a ludicrous dream. We laughed out loud while we typed it in, but it doesn't hurt to shoot for the stars. Turns out the joke was on us. When the GoFundMe closed, we had raised more than $30,000. That didn't include income from independent bookstores or zine distributors, which came in one order at a time. Two months after the release of our zine, *Electric Dirt*, we found ourselves ordering a second printing. When you add that profit with the fundraising we did in the first half of the year through GoFundMe, our Instagram account has made over $60,000 in profit in 2019. We're not a business or nonprofit; we are a group of artists who like to make things, especially change. We are friends who love our mountains very much and want to be able to call them home. We came together because we missed Bryn, and we are reminded that for so many, queer histories get lost even in these digital times.

Without the archival work of Reina Gossett, we would have no idea about the life of Marsha P. Johnson. We thought Bryn was worth a zine, that she deserved to be at least a footnote in rural queer history. Her art and activism reached national acclaim in multiple disciplines from hanging in museums all over the country to winning literary awards. We made more money than we could have ever imagined with this project. What's an ethical, responsible thing to do with this money? We feel lucky to be able to support ourselves through our vocations as regional artists. Creating a community micro-grant program gives us the opportunity to directly invest that money back into queer Appalachia. To qualify for one of our grants, you don't have to have a 501(c)(3) status or a website; all you need is an idea to create accessible queer Appalachian community. Our proposals range from medical clinic training for antifascist actions to pop-up interactive art installations. For far too long, limited grants in the region are the very definition of scarcity of resources. Sparse resources combined with the conservative religious nature of our community and regionally specific phenomenon such as brain drain mean there are not many opportunities for big, bold, queer ideas to get funding in Appalachia. We aim to change that. We want to be economic training wheels for our followers' big, queer Appalachian ideas. Through micro-grants, we hope to change the queer cultural landscape of the region.

This is only our first year. We get pretty excited wondering how much the queer Appalachian cultural landscape will change after a decade of us giving our profits back to the community, Queer Appalachia growing with every issue and opportunity. This has become so much more than we ever thought it could be. Not just financially—we can make and post a meme about toxic masculinity in the coalfields in the morning and before noon a teenage girl in Kentucky can literally be interacting with Dorothy Allison in the comments of that post. We have been able to raise more money in our first year than some local nonprofits have in their annual operating budgets. With this incredible resource comes responsibility. When we listen to the people who support us and follow us talking about the biggest problems in their lives, they usually involve the following: money/funding; addiction/recovery (living at ground zero of the opioid epidemic); and racism/the contemporary civil rights movement. Queer Appalachia feels it can best serve our communities by focusing our work and intentions in these three areas. Our micro-grant program addresses money/funding. When we describe the program, we explicitly say it is an intentional redistribution of wealth and QTIPOC are highly encouraged to apply. We wondered how we could redistribute power within our project's internal structure. Everything submitted to the Instagram page gets published without curation, but we can't promise that in the print zine *Electric Dirt*. We set about to the task of finding a way to reduce the role of white people gatekeeping within our project.

One solution to decreasing this gatekeeping was by having a new editor for every issue. This way, we get to explore power structures valuing underrepresented communities and cultures while they represent themselves and have creative control and freedom. Even though the collective is not all white, we understand the privilege white folks in the collective have, especially in the numbers we carry. We maintain the infrastructure and the selling and shipping of goods, which enables Queer Appalachia to hire an editor to come in and take over each issue. A staff is waiting for each new editor the second they take the job, ready to build their vision and bring it to life. The editor selects the photographers and consultants for their issue, and they make sure the small, paying creative jobs get dispersed in the community of their choosing. We want to defer to and support leadership by people of color at every opportunity. We want to explore different types of organizational hierarchies internally; we don't want to invest any energy and time in structures that have gotten the region where it is. We believe in reparations.

Every issue of *Electric Dirt* will include two ads. The first encourages queer Appalachians to run for public office at the city, county, and state levels; the second is a call for reparations. We can't ask people to challenge white supremacy and make reparations if we are not making those changes ourselves. The money we raise through this project is given as reparations. We hope others in the region will join us as we explore liberationist leadership structures and make reparations. We dream of a day where reparations are taken seriously, not just racially but through a lens of corporations and capitalism also. Many people reading this can think of industries that have taken advantage of Appalachian communities, and the people reading this are to take an opportunity to try to make it right.

The last item on that list was the opioid epidemic; we're not really sure where to fix that. We got to thinking maybe that's some of the problem—it's so big, we don't know where to start. Much like reparations, it feels like a lot of people in the region are waiting for the government to step in and fix this, but government at every level passes the buck while avoiding the conversations that need to happen around intergenerational poverty, dying communities, systematic racism, toxic masculinity, and so on. Due to rates of overdose and prescription use, many refer to our home as ground zero of the opioid epidemic. Queer folks are at an even higher risk of addiction and overdose. Why is that? We ask people who follow us to tell us what it's like navigating addiction in the region, and they all had very similar stories.

A lack of resources and support was obvious from the start. Can you imagine what it's like to try to find a twelve-step sponsor if you are a gender-nonconforming queer person in Appalachia? Think about that—a young, gender-nonconforming queer person, in Trump's America, in the buckle of the Bible Belt, trying to find a sponsor; it sounds like a Michael Moore documentary before we even get started. Even if you can make it through a few meetings with everyone staring at you and talking about you under their breath, would you ever feel comfortable sharing in those meetings? Even if you can muster up the courage to ask someone who you think might be a good fit to be a sponsor, how receptive do you think they're going to be? Remember, in more urban areas, the twelve steps have a broader concept of the totality. Not in Appalachia. Here it tends to be fire, brimstone, and an imaginary abacus in the sky. The faith that is helping get the straight community clean through step programs in Christian churches works against rural queers looking to find recovery in those spaces. Out of the one hundred people we spoke to, we could only find four who had sponsors willing to work with them.

Rural working-class queers seeking recovery are desperate for any resources. Even if they're lucky enough to be able to afford rehab with insurance, there's hardly a supportive community waiting for them on the other side of that deductible. There are few people (if any) who have battled opioid addiction and not made a complete mess of every aspect of their lives and relationships with community. The social network people have at the beginning of their addiction is often nowhere to be seen when they finally hit bottom. Small rural queer communities are isolating enough without the destructive behavior that goes hand in hand with opioid dependence. All of this means rural queers in recovery are more isolated than most, making relapse more likely. That's why our numbers are nearly double that of our straight peers. No one who wrote to Queer Appalachia about their addiction to opioids had a story about gateway drugs; all of them shared the same story of a having medically necessary reason for a pain medicine prescription.

In response to the need for resources addressing opioid addiction, on April 2, 2018, we launched a peer-led digital recovery space for queer Appalachians. Queer Appalachia Recovery is a secure, confidential online community connecting rural queers in recovery with one another and to rural queers in recovery who have substantial amounts of clean time and are willing to be a virtual sponsor. Not a decent meeting in a two-hour drive? It doesn't matter anymore. People who had to choose between their recovery and keeping the lights on won't have to make that choice; they won't have to come up with the funds to drive six hours round trip just to go to meetings more accepting of who they are. This is the beginning of an alternative, and we hope people will get involved and let us know about their experiences. We want to build this into whatever the community needs it to be. We have some great therapists and social workers who have helped bring all of this together, and we are very grateful to them.

Queer Appalachia Recovery started to get some press attention on a national level. Despite billions of dollars coming into the region annually, this was the first resource for rural queer addiction. Nan Goldin started following us on Instagram—Whitney Biennial Retrospective Nan Goldin. After almost losing her life to opioid addiction, she is interested in making art that explores education, awareness, and accountability of the opioid epidemic. Under the moniker Nan Goldin's PAIN (Prescription Addiction Intervention Now), she was engaging in political protest actions that were just as much art installations. Increasing masses of people from all over the world focused on holding the Sackler family accountable for their role in Purdue Pharma, the makers of OxyContin. The Sacklers were washing their money in plain sight and in a way that buys them social equity. After decades of her work hanging in Sackler wings and galleries all over the world, Nan made the connection of how they almost killed her and how the art in their sponsored museums was being used to wash their dirty hands. Nan started following the Queer Appalachia account because of the photography. She soon realized there was a whole other side to the opioid epidemic, a rural lens that is fundamental to the economics of big pharma and to its carnage. We've been given the opportunity to collaborate with PAIN and bring a rural lens and voice to it. The opportunity to make things at this level in the art world in a way that brings light and awareness to the things that are the most important to us in our home is exciting and overwhelming.

We were suddenly thrust into the art world spotlight two and a half years after the start of the project. In 2019 we have been featured in *Art Forum*, *Art Net*, *Hyperallergic*, *USA Today*, *Mashable*, MTV's LOGO TV, *Anthony Bourdain Parts Unknown*, Burnaway, CNN, *OUT Magazine*, *Curve Magazine*, *100 Days in Appalachia*, *Bitch Magazine*, *The Advocate*, *BELT*, It's Going Down, *THEM*, and Autostraddle. This little community zine project has a will of its own and is in a constant state of defying category, much like Bryn did.

Our first piece with PAIN was a public art installation called "Which Side Are You On?" that went up in Louisville, Kentucky, in October 2018 at Sheherazade Gallery. It is a riff on Zoe Leonard's "I Want a President," a countercultural manifesto written at the height of the AIDS epidemic. Leonard wrote the poem several years after the end of the Reagan administration, which largely ignored the subject of AIDS with devastatingly fatal consequences. The words of the original piece advocated for a society led by people with firsthand experience with the feeling of being powerless, and it circulated among artists for years like an analogue meme, before becoming resurrected in the digital age. "Which Side Are You On?" takes its title from a folk song by Kentucky social activist and poet Florence Reece; the song has become a celebrated Appalachian labor organization anthem. Reece's husband was a union organizer in Harlan County during the coal wars, before dying of black lung. Like Leonard's poem, Reece's song has taken on new interpretations and verses as it has traveled through time and place. They exist as parallel touchstones for present-day anthems of hope, converging in Mamone's expression of resistance to the continuing injustices of extreme class divisions.

The text of the installation "Which Side Are You On?" reads:

I want a survivor for Governor. I want a Governor whose home has been raided by ICE. I want the child of a public school teacher for Governor, and I want someone who knows what days to hit what food pantries. I want a Governor who has had experience heating a home with its oven, knows what a cruel joke rural public transportation is, and who never had the option to go to college. I want a Governor who knows what it's like when your utilities are cut off, knows the game of not if but when. I want a Governor who drinks the city tap water, only knows what it's like to have fresh vegetables because they grew them themselves, and takes better care of their community than they do their cast-iron skillet. I want a Governor who knows what Coinstar is because they've had to, what it's like for SNAP benefits to decrease annually as they see their children get bigger and bigger. I want a Governor who calls out the predatory economics of cash-to-payday loans in our strip malls, talks candidly about the violence capitalism causes in our community, and who knows what it's like to not be able to afford a security deposit. I want a Governor that knows it's ALL scrip. I want a Governor that had a tooth extracted in a large animal stall at the state fairgrounds because it was the only option, that grew up going to the Health Wagon, RAM & Mission of Mercy clinics. I want a Governor who detoxed alone without the support of trained professionals because that's all they could afford. I want a Governor who knows what it's like to share a bedroom wall with someone that has Black Lung . . . for decades, so they know what it sounds like at every stage. I want a Governor who has been denied disability on multiple occasions despite documentation and need. I want a Governor who flies a #BLM flag at the capital, refuses to call our home an extraction state and feels there is no reason to have a "dialogue" about what to do with all these Confederate Monuments. I want a Governor that believes only women should speak at women's rallies and that feel it's their duty to chain themselves to heavy machinery in the path of pipelines in our backyards. I want a Pro-Sex Worker Prison Abolitionist Governor who isn't afraid to say the word R-E-P-A-R-A-T-I-O-N-S. I want a Governor that still catches fire flies, sings Jolene & Fancy at karaoke, has bell hooks on their bedside table and Narcan in their pocket. I want a Governor who knows words like Harm Reduction & Restorative Justice should be seen in places other than just in our states grants, that will promise us a needle exchange for every McDonald's / Pill Mill in the county. I want a Governor that doesn't see addiction & poverty as moral failures, that doesn't see stewarding our community as a steppingstone in their career. I want a Governor that believes we've had a near-fatal amount of politicians and are desperate for leaders. I want a Governor that understands that the Civil War never ended; we just traded in our cannon fodder & muskets for more deadly weapons, like school district zones, mortgage rates, and being so poor you literally live on top of poison—from the coal slurry in West Virginia creeks to the streets of Flint Michigan. I'm tired of asking the people whose salary we pay: Which Side Are You On?

Gina Mamone, a founding member of Queer Appalachia, posted the following on their personal social media on the first anniversary of Bryn's death:

One year today. Grief is complicated and nuanced. The most healing thing I did for my grief over Bryn's death this past year was spend copious amounts of time with it. Myself and a handful of West Virginia and Ohio friends from Bryn's youth started making one of her ideas a reality—a zine about Queer Appalachia. Her vision was an intersection of country queer porn, art, homespun traditions, badass intersectional politics, pop culture, and accessibility. We are trying hard to do her vision justice. The grief has been miserable, but getting to make something that Bryn is a part of has been a godsend. Having an outlet and being able to make something has made all the difference in navigating my grief. I encourage everyone to make something for Bryn: a pie, a poem, a quilt, a pan of cornbread, color your roots, etc. A year without Bryn has taught me how short life is, that maybe the best thing we can make is room for each other, to actively engage in kindness, empathy, forgiveness, support and inclusion, with each other and ourselves. Keeping in the spirit of making things, I made this holy image of Bryn [fig. 11.10], biscuits, and an autoharp. It's designed to be printed out for a tall votive candle.

I got this picture (fig. 11.11) in a text message a week later.

Figure 11.10. Bryn: Our Lady of the Mountains (Photo by Mamone)

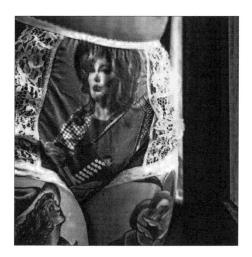

Figure 11.11. Via text message, on May 23, 2017 at 5:04 a.m.:
Author: "WOW, those are beautiful! Bryn would be beside herself! Did you know her well?"
Anonymous: "Only through legend!" (Photo courtesy of Anonymous)

BIBLIOGRAPHY

Ingraham, Christopher. 2017, March 31. "The Entire Coal Industry Employs Fewer People than Arby's." *Washington Post*. https://www.washingtonpost.com/news /wonk/wp/2017/03/31/8-surprisingly-small-industries-that-employ-more-people -than-coal/?utm_term=.6268cb6531b6. Accessed May 15, 2017.

Contributors

delfin bautista is an activist scholar of faith who explores the intersections of religion, queer theory, activism, resiliency, and intersectionality. delfin has a master's in divinity from Yale University and a master's of social work from the University of Pennsylvania. delfin is coauthor of "Religion and Spirituality" in *Trans Bodies, Trans Selves* (Oxford University Press, 2014) and a contributor to Believe Out Loud, Young Adult Catholics, and La Lucha, Mi Pulpito. delfin's eclectic background includes trauma therapy, chaplaincy, case management, advocacy, child welfare, and adjunct professorship. (delfin does not capitalize their name and uses they/them pronouns.)

Tijah Bumgarner is a filmmaker and professor. She teaches narrative and documentary video production at Marshall University. Bumgarner holds a BFA in film/video from the California Institute of the Arts and a master's in media studies from West Virginia State University. As a doctoral candidate at Ohio University, her dissertation "Examining the Ground: Shifting Narratives in Post-Coal Appalachia," explored how extraction is narrativized. Bumgarner's experience growing up in West Virginia has inspired much of her work. In 2017, she completed her first feature film, *Meadow Bridge*, a coming-of-age narrative set in rural West Virginia. Currently, she is working on a documentary about family structures in the opioid epidemic in Appalachia. In scholarship and practice, Bumgarner seeks to disrupt stereotypes that conform to a single defining narrative of the region.

Adam Denney is an advocate, educator, and writer from Monticello, Kentucky. His work seeks to explore the in-betweens of place and space in both the natural and built environment.

Justin Ray Dutton is a queer guy from southwest Virginia living in North Carolina. He has a master's of divinity from Wake Forest University and explores the intersections of Appalachian, queer, and religious identities.

Responding to a call for intergenerational mentorship and a need for codifying queer Appalachian resources, Justin Ray is the founding chairperson of the Appalachian Studies Association's Queer Caucus. He most enjoys dogs, board games, and laughter.

Savi Ettinger is a queer and trans writer, artist, and zinester. They are a recent graduate from Salem College with a bachelor's degree in English and creative writing, with a concentration in poetry. Their interests include multimodal writing and visual literature, as well as zine studies and LGBT media. Upon graduation, they completed two years of work as a writing consultant with previous volunteer experience, at the Salem College Writing Center.

Hillery Glasby is an assistant professor in Michigan State University's writing, rhetoric, and American cultures department and a faculty fellow for MSU's Center for Gender in Global Context. She teaches writing courses focused on rhetoric and culture, sexual literacy, environmental sustainability, women's studies, and LGBTQ studies. Her research interests include LGBTQ and feminist movements; digital, DIY, and queer rhetorics; and writing center and writing program administration. She adores cats, coffee, street art, 1940s music, and the Grateful Dead.

Sherrie Gradin is professor of English and director of the Ohio University Appalachian Writing Project. Her research interests include rural queer identities, composition theory, trauma, affect theory, and feminist studies. Her life is enriched by many dogs, a cat, and her younger queer colleagues who consistently remind her why we gotta stick together.

Kimberly Gunter is an associate professor of English and director of Core Writing at Fairfield University. Her research interests include queerness and intersectionality as they inform the teaching of writing, writing program administration, public rhetorics, and rhetorical agency. She lives in the wilds of Connecticut with two septuagenarian parents, a long-suffering partner, and a three-legged dog named Levon. Both she and the dog regularly threaten to pack their harpoons and start walking toward the state line.

Amanda Hayes is an assistant professor at Kent State University's Tuscarawas campus. A multigenerational Appalachian, she grew up on a farm that's been in her family for 150 years. Her work explores intersections of Appalachian identity, rhetoric, and literacy. These issues form the backbone of her book, *The*

Politics of Appalachian Identity (West Virginia University Press, 2018), which won the Nancy Dasher Award.

Michael Jeffries is a senior at Appalachian State University studying adaptive special education. His accelerated master's is in special education: double concentration in emotional behavioral disorders and specific learning disabilities, with a certificate in autism spectrum disorder. Michael's research involves recreational therapy and the implications for individuals with autism spectrum disorder, presented at the North Carolina Conference for Exceptional Children in Wilmington.

Logan Land is an undergraduate student at Appalachian State University. They are studying secondary education, English with a minor in gender, women's and sexuality studies; Logan is also pursuing their master's in English at Appalachian State. Their studies center around queer theory in various realms of literature. They also work to maintain a focus on pedagogy and activism in- and outside of the classroom with particular care for transgender and non-binary bodies.

Mamone (Gina) is an audio engineer and maker living in the coalfields of West Virginia. Mamone engineered and produced some of the first riot grrrl albums to come out of the Pacific Northwest. Until 2014, Mamone was president of Riot Grrrl Ink, the largest queer record label in the world, with a roster of more than 200 artists that ranged from the Gay Ole Opry to Andrea Gibson. In 2014 in an act of solidarity with the emerging #BLM movement and in an intentional act of reparations and redistribution of wealth, the record label was given to Awqward, the first queer POC/indigenous talent agency. Mamone is the creative director at Queer Appalachia, which communicates through social media with more than 250,000 rural queers and allies daily who call home below the Mason-Dixon Line. Mamone is also an editor at the Looking at Appalachia Project. Mamone has recently been in collaboration with Nan Goldin's PAIN project, bringing a rural lens to their opioid work focusing on accountability and reparations from the Sackler family.

Katie Manthey is an assistant professor of English and director of the Salem College Writing Center. Her research and teaching are focused around professional writing, fat studies, cultural rhetorics, dress studies, and civic engagement. She is a body-positive activist and moderates the website Dress Profesh, which highlights the ways that dress codes are racist, cis-sexist, ageist, classist, and so on. Her work has appeared in *Peitho: The Journal of the Coalition* *of Women Scholars in the History of Rhetoric and Composition, Jezebel,* and *The Journal of Global Literacies, Technologies, and Emerging Pedagogies.* She is currently working on *Writing the Body: Fat Fashion, Body Positivity, and Ethical Reading* (University of Nebraska Press, forthcoming).

Lydia McDermott is associate professor of composition and director of the Center for Writing and Speaking at Whitman College, in the rolling hills of eastern Washington.

Sarah E. Meng is a dirt femme, a creative, and a mental health therapist at Georgia State University. Sarah's research interests include resilience, queer and trans mental health, and fat liberation.

Caleb Pendygraft is an assistant professor of humanities at Massachusetts Maritime Academy. He earned his PhD from Miami University, in Oxford, Ohio, where his dissertation examined affect, trauma, spirituality, and embodiment of queer literacy in Appalachia. He was recently published in the inaugural protest issue of *Killjoy* and has a forthcoming book chapter on queerness, embodiment, and Grindr. His research interests overlap with queerness, rurality, and place in literacy studies.

Sonny Romano is a blue-haired bisexual trans boricua in his sophomore year at Salem College, currently working on his bachelor's in race and ethnicity studies and rhetoric and composition with a concentration in zine history, preservation, and archiving. He's in his second year of consulting and volunteering at the Salem College Writing Center, where you can usually find him listening to new wave music and knitting.

Travis A. Rountree is an assistant professor in the English department at Western Carolina University, where he is happily nestled among the mountains. In spring 2017, he earned his PhD from the University of Louisville. He teaches first-year composition courses and online graduate courses in composition and rhetoric. His research interests include archival research and pedagogy, Appalachian rhetorics, place-based pedagogy, and public memory studies. He has been published in the *North Carolina Folklore Journal, Journal of Southern History,* and *Appalachian Journal.*

Rachael Ryerson is a lecturer at Ohio University and director of their composition program. Her research interests include (queer/ing) writing pedagogies, multimodal composing practices and processes, and comics rhetoric and composition, especially their relationship to sexuality and gender. Her most recent scholarship considers queer, multimodal rhetoric in queer comics. In her free time, she thinks about teaching writing, drinks copious amounts of coffee, reads and writes about comics, and experiments with vegan cooking and baking.

Cynthia Suryawan is a queer and trans student with a bachelor's degree in mathematics who is currently working on a master's degree in statistics. In addition to using their math degree, they are interested in pursuing writing and are currently working on screenplays. During their undergrad years, they were a volunteer writing consultant for the Salem College Writing Center after completing a semester-long internship.

Matthew Thomas-Reid is assistant professor of educational foundations and affiliate faculty with gender, women's, and sexuality studies at Appalachian State University. Matthew is faculty advisor for GAPP (Gay and Progressive Pedagogy) and is editor of the *South Atlantic Philosophy of Education Society Journal*. His areas of research include philosophy of education, social justice education, and queer pedagogy. His current research projects focus on using LGBTQIA histories and narratives with a view toward "queering" pedagogy, praxis, and, most recently, digital literacies.

Index